Pigeon
Trouble

Pigeon Trouble

Bestiary
Biopolitics
in a
Deindustrialized
America

Hoon Song

PENN

UNIVERSITY OF PENNSYLVANIA PRESS

PHILADELPHIA · OXFORD

Published by
University of Pennsylvania Press
Philadelphia, Pennsylvania 19104-4112

Printed in the United States of America
on acid-free paper

10 9 8 7 6 5 4 3 2 1

Library of Congress Cataloging-in-Publication Data
Song, Hoon.
    Pigeon trouble : bestiary biopolitics in a deindustrialized America / Hoon Song.
        p. cm.
    Includes bibliographical references and index.
    ISBN 978-0-8122-4242-3 (hardcover : alk. paper)
    1. Pigeon shooting—Moral and ethical aspects—Pennsylvania. 2. Pigeon
shooting—Political aspects—Pennsylvania. 3. Animal rights activists—
Pennsylvania. I. Title.
SK325.P55S66 2010
179'.3—dc22
                                                                    2010004928

CONTENTS

INTRODUCTION

On one Labor Day afternoon, I fell into gawking at an old man crossing
the sparsely peopled part of Hegins Community Park, so abnormally
laborious and faltering was his trudge. He was pulling his grotesquely
stooped and feeble body along in tiny steps, his gaze fixed on the
ground a few feet away from a wounded pigeon fluttering in the dust.
Then, out of nowhere appeared several animal rights "rescuers,"
followed by a television camera and its crew, closing in at full speed.
The old man, spotting the storming pack out of the corner of his eye,
instantly came to his senses. He sprang forth on swift feet as if seized
by an alien creaturely animation, and relentlessly stomped on the bird
over and over, until its body went limp, trails of intestines exuded,
and an eye popped out. Then, spent and out of breath, the man stood
pale awhile before going back to his ever-so-laborious walk as though
nothing had happened, heedless of the cheers of the belatedly gathering
onlookers and the rescuers' cries of protest.
—Revised Field Note, the Labor Day Pigeon Shoot, Hegins, Pa., 1994

Take One

I have what you might call bird phobia or ornithophobia. My heart races
uncontrollably at the tumult of a legion perched on electric wires, like too
many musical notes in too rapid a rhythm. My hair stands on end at the
imagined feel of the cold, flinty beak materializing out of a soft, warm body;
at the unsightly shape of the wrinkled, sinewy fork of legs wired to the fluffy
torso with its unfathomable mass in disguise under the feathers. And of all
the monstrous combinations, there is the feral pigeon: its rapid red eyes of
rapaciousness, its bobbing, craven curiosity, and its shiny shell of a plump
heteropterous body, threatening to burst under the most innocent misstep.

Thus there was that splitting sense of part of me watching my own reckless undertaking in disbelief when I chose none other than the business of pigeons as the excuse with which I was to circumspectly approach the delicate theme of whiteness in rural America. I was to confront two sources of my deepest anxiety at once, hoping that my intimate knowledge of the irrationality of the former might illuminate the same in the latter.

But the unspoken plot and frame of fieldwork is such that one often finds oneself, as a matter of course, expected to put on a heroic face with respect to the professed subject matter of his or her pursuit. In the field, I came to hide my fear of pigeons behind the science of the pigeon I had amassed from books; I talked about them impressively and profusely whenever I had to touch them. Then there was a certain irritable bigot of a man everyone called "Farmer"—for being the only farmer in the miners' country around Ashland, Pennsylvania—who seemed to intuitively recognize a birdphobe in me. From our very first encounter, he was different: others, at my appearance in their territory, became agitated and voiced their displeasure aloud—with these I could argue, disagree, and, often, compromise—but Farmer held me in silent surveillance. In the unassuming presence of his stooped, skeletal posture he hovered about me, always stealing sidelong glances filled with the serpentine instinct and taste for the struggling victim—lying in wait for an opportune moment to strike. Thus when Farmer quietly approached me in an intimate fashion for the first time one day at a private gun club (where an informal pigeon shooting was taking place), I was apprehensive but was at the same time relieved that the uncertain wait for his attack was over. Besides, since I knew not when, I had come to harbor a vague expectation that behind his eerie silence might lie an incredible wisdom—wisdom that might hold secrets to understanding my feelings of vulnerability and loss in the field. Thus, like a perfect victim in sadomasochism, with mixed anticipation and fear, I awaited his *pharmakon*, a simultaneous poison and cure. And as if delivering the answer to an enigma long brooded over, he released his venom simply and effectively: he asked me to kindly bring a crate of pigeons from the club pen.

Moments later, I found myself teetering toward the pen some thirty yards away, all my senses focused on the plastic crate uncertainly dangling at the farthest possible grasp of my limb, slippery with the smear of droppings, fine feathers, and cold sweat. A throng of bemused men looked on in suspense, awoken from the gun club routine at this refreshing spectacle that Farmer had ingeniously facilitated. The pen was a temporary holding station before the pigeons were carried to the shooting ground. It was a wire cage the size of a tiny bathroom with a very low ceiling. It now held the incredible number of two hundred pigeons—each enough to turn my stomach. There was a shelf about mid-height, and most seemed to be perched there shoulder-to-shoulder (or wing-to-wing) in an orderly fashion like a single many-headed monster. At least, that was my perception from some ten yards away; now that I was to open the door, general panic ripped through the whole crowd and they clambered to the four upper corners of the cage, the farthest possible points from the intruder, forming hives of pulsating dark gray masses on top of each other. Given the low ceiling, and a small misperception by the leader of the hysterical pack, any of those hives could easily become my hat.

At the gate, I hesitated and, despite myself, looked through the wire cage in the direction of Farmer (in a desperate search for signs of his unlikely change of mind). Far removed from the others' engrossed attention on me, he was turned to the side, in the direction of the inertness of the forest, and was quietly grinning to himself—apparently in deep satisfaction with his own thoughts. Meanwhile, between Farmer's serenity and me was the riot of a beastly fracas, like the obstacle of an epic trial in the way of blissful self-satisfaction. The realization of this insurmountable separation of our lots—his careless self-possession on the one hand and my bestial anguish on the other—suddenly began to engulf me with blind fury.

I, or whatever possessed me, flung the cage door open, strode in, and closed it behind me—leaving my usual self outside in shock. The hives instantly broke and all two hundred pigeons were simultaneously airborne, or so it seemed. Blissfully, I was prevented from seeing anything—other than a constant flap of wings across my face. In compliance with the seasoned pigeon handlers' adage, or bewitching myself into their possession, I did not try to catch them in midair barehanded but drove them into my grasp. The congestion helped my first practice of this adage not go terribly amiss. My furious grabbing hardly ever failed to repeat the mechanical operation of opening and closing the crate door without the shoving in of a wriggling handful in between, like so many socks into a laundry sack. My arms stiffened with goose bumps and yet mysteriously became more effective with the increasing petrifaction. The birds' resistance was beginning to no longer touch me; I began to feel only the reward of the increasing weight of a crate filling with willing submissions. For a flickering moment, I caught myself desiring this paroxysm of abandonment to continue.

When my nauseated senses recovered once I was outside the pen—in my newly acquired plumage of sweat and feathers—I shuddered at what I had done. Not so much at what had transgressed within my body, but at the result of my own transgression: in the crate, a few pigeons had had their wings and legs broken and one had been poked to death on the side of its stomach, leaving traces of bloody flesh under one of my fingernails. I staggered back to the crowd, half dragging my reluctant trophy, dizzy with the sense of rapidly draining lust, impotence, and an utter emptiness. The others were sheepishly quiet at the unexpected assault of my fiendish bravado; Farmer the sadomasochist tormentor had already forgotten about me, occupying himself with something else in total disinterest.

Thus I was abandoned to the lonely company of my crated prisoners. More precisely, I was abandoned to myself, made ever so strange and ecstatic by the artificially assumed impetus of fiendish devotion to Farmer's whimsical demand. But it was now a devotion that had lost its command, an execution without its authorizing injunction. No one now paid attention to my hard-won prizes. In that limbo, I could neither approach them nor go away: it seemed too childish to insist upon my feat; it appeared too disobedient to take Farmer's oblivion at its face value and go away. I knew not where to place us, the pigeons and me. I knew not whether to stand or sit. So I kind of cringed into a squat next to the crate, somewhere in between Farmer and the pen, and blankly watched the injured pigeons trying to stand up with their broken bodies again and again. That way, I became my own ridiculous material embodiment of the failure of "assimilation," of an overshot eagerness to please. There was something amazingly efficient about how my desire to be "in" had so directly acquired a stark "out"-ward manifestation, like something legible directly written all over me; like a hieroglyph of an impossible injunction (I was bound to fail) tattooed on my very body. At one moment, I was a meek servant of authority; in the next, an outlaw. At one moment, I was a protesting victim of bird phobia; in the next, a fiendish bird-goring victimizer. I slowly realized what a terrible zone of confusion I had gotten myself into.

Take Two

In August 1999, the annual tradition of the defiant showdown at the Labor Day Pigeon Shoot unwound itself just as it used to flare up—with baffling speed and abandon. The excitable vigilante supporters of the event now hastened to pronounce their enemy's victory with a sadistic pleasure and righteousness at the first sign of hostile moves by the Pennsylvania Supreme Court.

"It is not as if this took us by surprise," said the shoot organizer Bob Shade, referring to the Pennsylvania Supreme Court's decision to uphold the jurisdiction of a Philadelphia-based SPCA (Society for the Prevention of Cruelty of Animals) office within Schuylkill County, Pennsylvania—the home of the Labor Day Shoot.[1] He continued with a mysterious confidence: "There is no way we can stand up against the money machine of animal rights organizations and the liberal judges and politicians in their pockets. But we put up a good fight. It came out exactly as we have foreseen."

Here I was in the end, after seven years of belabored chasing after the Labor Day Shoot, now finally catching up with its sudden death. I suspended everything at the first hearing of the shoot's doom from the national news and rushed back to the field with mixed emotions—the relieved sense of closure, the drama of denouement, and shuddering at the renewed memory of the pigeons I had wrung and gored. I was driven to hopeless sentimentality when I paid what was likely to be my final visit to Bob and grimly threw a naive rhetorical question as our parting neared: "What do you think *I* could do?"

Instead of the expected niceties, such as an invitation to put the heroic preservation of the now-passing tradition in writing, he muttered with cold indifference after a pause: "You *will* do what you have to do; I don't think you can do much more than what your boss expects you to do."

Then came this, like an afterthought: "You have your green card to win."

I was paralyzed, despite Bob's benign countenance. On the surface, I must have worn a puzzled face at this bizarre association: what in the world do my bosses and their expectations have to do with the green card I was supposed to be interested in? But, somehow, I perfectly understood him, like a familiar summons or an accustomed name. Factually, he was wrong, but it was as if he knew me. Part of me wanted to protest and correct him, but the other part was already dangling out from under me—exposed, rendered familiar, and irredeemably culpable. I did not know how to respond: it seemed excessive to try to verbalize my innocence—what exactly am I innocent or guilty of? Yet it was too incriminating to keep quiet. His gratuitous summons thus magically held me in total indecision and helplessness—pinned down like a dumb object.

Speaking of facts, I had never mentioned my immigration status to anyone at any point during my entire fieldwork. Nor had anyone ever shown interest in the matter. If I did anything, during the seven years of getting acquainted with the enthusiasts of an event sponsored by the NRA and the Ku Klux Klan, it was toward (desperately) establishing myself, already suspect due to academic affiliations, as a politically disinterested outsider, an impartial observer, and more than anything else, a foreigner innocent of immigration ambitions. Nonetheless, out of nowhere, out of no sort of relationship I had developed in the field, no context of conversation I had established, emerged this sudden recognition.

This was not the Bob I used to know: amid occasional death threats and regular intimations of insult hurled in my direction, he was the only one, among the prominent figures in the community, who did not flinch from the liability of treating me like a regular human being, and the only one sagacious enough and willing to diffuse tension on my behalf. I begin my narrative from a sort of postscript, with an episode from my "post-field" return to the field, so surprised was I by Bob's proclamation and my vulnerability in it. My ethnographic past will never be the same with Bob's prophecy, having now been mortgaged between his prediction ("You will do what you have to do") and the haunting echo of his cocksure avowal ("It came out exactly as we have foreseen"). His prophecy feels hot on my forehead still as I write these passages, as I pursue credentials and advancement, that is, as I strive toward making do in Bob's nation. I have done exactly as he foresaw.

I was not intimidated or insulted by being associated with the wretched business of a green card. Nor was I exceptionally heartbroken by the possible signs of a seven-year-old friendship with an extraordinary informant falling by the wayside. What disturbed and simultaneously fascinated me then was the total confidence with which Bob caught me and my then yet-to-be-written narrative in the mode of always-already, as if coming back from the future. He precipitously confirmed and recognized, as if he has all too often seen my kind of narrative completed somewhere, and my kind of person issued a green card. Why this sudden banishment of our venerable friendship to an imaginary future "somewhere," where things will have taken place "exactly as he has foreseen?" Bob was not bitter or defensive. Far from it, he seemed as self-assured as ever, upright like an ascetic (having renounced the "money machine," perhaps) and elevated by the glamorous alliance of "Supreme" forces (from the mass media to the state's Supreme Court judges) that supposedly had to conspire together to put down his austere defiance. He was apprehensively self-possessed to the extent of being prophetic; self-satisfied almost to the point of being carelessly prophetic. Within the vaticinal spatiotemporality he has caught me thus; Bob's free movement in time was my fixity, his unmarkedness my markedness.

Take Three

But what does it mean to say that I was "caught" in Bob's chronotope of, shall we say, whiteness? Was I a willed-upon patient of someone else's action, an innocent but duped accomplice, a reluctant but obliging hostage, or a tolerant spectator? Having never been (mis)recognized as "white," I have thought of whiteness as some kind of positive membership from which I, a "non-white," was marked to be excluded. Having been trained in the scrupulousness of anti-racist liberalism in American higher education, I have grown to carry my reputed non-whiteness as a pious truth—a mark of entitlement to rigorous objectivity, to the point of embarking upon research as though to sequester and detain the scandalous felony of whiteness. It was as though we belonged to two externally opposing camps, "whites" and I, and my job was to throw light on, expose, confront, and, ultimately, overcome the positive actuality of the other camp.

The first complication announced itself in the following realization: My look that probes and objectifies whiteness is never an innocent means, because the look is already "included" in the picture it tries to decipher. My look is already caught, as it were, in none other than the look that recognizes me as non-white. Thus, my act of deciphering whiteness is in a way already "indebted" to another look. How can one conceptualize the relation between the two "looks?"

It is said that the eye of the Other returning my gaze from inside the picture I behold carves out a gaping hole, a shadow, within my own field of vision (Dolar 1996). If this were true, probing and understanding this picture would take more than illuminating the positivity of things in it. It would require seeing what necessarily evades my vision, as though making out darkness itself rather than outlining manifest figures. Jacques Lacan observed that the weight of the gaze of the Other—whether real or imagined, internalized or positivized in the other person—opens up a lack, a gaping hole in our consciousness: "When in love, I solicit a look, what is profoundly unsatisfying and always missing is that—*You never look at me from the place from which I see you.* Conversely, *what I look at is never what I wish to see*" (Lacan 1978:103; emphasis in the original). The passage captures the "traumatic" limit posed by the Other subject; the maddening inaccessibility, or the given condition of the non-coincidence of Other consciousnesses to which we are irreparably thrown—"You never look at me from the place from which I see you." Insofar as I am conscious of my being gazed at, which is given in any socialization, my own gaze is deprived, limited, and a shadow is cast upon it—"what I look at is never what I wish to see." This does not mean that a vision could have been once complete and is now stunted through socialization. We could just as well prioritize the negative: the experience of being seen is a precondition for any seeing act; making out shadow is a precondition for any act of "illumination."[2]

The "maddening non-coincidence" is precisely that, a madness. The thesis of negativity is not just a theory of epistemology but an intuition about our ontological condition/limit: a brutal cry of existential protest. It is an intuition that stalks only as the aftermath of a "gag," a maddening inability to find words in the first place. Negativity, in other words, is not a neutrally necessary "shadow" generally available to any articulated experience. Some see this shadow directly and make out the darkness itself, others do not, and some even deny its existence. This varying capacity, rather than positive membership, in time, became my measure of whiteness. One should not bargain away the weight of this existential burden that is unequally distributed in society with so contrived an embellishment as in the motley theories of "identity." It is in an attempt to give an austere testimony to this opacity, this "gag," that I turn to my most intimate, my most opaque madness: bird phobia. What do I mean by this?

Introducing the gaze of the Other (qua limit experience) should complicate the issue of identity or identification. For the idea of the Other is meant to inaugurate opacity that is beyond intersubjective (un)shareability. The gaze of the Other—as in Lacan's exegeses—is not simply unavailable for "identification"; it simultaneously invites it and denies its possibility. This double-bind structure is fully repeated in the rhetoric of assimilation: "Be like me! You can't be like me" (Santner 2006:39). The limit experience signaled by this formulation testifies neither to inclusion nor to exclusion alone—either possibility or impossibility of "identification." Its structure is a paradoxical inclusive exclusion; how, to stay with the motif of assimilation, one gets excluded precisely on account of acting on the solicitation to be included. There is, in that strange zone of inclusive exclusion, more at issue than (un)identifiable "worldviews"—that is, the dimension Lacan named the imaginary. What becomes painfully visible is the body. I put the same experience of the body this way earlier: "I became my own ridiculous material embodiment of the failure of 'assimilation' "—I became a hieroglyph of Farmer's impossible injunction, which held me "outside" even as it beckoned me with a possibility of "inclusion." Such a limit experience—whereby an (injunctional) impossibility directly acquires the opacity of the body—Eric Santner calls "creaturely life" (2006). Bird phobia finds its full relevance in this creaturely dimension.

Take Four

In the gaze, pigeons hold me. Behind the disguise of their sewed-in, button-like eyes, the creatures regard me in sidelong glances of apprehensive familiarity. No matter with what flock and in whatever climes the encounter might be, there is a sense of my being primordially given to their recognition—the recognition of none other than a birdphobe in me.

But the cruelty of such a gaze consists not in discrimination but in incrimination. For me, what is so intolerable about pigeons is the fact of our being bound together in a complicity of mutual recognition, an intimate recognition. What is so dreadful is the imminent prospect of this fretful recognition uncontrollably spiraling into a mutually invoked eruption of convulsive panic, on account of no party's willing such a turn. I guess what I really fear about pigeons, then, is not some unbridgeable difference or self-same otherness—from which I might protest my birdphobe victimhood—but my own fear reflected and threatening to be multiplied in them. It is as if my fear of them is never in the present tense, but rather takes the form of a precipitous anticipation of what scene of commotion might transpire in our encounter; not only fear *of* them but, shall we say, fear *for* both of us. Thus, in front of the pigeons, I split into two roles at once: the actor (of fear) and the spectator (of the fearful encounter). It is as if the encounter is organized in my anticipation on account of an absently present "third gaze." I suffer and endure that gaze. It is everywhere. (Pigeons? How can I resist suspecting their conspiratorial alliance with the imaginary spectator? Are they trying to entrap me in their association? To embarrass me? I don't know.)

Disgust, wrote Giorgio Agamben, quoting Walter Benjamin, not only involves an (active) repulsion but accompanies an anxiety over being seen in that condition: "The horror that stirs deep in man is an obscure awareness that in him something lives so akin to the animal that it might be recognized. . . . Whoever experiences disgust has in some way recognized himself in the object of his loathing and fears being recognized in turn" (Agamben

1999b:107). In this counterintuitive observation, the philosopher defines disgust as something other than the problem of self and other—the crisis of the "intersubjective" indistinction. That is, disgust pertains to more than the problem of "the other in me." Rather, disgust requires two contradictory movements whereby what is most intimate turns out to be also most alien, most "animal"—like "the other part" of me that "dangles out from under me." What is crucial is that for Agamben, too, what organizes this contradictory movement is what we might call the gaze of the Other—which (mis)recognizes what is the "animal" as part of me. On account of this *exposure* (to the gaze of the Other), I am held in limbo, somewhere in between "inclusion" and "exclusion." It holds me precisely insofar as I am already other-than to myself—that is, the "animal." An inclusive exclusion or exclusive inclusion, creaturely life, then, is the proper realm of disgust. Doesn't disgust, then, also carry the elemental bodily sign of opacity, which is the by-product of the injunctional impossibility of "assimilation"?

In the novel *The Pigeon* (1988), Patrick Süskind confirms the centrality of the unassumable presence of a gaze as that which frames the world of a pigeonphobe. The story depicts the span of twenty-four hours in which a certain Jonathan Noel's life is ruined because of a pigeon perched right in front of his apartment door, blocking his only exit to the world. Immediately, it is the gaze that grips his terrorized attention:

> It had laid its head to one side and was glaring at Jonathan with its left eye. This eye, a small, circular disc, brown with a black center, was dreadful to behold. It was . . . lashless, browless, quite naked, turned quite *shamelessly* to the world and monstrously open; . . . it seemed to be . . . lifeless, like the lens of a camera that swallows all external light and allows nothing to shine back out of its interior. No luster, no shimmer lay in that eye, not a spark of anything alive. It was an eye without sight. And it glared at Jonathan. (1988:14–15; emphasis added)

But the key is that this gaze, which he describes as "shameless," turns out to be besetting for Jonathan Noel, not circumscribed in the creature's dumb ownership. For what transpires from the introduction of the pigeon into his life, as the narrative progresses, is a faux pas of ultimate cruelty for the hypochondriac: he is reduced to pissing into his washing basin (the only public toilet being outside); when he manages an escape from his apartment Jonathan the bank security guard is forced to endure the embarrassment of having to stand in public with torn pants, et cetera. In the end, he finds himself virtually indistinguishable from a shameless beggar (known for public defecation) he used to so despise. "Tears flowed from his eyes . . . for the shame" (21), the author writes, as Jonathan watched his piss flow totally uninhibited and unchecked down his beloved washing basin. The "shameless gaze" ends up forcing an overwhelming feeling of shame on the protagonist.

In the end, then, bird phobia turns out to be more than the relation between the phobe and the bird, more than, shall we say, intersubjectivity. Once again, the escalation of Jonathan Noel's tragic confrontation with the pigeon takes place on account of no party's willingness particularly; the agency of the phobic encounter turns out to be "external" to both—insofar as the scene is organized around a third gaze, a shameless gaze.

But the truly irrational aspect that often escapes a non-phobic observer is still something else. It is the fact that there is a certain necessity about such a pandemic gaze, as if the gaze is "meant for me." It is pointless, for example, for a birdphobe to try to console him- or herself that an encounter with a bird is always *contingent*, that the bird could have been elsewhere and otherwise, that the world could be this way rather than that the next time around. As if facing present-at-hand choices, the phobe cannot afford to place him- or herself "before" the contingent possibilities of the world. Rather, as if by fate, the phobe always finds him- or herself already "there," thrown into an (phobic) encounter irreparably and senselessly. It is "by fate" because the script for *this* particular upstaging seems to have been intended for the phobe, with the whole world watching in complicity. The phobe *knows* perfectly well that it is absurd to imagine so; that, from the "natural" scheme of things, his or her particular encounter with a bird is just as insignificant and just as contingent as any other encounter between intraworldly things. But no matter, it is as if each encounter is a privileged moment that warps and pulls the whole world as an irreducible necessity—"necessary" to the precise extent that it is "subjective," un-natural, as if made up, and in violation of the inert indifference of the world of things.

Take Five

Just as in bird phobia, so it is in whiteness. A birdphobe cannot declare him- or herself the victim of avian kind, just as I, in time, found myself incapable of accusing anyone of the "crime" of whiteness. The bird, after all, is not

"responsible" for my phobia. There are neither factually describable positive memberships nor externally opposing "camps" here. So, phobia does
not belong in the juridical realm; there is no responsibility, guilt, or the factual truth of justice. But there is only, if I may dare use Primo Levi's term,
"brotherhood in abjection" (quoted in Agamben 1999b:17).

What we might call the shameless gaze of whiteness that organizes that
abjection is not agentivized in the white person—he or she does not "own"
it. Rather, the gaze around which the white racial scene is organized remains
that of the third party. What is impenetrable from the point of view of a
"phobe" is that that gaze, which belongs to a third party, instead of taxing
self-loss seems to *warrant* the white subject *self-possession*. Let me explain
this matrix of self-possession via a third party. Let us see how peculiar this
fantasy is, and, by comparison, how it is worthwhile to defend what one
might call the "ethical (in)sanity" of the world of a phobe.

Allow me to return to my last interview session with Bob Shade. On that
day, he was impenetrably removed, as if standing beside himself spectating.
He laboriously spat out words in my general direction—almost in the manner of careless monologue, as if forced into a tiresome regurgitation—in a
kind of semi-address. The manner, however, radically betrayed its content—
a flash of biting, abject, and prophetic "intuition" that riotously flared up at
the precise moment of his (the Labor Day Pigeon Shoot's) awesome defeat.
There was a distinct feeling of this discourse having been "spent," as if the
lines had been spoken already, and the script already tried with some previous audience. I felt as though my reaction was being tested, and a whole
crowd of Bob's invisible (erstwhile) interlocutors were listening in. Gone
was his habitual avoidance of eye contact; now, he was blankly staring at
me across the table with a faint smile, as if bemused by his own unfamiliar borrowed forwardness. His stare seemed not a bit interested in what it
saw, but was rather soliciting a look from elsewhere, showing rather than
looking—displaying a scandalized reaction rather than being scandalized
himself. There was something cruelly comic and unpredictably violent about
this disingenuous reflexive doubleness at my expense, like some kind of joke
that was always already rehearsed and set to be repeated.

According to Sigmund Freud, the joke or, more precisely, the tendentious
joke calls for at least three people: the joker, the butt, and the inactive third
listener in whom the joke is imagined to be registered (Freud 1964[1905]).
For him, the presupposition of the third listener was the reason the witticism
of the (tendentious) joke did not lose its power in its transmission and repeti-

tion in the form of indirect speech. Its presupposed but unspecified audience of "consensus" proves politically potent in building affective conformity and mobility, if not rational persuasion. The examples he considered were subversive practices in the fashion of "weapons of the weak" (Scott 1985). Kalpana Seshadri-Crooks, however, identifies the productivity of this structure at the core of racial violence, paradigmatically lynching (Seshadri-Crooks 2000:88): its theatrical collusion with the audience, its sportive indulgence as if in warrant, its ready transference of responsible agency as if on no one's account, and (as the result of the evacuated agency) the self-aggravating and reciprocally encouraging victim-victimizer deadlock. Something like the "madness" of auto-affection can we invoke here for both cases, the joke of the Freudian kind and Bob's, in that the joker "stands beside" as if passively in order to interpose him- or herself as an instrument for the amusement of an absent, inactive audience. Shameful and phobic madness this certainly is not. Here, an act of "active privation" (of reducing oneself to the status of an instrument), instead of affecting self-loss, *perverts* into an artifice of taking possession of oneself "objectively," as though through the eye of the Other.

In perversion, Joan Copjec writes, "the gap between the eye and the gaze that opens vision to the presence of the others as such has vanished. The difference between the eye and the gaze collapses, or as Lacan once put it, 'the contemplative eye' is confused 'with the eye [gaze] with which God [the Other] looks at [us]'" (2004:230). Here, we are no longer in the presence of "some" (indeterminate) other consciousness, of a public with which we maintain a relation of "uneasy indetermination," but of an infallible *law* with which we maintain a relation that leaves no room for doubt (230). This *coincidence of the eye with the gaze* (of the Other)—as though looking through the eyes of the Other, thus freed from the double bind of the assimilatory interpellation mentioned above—I take in this book as the most convincing figure of whiteness.

To continue with Freud's lesson, that "Other" is an unspecified consensus à la the silent majority on whose account the joke consummates. The joker, in other words, not only cracks a joke in itself but does so for itself, that is, he or she "doubles" and posits him- or herself as a joker in the eye of the Other. The joker, still in other words, not only makes a joke but performs being a joker, establishes and "takes possession" of him- or herself as a joker—"objectively," under the projected authority of what we might call the silent mainstream as the guarantor of "the objective." For the same reason, Kalpana Seshadri-Crooks points out that it is not enough to say, concerning racial violence, that the perpetrators spontaneously react to *seeing* the bodily "evidence of the eye" to which racism obsessively turns, that is, the skin, the hair, and so forth; as a prelude to violence, the perpetrator has to *see himself seeing* (2000:6–19).[3]

Take Six

White subjecthood defined so broadly attempts to respond to the most incisive challenge made by critical whiteness studies (for example, Frankenberg 1993, 1997; Rasmussen et al. 2001; Hill 1997): on whose account is a racial practice allowed to go on unimpeded, external to the everyday person or conscious agency? The question calls for raising the issue of race where no race is either explicitly spoken about or consciously identified. What the question draws our attention to is the fact that a rigorous commentary on whiteness cannot afford to overlook what we daily come to grant as the most objectively, consentaneously, factually, or, to use Süskind's expression, shamelessly, real. The goal of such a questioning is neither to reveal racism everywhere indiscriminately, nor to blunt the question of moral answerability. The goal for me, as I will elaborate in conclusion, is to return the testimonials to racism where they properly belong—the ethical realm.

For the notion of the ethical, let me re-invoke the motif of "brotherhood in abjection." Call this query a phobe's biased commentary on whiteness. A bestiary experiment, this query is bound to disappoint scholars of whiteness insofar as one subscribes the notion athropocentrically. What was so intolerable about my final encounter with Bob—if I may paraphrase my own descriptor for bird phobia—was the fact that we suddenly and uncharacteristically found ourselves bound together in a complicity of mutual recognition. What was so dreadful for me was the imminent prospect of this fretful recognition uncontrollably spiraling into a mutually invoked scansion of "misunderstandings," on account of no party's willing particularly. If I may continue paraphrasing: my fear of him that day took the form of a precipitous anticipation of what scene of commotion might transpire in our encounter; it was not only fear *of* him but, shall we say, *fear for both of us.*

The phrase "brotherhood in abjection" Primo Levi employs in reference to Auschwitz. "Brotherhood" because the death camp, in Giorgio Agamben's words, is a "zone of indistinction," where "victims become executioners and executioners become victims" (Agamben 1999b). In the chapter titled "The Gray Zone" Primo Levi himself writes: "The arrival in the Lager was indeed a shock because of the surprise it entailed. The world into which one was precipitated was terrible, yes, but also *indecipherable*: it did not conform to any model; the enemy was all around but also inside, the 'we' lost its limits, *the contenders were not two*, one could not discern a single frontier but rather many confused, perhaps innumerable frontiers, which stretched between each of us" (1988:38; emphasis added). Agamben annotates the meaning of the phrase the "gray zone": "It is the zone in which the 'long chain of conjunction between victim and executioner' comes loose, where the oppressed becomes oppressor and the executioner in turn appears as victim. A gray, incessant alchemy in which good and evil and, along with them, all the metals of traditional ethics reach their point of confusion" (1999b:21). Given this state of terrible "indistinction" or "indecipherability," Agamben challenges us to think of the possibility of bearing witness to the "darkness" called Auschwitz. What could he possibly mean by the claim of such a shocking indistinction, where the author and the patient of the ultimate horror are confused? A careful unpacking of his bold experiment will prepare me to envision what an ethical testimonial to—rather than a factual illumination of—the "darkness" of bird phobia might be, and, in turn, hopefully, that of whiteness.

What Agamben's reference to indistinction turns on is far from anything like a victim's complicity, let alone a second guessing of the verity of the willed wholesale butchery. Rather, Agamben's intervention—closely following that of Levi—aims to have us assume a responsibility that is far greater than any juridical judgment, with its supposed factual settling of the score between guilty parties and innocent victims, would have us resort to. He does not deny the need for juridical judgment; his only objection is that law should not be allowed to exhaust the matter—that an *ethical*, rather than factual, bearing of witness to the horrors of Auschwitz remains to be envisaged. The first step for him is the acknowledgment of the impossibility of factually signifying the experience of Auschwitz, as through a neutral, third-party gaze. Factuality, having to abandon the "first-person" testimonial to the libel of the subjective (or as a logical impossibility in the case of death), only admits to its terms the unbroken agency of the moral—that is, who did what to whom, who survived and who perished, and so forth. But what took place at the camp was the exact opposite: an arbitrary summoning of culpability based not on the agency of the person but on the groundlessly branded collectivity (as when a birdphobe meets his birds). Precisely because of its failure to come to terms with how subjects are thus "broken," senselessly and "madly," factuality invariably leads to the sterile lamentation for the unilateral passivity of the victim—senselessness finds a makeshift sense in a pathetic plea to "innocence."

Factuality, in short, fails to convey the full story of the profundity with which the dignity of the human being is violated at the camp. It fails to listen to, if I may repeat the expression, the brutal cry of existential protest gagged. The fact-finding vision only deals in illuminating the positive and does not comprehend our "madness" of seeing darkness itself. But, as Agamben argues through Aristotle, the truly human potential resides precisely in our ability to see darkness and to hear silence: "If (human) potentiality were, for example, only the potentiality for vision and if it existed only as such in the actuality of light, we could never experience darkness. . . . But human beings can, instead, see shadows, they can experience darkness: they have the potential not to see, the possibility of privation" (Agamben 1999a:181). Agamben continues: "The opposite of actuality for humans is not simple fading away, because (human) potentiality can maintain itself in relation to its own privation" (180). Thus, any positive potentiality in humans is a dialectical one: we can see only as a counterpoint to our ability to not see; we can illuminate the positive only as a counterpoint to our ability to see darkness itself. To bring back Lacan: being caught in the experience of being seen is a precondition for any seeing act; shadow is a precondition for any act of illumination. For this reason, human suffering is not simply a destruction through an opposing principle or force; what is destroyed at Auschwitz is not mere positive potentiality—in the form of unilateral passivity—but the potentiality that is also a potential for privation, that is, the being that *actively suffers its passivity.*

Hence the scandalous complacency of settling the accounts of Auschwitz's atrocity in the familiar terms of the oppressor versus the oppressed, as if the agency of one cancels out the other without a remainder. But Agamben's aim is not to make an exact estimation of a price of humanity paid at the camp but to find, to remind ourselves of, a properly *ethical* way to bear witness to the camp's destruction in terms other than juridical calculation. One of the most illuminating moves he makes toward this task, almost in passing, is his recovery of early Christianity's notion of witnessing: *martis* in the Greek, or the martyr (1999a:26–27). Martyrdom was where a Christian *bore witness to* his or her faith through death. The notion was used by the first Church Fathers to take account of the *senselessness* of the persecution of the Christians, who were the innocents put to death by the human law of the heretic. Why would God allow such a "meaningless" death? How does a Christian bear witness to his or her faith by being so unjustly and senselessly persecuted under the human law? Or, how does one bear witness to one's own death in the first place? The answer allows us to overcome the false (juridically conceived) choice between the first-person testimony and that of the third person.

The factual bearing of witness would not solve the scandal of the "irrationality" of martyrdom. To repeat, the factual witnessing, with its presumed access to a neutral, third-party point of view, in turn presupposes the positive coherence of the agent/patient of an action, as though they were mutually repelling, opposing forces. But martyrdom, precisely because it is without the pretense of direct access to a neutral point of view, solves the problem of "irrationality;" *the martyr is both the patient of persecution and the author of its witnessing, to which the action of the persecutor is, in a way, enlisted.* The martyr actively suffers his or her passivity. This does not in any way mean that the martyr is "in control" of the situation. It is, as it were, that the persecuted, rather than fearing the persecutor, fears *for* both of them. That way, the martyr's "passivity" is redeemed, its meaningfulness delivered over, if not accounted for, to a greater truth that is but still within the horizon of "subject-language."[4] The "irrationality" is resolved, thus, if not by some intervention from outside and beyond, but in excess of what the individual agency and knowledge would allow. That way, the "meaningfulness" is undying with the person of the martyr.

At this precise location of the passivity/activity indistinction, Agamben situates the ethics of witnessing. In other words, the ethical witnessing is only possible at a moment of the madness of *self-loss*, the moment when we are consigned to something that cannot be fully assumed by the agency of the person. "Shame" is the name Agamben gives to the "emotive tonality" of a being exposed or abandoned to such an unassumable force, a loss that is paradoxically an excess, a disempowerment that is also an empowerment.

I do not know what word better describes the "emotive tonality" of my being caught in Bob's chronotope of whiteness than "shame." As the expression goes, it is a shame that he did what he did that day. To the extent that I say that, I do not fear the person of Bob Shade—I fear for both of us. Finding myself "bound together in a complicity of mutual recognition" with Bob, I find myself blushing. It is as if in this uncontrollable blushing I effortlessly trespass Bob's innermost interiority and from there can be ashamed for him as he himself is momentarily unable to be, having been lost in the perversion of whiteness. My only reference is to my inability to accuse—*impotentia judicandi*, as Primo Levi would write (1988:60)—even as I feel "gagged." It is as though this shame will survive my clumsy attempts at accusation. So it is from the darkness of self-loss and from the groundless feeling of liability, rather than from the entitlement of innocent victimhood, that I wish to open my "testimonial."

CHAPTER ONE

Cruelty through Glassy Eyes

They drink, smoke, kill animals in front of their children. They are
wife beaters, they beat their children, praise their children for killing
animals. They said to me, "Wring her neck," asked for my number,
and sexually harassed me. There are KKKs. I see Nazis. I hear racial
comments toward blacks. They will kill anybody if they get the chance.
—An animal rights activist from Ann Arbor, Michigan, on her
experience at the Labor Day Pigeon Shoot

I could not have missed the Labor Day Pigeon Shoot controversy while con-
ducting fieldwork among Chicago-area animal rights groups in the early
1990s. Though a relatively minor event in terms of the number of animals
involved, the event's gratuitous exhibitionist inclination was widely anticipated to stir up a new level of passion in the entire animal rights movement
(*Animal's Agenda* 1992). In response to my curiosity, my informants flooded
me with videotapes and newspaper clippings on the shoot and the protest
against it. I studied them carefully, at first because of the singular emotion
this decidedly working-class slaughter of a few thousand birds seemed to stir
in my informants. It is a passion, for example, unmatched by the plight of a
million cows.

Regardless of the medium—whether from the mouth of an animal rights
activist, television news (local or national), or newspapers—views on the
Labor Day Shoot expressed from a distance seemed to return to the same
point again and again. They all seemed to agree that the controversy was,
to use an expression in an article in the *Washington Post*, a quintessential

moment in the ongoing "war of philosophies" that divides the nation in half today (1992): a war between "liberals" and "conservatives," urbanites and rural populations—or in the brusque locution of animal rights activists— between "the enlightened" and the "barbarians." The model after which the images were conjured up was the abortion issue: two sides drawn up neatly and passionately in a duel between pros and cons, one side just as unyield-ingly committed and resourceful as the other. News clips I was given went back and forth between shots of pigeon deaths and those of screaming fa-natics, and topped them off with an obligatory course of interviews with "spokespersons" from each side. It was a readily recognizable spectacle: an eye-catching scene of clashing cultures but nonetheless suggestive of an in-tegrated social order with each side connected to the "centers" of the society (Shils 1975), represented by spokespersons of liberalism and conservatism. It was a ritual of political contestation in a "democratic society," a case of a "media event" (Dayan and Katz 1992a) with all its sensationalistic details and overarching prudent rationalism.

However, the more I looked at those news clips, the more frequently and compulsively my eyes followed devious details. Why is that man giggling in the background? Why do some people glare at the camera? Who are the shooters, and why do they look so different (generally wealthier) and de-tached from the spectators? Why are animal rights activists standing side by side with supporters of the shoot? Are they allowed inside the place of the shooting?

I made my first trip to the Labor Day Shoot with an excitement not unlike that of flocking to a neighborhood disaster reported on television. On Labor Day morning, I watched television in the motel where I was staying; the TV programs instantly brought on images from past shoots, as if they had been covering the pigeon shoot issue all along. Having been reminded of the im-pending "showdown" all morning, and having armed myself with the histori-cal literature on the clashes between the bourgeois humane sensibility and the plebeian "cruel customs,"[1] I headed for my first shoot expecting to find a carnivalesque blood sport with an engaged crowd and a sharply divided battle between "urban protesters" and "rural supporters" on the sidelines.

Hegins, the home of the Labor Day Pigeon Shoot, is a small town of about 900 residents located in the Appalachian Mountains of the central Pennsylvania coal mining region. The town is seated at the southwest fringe of Schuylkill County (fifty miles northeast of Harrisburg), once the nation's anthracite coal mining capital and a hotbed of early labor movements (Blatz

1994, Palladino 1991, Wallace 1987). Since coal's downturn as the nation's energy source beginning at the end of the Second World War, the region has been going through a steady deindustrialization and population loss, whose turbulent social effects are felt to this day (Dublin 1997, 1998; Marsh 1987). From 1930 to 1986, the population of the county dropped from 235,505 to 156,400. During the same period, employment in anthracite mining dropped from 45,800 to 8,500 (Schuylkill Economic Development Co. 1995).[2]

No one had suspected that the obscure Labor Day Pigeon Shoot would turn into a world-scale tradition of pigeon massacre, until 1985, when a notable Jewish family in the area complained of the "blood sport" (*New York Times* 1991). When word about the first protest traveled through the local media, thousands (five thousand to eight thousand) of blue-collar residents from surrounding areas of the county turned up at the shoot. They were predominantly working miners, ex-miners, or descendants of miners. In subsequent years, phalanxes of activists fortified the animal rights contingent, while on the other side, an assortment of nationwide conservative advocacy groups for gun rights, hunting rights, white supremacy, paramilitary survivalism, and the outlawing of abortion rushed to the pigeon shoot's defense—deeming the heritage of pigeon shooting a bastion of conservative values. Amid the lavish attention of the mass media, yearly battles have gone on ever since between those who support the shoot and those who protest, between those who try to "rescue" wounded birds and those who maim and decapitate as many birds as they can lay their hands on.

I gathered this much from the safety of distance. Now that I was entering the field-level confrontation for the first time, my mind was heavy with uncertainty as State Route 25 inexorably turned into Main Street of Hegins Township. Despite having received numerous discreet letters of introduction, Bob Shade, the shoot organizer, sounded impenetrably severe on the telephone; he did not waste a minute in abandoning me to the company of his sly mouthpiece of an attorney. As if in a concerted show of unapproachability, no lodging for an outsider was to be yielded within the entire Hegins Valley area (which includes Hegins, Valley View, Lamberton, and Fountain). At least, the twenty-minute drive from my lodging at the county seat, Pottsville, was soothingly picturesque and lonesome that morning. As that was about to end, and more and more houses pressed close to both sides of the road, I had that familiar sensation of splitting self in the face of mounting pressure: part of me was stepping aside to have a good view of the impending disaster from a safe distance.

As with most patches of inhabitance in central Pennsylvania, Hegins is sandwiched between the formidable fortresses of parallel mountains, running in a northeast-southwesterly direction. This parallel orientation gives an added sense of orderliness to the community of predominantly "Pennsylvania Germans," already known for their tidiness. Neat houses with scrupulous homely decorations pressed up against the Main Street as if to keep vigilance, assisted by the imposing mountains closing off on both sides from afar. It was a holiday morning, and a lot of residents were visible on their lawns, seemingly occupied with domestic chores but keenly apprehensive of the passing cars.

The car I was driving seemed to be causing a momentary general stoppage in the entire community lined up along Main Street: bodies bent on flower beds were straightened, lawn mowers were stopped at curvings, garage sales tables were momentarily abandoned, et cetera, all to cast bold stares at me or my car, until we were seen no more. These erect and adamant stares were very fresh to me, since I had gotten used only to quick and furtive glances in the city. It was an unusual experience to be stared at behind the privacy of one's car in the first place. Only much later did I come to realize that driving a Japanese make in Schuylkill County was just about the worst an anonymity-seeking Asian could do; you could not possibly wear a larger face of un-Americanism.

The eighty-acre Hegins Community Park, the location of the Labor Day Shoot, sits at the south of Main Street on a gentle slope that continues downward until it is embraced by the mound of a mountain thick with foliage. The homely statement the panorama provides is quite convincing: rolling hills, well-trimmed turf grass, sparse mushrooms of white homes, and the background distant hue of the mountain. The park unassumingly emerges in the middle of it behind the three-acre plot of grass that is used as a parking lot on Labor Day. On the morning of the shoot, the park itself is impeccably adorned with neighborly statements: new playground fixtures are installed and old ones are freshly painted with bright colors in childish patterns; a fire engine, that ultimate symbol of voluntarism in the American countryside, is carefully polished and positioned at the entrance of the park; a huge brick outdoor oven for the communal barbecue is built; a Stars and Stripes is raised during the sudden and boastful solemnity of the national anthem.[3]

It was close to eight o'clock and the parking lot was already half full. I parked at the end of an endless row of pickup trucks. Almost immediately,

I (or, perhaps, my car) was met with a group of curiosity-seekers. Astonishments and exclamations broke out as I emerged from the car: "Well, well, what do we have here!" smirked one man; "Man, them shoot is gittin' famous!" quipped another.

But none came close enough for a real inspection; we kept a respectable distance and went our separate ways. Near the entrance, I spotted a group of animal rights activists. They looked absorbed and purposeful—talking into walkie-talkies, eyebrows knitted, engaged in serious discussions—and all but ignored me after fleeting, somewhat irritated glances.

As I looked around, the animal rights activists were readily discernible in the crowd. Most of them were dressed in two kinds of T-shirts. The white shirts had the logo of PETA (People for the Ethical Treatment of Animals), and the blue ones that of FOA (the Fund for Animals). There were arm bands on some of the activists. From afar, they must look like chess pieces, I thought to myself; a display of team allegiance was half the battle for them. Clearly, the two groups were working together, but there was no confusing them because of the uniforms. As in the battle scenes of Akira Kurosawa's films, there was a feeling that an absurd emphasis was being given to the display of clannish identity over what is being claimed as the utmost importance: a life and death battle.

To one side of the entrance, the eastern stretch of the park's fence was littered with the motley placards and banners of the animal rights activists: "Killing just for the sport of it?"; "Vote to ban legalized murder"; "Hegins and the Klan go hand in hand"; "No cross burning, no bird shooting." And then, the voice of the nation itself followed: "Arizona is against the shoot"; "Utah protests this cruel sport"; "Michigan protests the pigeon shoot"; and so on. There was a lonely display of countering voices as well. Two men carried placards of much sturdier construction with a duplicated message: "Pigeons are rats with wings! Shoot 'em!!"

Inside the Shoot

Telling opponents apart inside the park was an entirely different affair. The ideologically divided "battle" I was driven to envision endured only up to the parking lot with its banners and placards. From the entrance, I quickly lost sight of the protesters in the sea of bodies milling around aimlessly but with a look of a thirst for trouble. And I lost sight of the ideological divisions in the suffused atmosphere of barely held mischievous ferocity ready to explode at anyone indiscriminately. Nothing was happening; the place was filled with eager and anxious onlookers-to-be, but there was nothing to see. As if in a disorganized ball, the entire body of the crowd seemed to be unsurely drifting about, eyeing each other uncertainly for cues that were not forthcoming. Of course, there were occasional attractions, like myself or sightly women protesters. But the crowd in general seemed to be quite single-mindedly preoccupied with vague anticipation of an indefinite future attraction, and their restless gazes quickly moved on from us after obligatory pauses. It was as if I were in a giant game of musical chairs, with thousands of willing players but no one to stop the music.

The shooting game itself was pitiably uneventful. According to a frequently used expression at the shoot, "It's like watching the grass grow." Six games go on simultaneously at the Labor Day Shoot, three double-barrel games facing south and three single-barrel games facing north, toward Main Street. In the middle of the two stretches of game is the spectator area, with food vendors, park facilities, a playground, bathrooms, et cetera. Since the protest in 1991, when a legion of protesters ran out to the shooting range in order to disrupt the shoot, high fences have separated the shooting and the spectator areas. I believe this move has sapped much fun out of the game. The shooter is far away, and the birds still farther. There are chances neither to become familiar with particular shooters nor to behold the gory details of pigeons getting blasted. Only when a shooter's turn is called is he admitted beyond the fence, past tight security.[4] He does a couple of practice sightings and steps up to the firing line. He yells "pull" and the puller (who is also the referee) chooses one of eight shoe-box-like traps, which are thirty-four yards away, and collapses the trap (by pulling a rope), at which time the pigeon in it takes flight. This repetitious scene of a feeble pair of wings rising and fainting motionless, or flying away unscathed, continues from dawn to dusk. It is only close to sunset that a mildly exciting tournament "shoot-out" takes place among a handful of contenders for a trophy. But overall, the crowd pays only intermittent and languid attention to the shooting game.

Toward noon, the mood of the crowd changed dramatically. The morning-long beer consumption might have been taking effect, the deterrence-efficacy of the state troopers' presence might have been wearing thin with the swelling crowd. But the most noticeable change was the arrival of the media personnel. Their debut at the shoot is always dramatic. First, there is the media bus, with its noisy generator, lofty satellite dish, and the familiar national network logo. Then, there are the relentless cameramen, the zealous equipment staff, and the star-complexed reporter. They will trample on anything, stop at no protest, and excuse themselves before no one. Through relatively few in number—altogether not more than fifty, including newspaper reporters—they possess a singular ability to stir up the crowd in movement and in spirits. Their arrival cannot be missed.

It seemed that the size of the crowd almost doubled around the time of the media's arrival. The midday air was sultry and dusty with the sheer number of people moving about. The aimless wanderings of the crowd continued, now, to be disturbed by regular outbreaks of commotion. They flared up out of nowhere in the idly milling crowd and disappeared just as quickly, leaving only traces of curious gossipers. They flared up when shoot supporters young and old raced and wrestled with animal rights activists for the wounded birds that fell into the spectator area; when members of the Ku Klux Klan got into shouting and shoving matches with reporters and protesters; when crowds of unemployed miners tangled with state troopers and vandalized park facilities and media crews' equipment. But, by far, the commotion caused by falling wounded birds was the most frequent and the most intense.

Caught by a supporter of the shoot, the pigeon is subjected to a celebratory theatrics of flamboyant lynching; by an animal rights protester, moments of soothing care by veterinarians, and most likely a comforting euthanasia at the Wounded Bird First Aid Station, a makeshift veterinary care unit at the parking lot. However, at moments of competition for a wounded bird, the apprehensive and timid handling of the rescuers is usually no match for the relentless clasps of the shoot's supporters. For protesters are generally awkward with pigeons; wounded pigeons rescued by protesters tend to put up all kinds of struggle, fluttering and rolling their panicky eyes wildly while being precariously hustled away at arm's length in an unhandy grasp.

In contrast, shoot supporters display an unflinching familiarity with the birds. It does not have to be someone especially charged with the handling of birds or someone of a weathered exposure to them; virtually any man on the side of the shoot supporters is a ready and willing handler of the beasts, which are often in grotesque condition. I could not help apprehending a certain cruel beauty in such a human-pigeon relationship. It is as if the helpless victims find comfort in the sure grip of confident and thick-skinned handlers. Birds are calm in the hands of their executioners, turning submissive and malleable as if giving up resistance in the face of irresistible domination and doom. Of course, skills vary and men tend to show off their artful ways with pigeons. An experienced hand never forces the bird visibly, never allows it to flutter and struggle while its life is cut short, but imperceptibly, with the smallest of motions, squeezes and snaps to let its breath drain out, almost despite itself. Stains of droppings or splashes of blood on hands and clothes go completely ignored, as pigeon handlers go straight back to their beer bottles and sandwiches.

But by far the favored method of killing is decapitation by mouth or fingers. These tend to be highly theatricalized acts that follow a tacit, albeit loose, convention. When a teenage boy secures a bird, for example, the captive is submissively and with much pride relinquished to a demanding nearby adult man. The newly charged paternalistic master of ceremony then would take his time, beating his chest, verbally abusing the bird, and hurrahing slogans until a good crowd gathers around in jestful cheer and anticipation, in horror, or with camera at the ready. As if to make a speech, the more flamboyant of these will seek a higher ground or a picnic table for a better display. The crowd responds in a rousing and rowdy cacophony of urges to kill, along with a few shrieks of threat and beseeching. Then comes the kill, with lightning speed, as an abrupt punctuation, as if nothing could be more insignificant and easier. Some simply fling the bird through the air with one hand, letting centrifugal force do the job. The head and the body are tossed their separate ways, onto the eagerly stretched spikes of arms. Heads are usually pocketed, and the body, still fluttering, is finished off some more by hands and feet that pull and kick in all directions. Some heroes of these theatrics are emotionally carried away, calling their children onto the "stage," cheering and hurrahing with them some more, hugging them, kissing them, and, with surprising frequency, lovingly smearing blood all over their faces in the process.

Such confrontations and theatrics suck in crowds, nearly emptying the rest of the space of the park momentarily. Media crews scuttling to and fro add to the pandemonium. And not to miss this gratuitous attention, politicians running for office stride in sashes and with big smiles, while in the sky their advertising Cessnas trail banners—"So and so for D. A." This indiscriminate and swarming mass of chaos assaulted my senses and overwhelmed my wit. The only "order" I could see, my intellect having been taken over by the instinct of self-defense, was the rule-of-thumb fact that "outsiders" in whatever shapes were targeted: next to the protesters, African American state troopers were spat at, reporters' cameras were grabbed, and my persistence was once ended with an epithet for the Asian race and a fierce shove.

Miming

For years, I could never get over these afternoon affairs at the shoot, with its sheer number of bodies and the intensity of movement. Usually, lost in the sea of unrelenting cold stares of curiosity, desperate to convince myself of "doing fieldwork," I too, busied myself aimlessly pursuing to and fro these rowdy entourages of frantic birds and human bodies. The intensity of the action and passion in such scrambling, as seen from the Introduction's epigraph, is enough to raise an old man nearing his deathbed. Consequently, however earnestly I inflated my professionalism, instinctively I always found my small body arriving at the edge of the solid wall of huddled onlookers too late—except one day.

It began with a scene quite common at the shoot: a protester or two chasing after a wounded pigeon and the spectators trying to prevent that. This time, it was an unbalanced competition between a stout female protester (the Fund for Animals' national director) and a nine-year-old boy:

> I froze as the bird, frantically avoiding the two pursuers, directly flew (or leaped) in my direction in several bounces. By I do not know what, I was knocked down to the ground and the lens of my camera was thrown in the air. A collision between the competitors sent the boy skidding underneath a parked truck. The boy's parents were on hand and verbal assaults broke out immediately. The parents cried attempted murder and exaggeratedly examined the boy from head to toe, heedless to the protests of the embarrassed victim. Onlookers, media crews, state troopers, and additional protesters quickly squeezed onto the scene. Left and right, there erupted the question "What happened?" among the latecomers who had failed to bear witness. Within minutes, several versions of what happened were made available, some embellished beyond recognition in the process of being told and retold, from mouth to mouth. . . . Because the incident involved a child, anti-abortion rhetoric seized hold of the crowd's imagination at one point and everyone began to drive at the theme of the animal rights activists as "child haters," "pro-abortion city slickers," and even "child molesters." They ranted that liberals

like animal rights activists were willing to "sacrifice" children for their decadent lifestyles of welfare, teenage pregnancy, drugs, promiscuity, and homosexuality.[5] As if holding up the evidence of an attempted child sacrifice by animal rights witchcraft, the crowd kept pointing at a deep dent on the fender of the truck in question (deep enough not to have been caused by a pushed child) whenever reciting the story of "what happened." The voices got louder and louder as a television camera began to roll. From behind the camera, some cried for a bloody revenge, some admonished the boy—who was by now wearing a terrified oafish grin—to stop smiling and look hurt. But even as the accused and the accusers were led away by the police, the crowd refused to disperse. Instead, people grew more agitated and rowdier even without the protesters' presence: a hand from the throng snatched a cameraman's hat, another pulled at the microphone cable, still another sprinkled beer at an interviewing reporter, tumbled over a garbage drum, and went on to hurl the bird in question (by now completely forgotten) by its neck until its headless body slammed on the dusty ground with a muffled thud. Then, he picked up the headless body, looked around, and spotting me, threw it at my feet. The bird, or what remained of it, landed upright facing me, a foot away from my feet, buttressed by a stub of grass underneath. The stem of bloody white spine quivered slightly at the missing head, glistening in dull red under the blazing midday sun. I thought I saw an attempt of a bob and froze in instinctive anticipation, perhaps to comprehend the "last gesture" addressed to me, or something—but it was not forthcoming. Very slowly and laboriously the wings spread to the open position. The body stooped as if in deflation and stopped. (revised field note, 1995)

With this incident, I felt I was made part of the shoot, not in the sense of being "accepted"—as the Geertzes would feel accepted into an already contained cultural scene after that fabled cockfight raid (Geertz 1973)—but as one would be implicated. This was the day the shoot, its madness, came over me in fluttering leaps and bounds in all its avian queasiness and hysteria. All in all, the incident was typical of the affairs at the shoot: its "out-of-hand" nature, its senselessness, its uncontrollable acceleration on no one's particular account. But on this day, I felt culpable, even as I felt violated, as though witnessing a fit of profligacy and violence unleashed on my account. It was downright horrifying to so helplessly watch the unending trails of sadism seemingly coming out of myself.[6]

If I were an animal rights activist, I don't think I would be capable of such a feeling of vulnerability, even if the whole menacing crowd confronted me with nothing but antagonism. For I would be blinded by the faith that how they act is what they are, that there is no distance whatsoever between their savagery and their "true nature"—their inherent violent essence. But to me, hooliganish behaviors are filled with what one might call parodic detachment. It is as if the shoot supporters are intoxicated in playing out the role that is expected of them by their opponents, precisely and excessively. We had a glimpse of this in the episode imparted in the Introduction's epigraph. In it, the shocking split between the old man's inactive everyday body and the sudden fit of spiteful energy he so flamboyantly displayed stands as a terse testimony to the detachable nature of the villainous character at the shoot. Through this transferable role-taking behavior, one heroically inhabits a momentary "spokesperson" when feeling the censuring gaze of an "outsider." Had the camera not been there or had the pigeon not fallen next to him that day, the old man could not possibly have become a villain whom the animal rights organizations later put on their "most wanted" list. The result is as though it were due to the combined effects of the extemporaneity of the camera-induced role-playing and the unpredictability of the animal mobility; the "cruel" subject that emerged through the old man is temporally and spatially removed from the person of the perpetrator. One can safely conjecture that an act of aggression at the shoot is not so much an ideologically informed, much less raw, "explosion" as it is a rehearsed mime.

This impression of a subversive detached air was prefigured by my first encounter with Bob Shade. I remember being shocked to find him a kind of cynic. A slender and elegant grandfatherly man in his sixties, self-collected to an extreme degree, exacting in speech but easy in manner, he silently made a mockery of the dreaded idea of "rural bigot" I had secretly come to harbor after viewing national media reports and after conjuring up such an individual as a reflected twin image of the relentless and demanding animal rights activists I had known. For one thing, he repeatedly used the phrase "this circus" to refer to his duty as the spokesperson of the shoot and expressed, with a perfect professorial air, a profound sympathy for a foreigner who was moved to devote a thesis to such a "phenomenon." He informed me that the shoot had been a humble social event for local pigeon and gun enthusiasts since the 1930s and was on its way to oblivion anyway when the animal rights activists showed up. But now the event had become by far the biggest money maker for the upkeep of the park facilities, the fire company, and other community services. He added that, not being a gun enthusiast himself, he would rather the village do something other than the "media circus" if an alternative would promise the same profit. But as it is, it continues, and more than anything else "the whole community came together" because of the opposition. Since our first conversation, Bob has remained to me a modest man reluctantly caught in an extravagant agitation, and yet all the evidence indicated that he was a spirited warrior leader.

Bob Shade was not alone in this strange mixture of cynicism and determination. All of his staff officers for the Labor Day Committee, which runs the shoot, were good-humored about their involvement in the event—except perhaps their attorney, Jim Schaeffer, who zealously stood guard over the feeble flame of hostilities he had fanned. No volunteer for the shoot (which all of the staff members were) seemed to be afflicted with a rabid commitment to the cause, and yet, amid habitual disclaimers verging on self-mockery, the preparation for the shoot always proceeded with a remarkably willing proficiency, and the event grew and grew. For an unsuspecting researcher—with a complacent adherence to cliché ideas of "ideological differences" and "clashing values," such as I was—this was a little disconcerting; it was as if there was no robust object on which to hang the purpose of fieldwork. The only tangible thing was the sudden and explosive "flourish" on the day of the shoot, without befitting arousals and rallying cries leading to it. The "consequence" did not add up from observable "causes"; the shoot magically flared up from the gentle hands of those who sounded serenely detached, as if staying above all the forays.

Hence, the source of my feeling vulnerable and stupefied when thrown in the middle of the shoot's furor was this: I was not "prepared" for it; the agitation was senseless, filled with, or emptied by, a sort of parodic excess. Miming breeds subversive impulses, almost naturally digresses into capricious hooliganism. Such a hooliganism is disconcerting to the extent that it is seemingly aimless, devoid of agendas, and singularly unconcerned with consequences, as if warranted by, and the responsibilities relegated to, some indefinite Other, a third gaze perhaps—be it a foreign anthropologist, protesters, out-of-county state troopers, or media personnel. What is miming if not Self-othering or Self-doubling in the name of the Other of the audience (Taussig 1993)? Such a splitting into two was the only way I could make sense of the general havoc wreaked on Labor Day, and on Labor Day only, by otherwise sensible and responsible men of the region I became better acquainted with later. Within this exceptional chronotope, I came to be fearful of possible intimidation even from proven congenial acquaintances. More appositely, I came to fear for all of us, for myself and the acquaintances alike; I came to be fearful of the imminent possibility of our encounter spiraling into a mutually invoked "scansion of misunderstandings." Thus my inquiry moved from the self-same agency I thought I could find behind the shoot-supporting crowd to some Other that seemed to cause a splitting in them. In this chapter and the next, I turn to the obvious Other: the animal rights activists. In Chapters 3 and 5, I turn to the mass media and conspiracy theories it inspires.

The Gaze of the Glassy Eye

. . . like the lens of a camera that swallows all external light and allows nothing to shine back out of its interior . . .

—Patrick Süskind, The Pigeon

See, them eyes are always glassy and wandering? They are high, they are drugged, man!

—Tom Klinger on the animal rights activists
at the Labor Day Pigeon Shoot

The gaze is concealed by an eye, i.e., by its very organ.

—Slavoj Žižek on Descartes's fantasy gaze

Around 1989, as the shoot protest matured, the participating animal rights organizations began to put more and more emphasis not on demonstrating but on "documenting" the event. My fieldwork did not begin until 1993, but Dan Nerle, a reporter from The Pottsville Republican, vividly recalled the year "Steve," that famous buffoon of an activist from Chicago, got into a fight with Tom Klinger (September 4, 1995). "Steve" showed up at the shoot not in his usual martial arts uniform but with an inordinate amount of elaborate video equipment, saying that he was now "documenting" the shoot.[7] Thus he embarked upon what was a meticulously plotted scheme to record the entire event on a scale comparable to telecasting, with the deployment of a massive quantity of still—and video—photography equipment.[8] Whenever there was action—altercations, arrests, shouting matches, illegal firing of a gun, excessive cruelty, et cetera—within minutes, the central command enclave of the protest dispatched a cameraman through walkie-talkies. In addition, a cameraman was designated to each troop of protesters assigned to rescuing wounded birds, to capture every possible close-up of the pigeon victims, every move of aggression on the part of the shoot's supporters, and every act of heroism by the protesters. It was as if the entire body of protesters were there now narcissistically to star in a documentary of their own authorship. Gradually, it became hardly possible to sharply distinguish animal rights protesters from the media crews, and accordingly, a new derisive epithet came into circulation among the shoot's supporters to designate those look-alike outsiders: "the media people."

Thus, when Tom Klinger remarked upon the "glassy, wandering eyes" of the protesters, he was merely voicing the charge that was already enjoying much currency among the shoot's supporters.[9] The individual protesters were specifically instructed to avoid face-offs as much as possible, and to concentrate their efforts on documenting.[10] This was carried out with such a remarkable discipline that when I had to follow a protester or two around, I was often amazed at how nonchalant, haughty, and abstracted an isolated activist could be while being surrounded by hundreds of menacing supporters of the shoot. They managed to wrap themselves in a coat of mysterious abstraction to the increasing irritation and frustration of the shoot's supporters, who seemed to become more disposed to taunt, yell, and shove.

For Warner Klinger, Tom Klinger's father, this new attitude of a reporter-like haughtiness and abstraction on the part of the protesters was more evidence of collusion between the media and the protestors. Thus he growled in total frustration one day: "When we have differences among ourselves, we talk it out or fight it out with each other—we don't do press conferences first." Curiously, as if in answer to Warner's complaint, Bob Shade added: "All them protesters are drugged before being bused in here. That's why they never look at you straight in the eye."

Hence, the "glassy eye" around the shoot became more than a metaphor or synecdoche for that focal apparatus of the Outsiders, the camera lens. It came to embody the general state of psychedelia indiscriminately infecting the outside world. These mutually reinforcing images were invoked again and again among the shoot's supporters, as if they were suddenly betrayed by the protesters who stopped fighting back—as if inscrutability was more offensive than insubordination. In terms of sheer quantity, it cannot be said that this change in the protesters' tactics invited more violence. But certainly, the violence turned more hysterical.

An instructional brochure from the Fund for Animals admonishes the individual protesters to use their cameras "like a weapon"—always to place them between themselves and the confronting adversary—to deter serious physical assaults and to provoke humiliation. I think this line of instruction captures (and prescribes) the dynamics of the shoot exceedingly well: it admonishes an inciting of action and the recording of it at the same time—some weapon that is.

What motivates what one might call the "theatrical awareness" of the protesters, which drives them to prioritize press conferences, avert face-offs, and indulge in self-image making? The overriding prerogative in the "documentation" is to use the collected images in the organizations' mass fundraising efforts (and in political lobbying to a much smaller extent). Thus, the protesters' behavior "in the field" is governed by the fact that their critical mass, their patrons and sponsors, are imagined to be *elsewhere*—an abstracted and homogenized category of tens of thousands of spectators, whose transcendent existence is conceivable only through electronic media technology and who are reachable only in terms of an encapsulated imagery fit for mass circulation. In Hegins, in the abstracted disposition of the protesters, we glimpse a mass-media-driven politics of image and affect in the making; what we witness from the clash at the shoot is the "raw material" of a political conflict before it is pre-packaged and made fit for mass circulation for privatized, intimate consumption elsewhere.

This requires us to explore what might be called the political culture of animal rights activism from an uncommon angle: by identifying and analyzing the main conduit through which its public sphere of supporters is solicited into existence. The focus here is on the crucial historical and sociological events and moves in the formation of such a conduit as a *genre*, to which the issue of the Labor Day Shoot is merely one instance. This will be the subject of Chapter 2.

The Camera and the Glove

Situated outside Hegins Community Park on the high slope of its parking lot, the Wounded Bird First Aid Station is the headquarters of the protesters. Standing there, one gets a good command of the entire northern side of the park where the shooting games take place. It is made up of tents and a van, and it is surrounded by a caravan of automobiles. It is readily recognizable amid a sea of cars not only because of its showy sign, which is almost the size of a van, but also because the vehicles surrounding it and demarcating the territory are the kinds not normally seen in the area: lots of foreign makes and the latest model sport utility vehicles. Wounded birds collected inside the park by the rescuers are sporadically brought in here all day long, where three or four veterinarians busy themselves tending them. Despite the continuous gory scenes and frantic resuscitation efforts, the station is eerily peaceful, except for very occasional sounds of distressed humans and the taunting of a passerby. It is even a nice place to quiet one's nerves—rubbed raw from the ubiquitous mayhem and hostility inside the park. One is reminded how quiet these birds are, even when they are torn up and dying.

It was here that I was to meet Joe, one of the directors of the Chicago Animal Rights Coalition, on one Labor Day afternoon. Joe, a man of extraordinary patience and moderation, and an old acquaintance of mine from Chicago, was the person to turn to when the antipathy and suspicion between the two sides became unbearable to me. Joe was so uncharacteristically mild and sensible for a protester at the shoot that he was well liked even among the shoot's organizers—Bob Shade once said that if he were to ever make friends with an animal rights activist, it would be Joe.

Joe was somehow different that day. I could not say that he was agitated, but he looked occupied and wore a stern, determined face, to the point of making me feel guilty for trespassing upon his rare break from hectic duties. After a distant greeting, he sat next to me on the lawn, where we had a panoramic view of the north-side firing ranges. Immediately, Joe fell into a stupor, grew meditative and profound, even as I tried small talk to distract him, to thwart my own feelings of becoming small. Joe responded occasionally, but he was not there. As I fell to guessing the reason for his mood despite myself, a heavy silence fell between us, and we began contemplating the mechanical rising and falling of birds from afar—that grand spectacle of execution so extravagant and yet so mundane by now. Minutes passed in the oppressive silence, Joe nervously twiddling his camera with hands flung over his bent knees and I playing with the audio recorder that stayed put in my pocket. Finally, as if struck by something, Joe perked up, inhaling deeply and his eyes still glaring wildly at the firing line. He laboriously uttered these words with a shudder, like a solemn judgment: "Look hard and don't ever forget this scene. This is what we have to remember and deal with, this violent instinct in all of us."

Joe emphasized "in all of us" a couple of times. And I nodded enthusiastically, quite moved by his magnanimity in refraining from pointing fingers at others—a genuine rarity at the shoot. Joe suddenly looked to me not like a self-righteous and self-serving petty bourgeois zealot, but like a pilgrim on a spiritual quest, expiating sinners along the way. Admiringly, I stole a look at him: his watery and melancholy eyes, the determined look on his forehead, his weathered skin, and so forth. But two things caught my eyes and disturbed my reverie: a rather expensive-looking camera (noted earlier) and a pair of surgical rubber gloves peeping out from his pocket.

"A pilgrim with rubber gloves and a camera . . . ," I thought, searching in my mind. A camera may be a cliché image at holy sightings, but not at a spectacle of gleeful slaughters. Rubber gloves, I know, are distributed among the protesters for the chance encounter with wounded pigeons for the rescue-minded. But neither was characteristic of the usual Joe, because he was someone with a disregard for appearance and who abandoned commitment to action, always in a worn-out pair of sneakers, a sweatshirt with an illegibly dilapidated logo, and with cracked and grimy fingernails. It was difficult to visualize Joe fitting his shoe repairer's hands into a pair of silken surgical gloves before securing a pigeon in distress, or wielding a camera for that matter.

As I turned this thought over in my mind, now almost oblivious to Joe's continuing monologue, the first aid station behind us was continuing to bustle with rescuers hurrying in with mangled pigeons and veterinarians stirring about. Everyone was wearing a pair of surgical gloves.

Relating Joe's magnanimous pronouncement to his prudent instruments is the task at hand here. What is the relation between the self-abnegating and self-incriminating lament over failings "in all of us," on the one hand, and sanitizing rubber gloves and witnessing/objectifying cameras—which must be related to Joe's admonition to "look hard"—on the other? What of this "scene" so familiar that Joe recognizes it with a shudder, and yet so foreign to him as to warrant a photographic recording on the one hand and disinfecting protection on the other? If the problem is "in all of us," one might naturally be led to wonder, what is driving Joe to be some seven hundred miles away from home with his camera, and from what does he seek gloved protection? Commonsensically, these might be moot questions and perhaps too impressionistic an association, but considered together, I believe, these figures—the distant location, the desire to see and record, and the horror of contagion—conjure up the affects beneath the currency of the term "cruelty" in modern sensibility within animal rights activism and beyond.

The camera-glove co-occurrence here suggests something other than a camera's representationality (which we are going to dwell on in earnest in the next chapter): the materiality of the scene of cruelty somatically inscribed by the pair. From early on, both sides of the controversy tried to cash in on the perceived "public" nature of the Labor Day Shoot. *The Animal's Agenda*, the nation's leading animal rights magazine, confidently predicted, echoing many organizations' leaders, that the shoot will have a "radicalizing influence on the entire animal rights movement." The reason provided was this: "Hegins is one of the only public shoots where media representatives and the public can actually record the images of pigeons being so gratuitously slaughtered" (*Animal's Agenda* 1992:13).

It was the shoot's flagrantly visible nature that at once shocked and animated the most enterprising national animal rights organizations. For them, the shoot was simultaneously a valuable resource and a target of elimination. Their welcoming elation at the discovery of the shoot was barely disguised by the horror the event inspired: "the public" is finally allowed a chance to "actually record." Hegins thus debuted as something simultaneously so shocking, yet so familiar, and so primordial, which finally revealed its face for the whole world to examine—something like a hypostatization of a normally invisible part of our selves. In public discourse, it followed the familiar trajectory of censorship controversies. And like other censorship issues, its most hideous Otherness consisted in its suggestive affinity with the Self: the monstrous conflation of subject and object, of victim and victimizer, and children's innocense and their natural attraction toward "mimicking" the evil.[11] And like other censorship issues, the shoot was perceived as "for fun"; its willed staging of a contagious threat was utterly indefensible in utilitarian terms. Slaughterhouses may kill animals a hundredfold every day, but no "radicalizing influence" is to be expected from their discrete, sanitized existence.

In contrast, the shoot's supporters took great pride in the fact that the event is the only "public" live-bird shoot in the nation, meaning that it is held on public property (Hegins Community Park) and is accessible to everyone (unlike the ones held at private gun clubs). They took pride in this "democratic" visibility of the shoot; it was "family fun" that indiscriminately welcomed rich and poor, young and old, men and women. The magic word was "for the community," to which the pigeons themselves were made to sound like willing contributing members. It was argued that pigeons are pests "in the community": they live off farmers' grain yards and make hay go moldy—they are "dirty birds," "rats with wings." Shoot supporters were particularly self-righteous about the point that dead pigeons were used as fertilizer for local soil. From the community and to the community, pigeons are locally held culpable and locally punished.

Cameras and rubber gloves were not prominent in the first stages of the protest. It was only after several years of unfruitful, violent annual demonstrations and clashes that animal rights organizations turned to those "symbolic" arms. The year was 1989, when the pigeon shoot was first accused of being a scandal of reckless "health risks." Recall that 1989 was the same year that the phase of "documenting" began. Avian flu was the scientific name given to the scandal, and the protest began to focus on, first, the legal issue of transporting thousands of potentially diseased animals across county lines, and second, "trapper boys," teenagers who run out to the field after the buckshot subsides to retrieve dead pigeons and dispatch wounded ones bare-handed. Animal rights activists recruited veterinarian after veterinarian to testify (in the media) about the dangers of touching the birds with bare hands. Among the protesters themselves, rubber gloves became the rule for all "rescuers" at the same time.

Protesters' insistence on rubber gloves at the shoot, amid thousands who promiscuously mix with pigeons bare-handed, has a doctor's haughtiness and patronage about it. On Labor Day, it is as if the whole town of Hegins wallows in an unnerving intimacy with pigeons—more accurately, pigeon members, bloody particles, pigments, and that distinctive, nauseating, musty stench. In the midst of some twenty acres of broken pigeon debris, the undaunted efforts of ceaseless stitching, resuscitating, and antisepticizing by a handful of veterinarians in the mere shack of a first aid station impress one as noble, to the extent of being vainglorious. The nonchalant and steadfast rescuers in rubber gloves seem like so many self-abnegating nannies cleaning up the accustomed mess made by uncivilized but perfectly familiar children. Rather than the reaction of hysterical horror and shock often associated with early humane reformers (Stallybrass and White 1986), the predominant air assumed by today's animal rights activists at the Labor Day Shoot is that of self-possessed and learned condescension reserved for something familiar—perhaps something "in all of us."

Rubber gloves visually index the presence of (invisible) pathological threat to *all* bodies, protesters and supporters alike. To that point, the "fact" of hygienic science embodied in the gloves in turn inscribes the common humanity in the vulnerable bodies and in one leap surmounts (and neutralizes) the social specificity and markedness (for example, city versus countryside, liberals versus conservatives) that effectively united the shoot's supporters against the protest. Rather than unfruitfully prolonging the socially all-too-contingent insistence on the dignity and value of a "third party" (that is, animals), the protesters introduced the universalizing authorities of science and nature that implicated "you and me" equally. Hence, by mobilizing two of the most rational-humanistic appeals to the moderns—children and science—the argument proved at once invincible and species encompassing. Suddenly, the protest took on a new meaning: saving "our" children, saving cruel subjects from their own cruelty, saving "all of us."

This softening and "universalizing" of the argument worked. The counter-attack of the shoot's organizers to this newly emerged charge of "pigeon shoot as health risk" was surprisingly tame and self-conscious. This was especially exceptional given the fact that the protesters' novel warning of the dangers of avian flu directly reversed their earlier stance: the protesters first scoffed at the shoot's supporters' insistence that pigeons were "dirty." Back then, some protesters linked the very notion of pigeons as dirty to racism, saying, for example, that "the Irish were considered dirty." This glaring contradiction in the protesters' stance went totally unremarked by the shoot's organizers. Instead, Bob Shade weakly explained that "trapper boys do not seem to have any problem so far" and even required youngsters to wear rubber gloves one year—which were abandoned in no time by the trapper boys.

Dissatisfied with Bob's response, the Klingers prepared a list of ex-trapper boys who have become "doctors and lawyers" and delivered it to the media and the protest's leaders. At an interview Warner Klinger had this to say: "Those boys grow up to [sic] upstanding citizens—doctors and lawyers. They are not in jail. They are upstanding children with upstanding parents" (*The Citizen Standard* 1989).

This was fascinating: the charge was on the health risk involving avian flu, and the shoot's supporters self-consciously volunteered an intriguing translation into matters of moral hygiene. Protesters did not have to say anything to pronounce the radical provincial nature of their enemies. The discourse of science magically agitated and brought out the confessions from those who internalized modernity, that is, the world of doctors and lawyers, only as alienation, or, shall we say, as self-loss. What we have here is certainly not "self-possession via third gaze." I will return to this issue at the end of Chapter 3.

CHAPTER TWO

Gloved Love

There is more than the cleverness of protesters' change of rhetoric at stake in the presence of gloves. We have to appreciate a certain paradox in the protesters' demand for the hygienic relation with animals in all its strangeness. Simply put, the paradox is this: despite their professed "love" for pigeons, the protesters seem to require many provisions in their physical contact with them—in addition to rubber gloves, bird-catching nets, feeding tubes, and so forth. Gloves or not, protesters are generally awkward with pigeons, in radical contrast to the unflinching familiarity the shoot's supporters display. Wounded pigeons "rescued" by protesters tend to put up all kinds of struggle. Many pigeons break free in this manner on their way to the Wounded Bird First Aid Station. Every year, field directors from the Fund for Animals spend hours training rescuers how to tug pigeons tight underneath shirts to quiet them, but to no avail. At moments of competition for a wounded bird, the apprehensive and timid handling of the rescuers is usually no match for the relentless clasps of the supporters. I brought up this irony—of gloved love on the one hand and intimate cruelty on the other—to Wayne Pacelli of the People for the Ethical Treatment of Animals (PETA), to which he retorted: "The fact that doctors wear gloves don't mean that they don't love their patients, does it?"

Indeed, doctors wear gloves for reasons of protecting both patients from themselves and themselves from patients. But this precisely is the question: what kind of prudent "love" is this, love that fears, and fears for both the subject and the object?

There are more ways protesters' apprehensiveness about pigeons is manifested. Consider the fate of those hundreds of wounded pigeons saved by the protesters at the shoot. In addition, there are some five hundred "leftover" pigeons at the end of each Labor Day Shoot, which the protesters, amid publicity, are more or less forced to purchase (see Chapter 3). What do the protesters do with those pigeons, those inner-city "vermin," as the shoot's supporters would say? The animal advocacy organizations are elusive about the birds' destinations. Although they claim to "adopt" most of them, pigeon pets are foreign to urban dwellers, which most protesters are. An unofficial source hinted that they are released "back to nature" eventually after a process of "rehabilitation." In plainer terms, the birds end up returning to where they were supposed to belong, to the squalor of inner-city streets and their scraps and garbage. A strange justice it is: the shoot's organizers' "illegal" practice of transporting and displacing potentially diseased birds is corrected by sending them back to their sickly origin.

"Killing for Fun"

It is the willfully and cold-bloodedly carried-out nature of the shoot, such as the coordinating of massive transportation, that outrages. A typical lament of protesters goes thus: "[At least], hunting in the field is different than this. Out there, 90% of the kill is eaten and the *animals are taken where they live*" (a protester interviewed by *Pottsville Republican* 1989, emphasis added). This quote negatively defines for us the concept of "killing for fun," which is central to the charge of cruelty. As indicated by the quote, the most glaring fiendishness of "killing for fun" is its indefensibility in utilitarian terms: it is killing for the sake of killing, not even for one's subsistence needs. This is contrasted to what is happening "out there"; out there, where the sanity of utilitarianism reigns, animals are "taken where they live" and are not made to transgress boundaries. The gloved protesters at the shoot seem to me like vigilantes who police animals and animality ("in all of us," as it were), a sort of clean-up crew (or nannies?) who stitch up, patch up, and wipe off "our" bestiality that has been childishly spilled all over the place, unsparingly correcting, rearranging, and returning displaced ones to where they belong.

This problem is irreducible to mere "classification" questions in the tradition of structuralist studies of human-animal relations (see Chapter 6). Investigating the proper "place" and "delimitation" of animals in human lives is not enough to make us understand the notion or image of "killing for fun." The horror of this category owes not only to displaced animals, for example, but to human traits; it reflects and constructs *human Otherness* that is not reducible to, for example, "those who do not maintain proper boundary with animals" (Tester 1991:55). This mundane insight is, however, often forgotten in the studies informed by the classic structural approaches to animal questions. The reason, I think, is as follows.

There is a certain assumption almost categorically shared by scholars on the subject of modernity regarding the maturation of the animal protection movement. The advent of modernity is suggested by the bourgeois activists' diminishing preoccupation with their cruel Other classes on the one hand, and the intensification of their love of animals for animals' sake on the other (Frykman and Löfgren 1987, Ritvo 1987, Tester 1991, Thomas 1983). It had been commonplace for studies of the subject to treat the earlier part of the movement as the period when the veneration of animals had been inseparable from the persecution of other classes. However, the same studies started to see the later, "modern" half of the movement, the beginning of which roughly coincides with the appearance of Henry Salt (Hendrick 1977), under a radically different light: despite the fact that the animal protection movement had remained as class-specific as before, the dimension of possible interhuman conflict was suddenly dropped and instead only a direct inquiry into the cultural value of animals was recommended (see Tester 1991).

This trend of turning away from the appreciation of the contribution of human Otherness, and the embracing of the cultural values of animals as an analytically independent positivity, parallels the rhetoric of modern animal advocacy. In a gesture to distance themselves from their class-conflict-ridden predecessors, the advocates insinuate that the modern valuing of animals had arrived simultaneously with the activists' abolition of class biases, which is embedded in the assertion that the modern movement has been made possible by recognizing a parallel between the victimized animals and the oppressed sectors of human beings (see Singer 1990[1975]). In the theories and the advocates' rhetoric alike, the alleged disappearance of the issue of human Otherness becomes a necessary assumption in order to construct the animal love that is pure positivity, independent of political contexts. The persistent privileging of the cultural value of animals as an autonomous positivity concerning the modern human attitude stems from an insufficient appreciation of the political-economical background from which the modern sentimental attitude toward animals has emerged. I will argue that this emergence of the animal as an autonomous positivity, this "humane" consolidation of human/animal boundary, has to do with our increasing self-possession vis-à-vis not only animals but animality.

The Other Side of Glassy Eyes

One of the two leading animal rights organizations at the Labor Day Shoot protest, the People for the Ethical Treatment of Animals (PETA), occupies a special place in the contemporary history of animal rights activism generally and in the construction of a dominant *genre* of direct mailing specifically, which most major organizations, including the leader of the shoot protest, the Fund for Animals, came to imitate.[1] The aim here is to sketch the generalized *genre* that thus came to bear on the disposition of the shoot protest (not the specific direct mail campaigns carrying the message of the shoot particularly).

During the height of the shoot protest, PETA was the fastest-growing and, arguably, the largest animal rights organization in the United States (*Chicago Sun Times* 1993; Jasper and Nelkin 1992:92; PETA 1993). The organization leaped into the spotlight in 1981 with a successful infiltration and exposure of the treatment of animals in Edward Taub's laboratory at the Institute for Behavioral Research, Silver Springs, Maryland, by PETA's co-founder, Alex Pacheco, who acted as an undercover research assistant. Its membership skyrocketed when fragments of Pacheco's diary that detailed his undercover experience circulated, along with the photographic images of the abused animals, through direct mail (see Pacheco and Francione 1985; Holden 1981; *Washington Post* 1981).[2] In 1984, PETA secured another boost with the case of abused animals at the University of Pennsylvania's Head Injury Laboratory. This time, a journalist was invited to witness the illegal break-in to the laboratory, after which PETA released sixty hours of videotape to the media and select images from it in a direct-mail campaign (Weil 1986).[3] These two cases of the photographic and diary-confessional exposé have been consecrated as the signature mode of PETA's investigative crusade and are still perpetually revisited as a set narrative trope for almost every case told in PETA's and other organizations' newsletters.

Another novelty was added to PETA's arsenal in the 1990s, which won for the organization a trendy currency among the younger generations: publicity by celebrities, which culminated in the smashing success of the campaign "I'd Rather Go Naked Than Wear Fur." The sensational success of PETA, and the rapid growth of the animal rights movement in general it stimulated in the 1980s and the 1990s, I believe, are due to PETA's introduction of the above three tactics, which are congenitally interdependent: direct mailing, photography, and celebrity.

PETA's Direct Mail

The primary material I will analyze here, PETA's *Animal Times*, much resembles popular news magazines such as *Time* or *Newsweek* in appearance. It is a bi-monthly magazine or newsletter mailed to all subscribers of the PETA membership that replaced the much smaller and less colorful *Peta News* beginning in June 1994. The founders of PETA introduced the magazine in the first issue with these words: "It's specially designed to reach out to people who are just learning about the ways animals all over the world are used. The large, colorful format, packed with information and ideas, should help newcomers to animal rights understand how easy it is to get active for animals. Best of all, PETA's *Animal Times* will come to your house every two months!" The magazine is filled with colorful photographs, starting from the cover, which features a full-page portrait of an animal and an inset picture of, usually, a celebrity. In each issue (each one a total of thirty to thirty-five pages), I have counted on average twenty-nine photos of "abused" animals, twenty-five of "happy" animals, fifteen of PETA's activists, and seventeen of some sort of celebrity. Every issue alternates between grim and delightful stories, between investigative articles on some cruelties perpetrated by big brand names, the government, the military, the entertainment industry, et cetera, and stories on "rescued" animals, tips for better care of animals, reports on humane celebrity-heroes and heroines and their vegetarian/vegan recipes, et cetera. Shocking exposés and feature investigative narratives are placed toward the beginning of an issue, with bold letters and half-page-size photographs in a colorful layout. The latter part is devoted to tidbits on the benefits of a vegetarian diet, cruelty-free products, boycott lists, and general news on how much of an impact PETA is making. The last page usually ends with a plea for donations. The secondary source to be consulted, PETA's *Annual Review*, is a smaller booklet, also mailed to members, that features all of the activities and achievements of PETA throughout the year, with as many photographs of animals and celebrities, only reduced in size.

   In the 1990s newsletters of PETA, no witnessing of cruelty happens by accident or with a pretense of spontaneity. Any uncovering of atrocity is made through a carefully planned, often clandestine, deliberately carried out "assignment." An "investigator" is dispatched "undercover" to the thick of the crime scene, with a disguised identity. Furthermore, over 75 percent of the investigative cases PETA tackles begin with whistle-blowers, who lead the investigator to the otherwise impenetrable shady burrow of cruelty.[4] The nether world of brutality exists as a disruption from everyday space, only approachable by undercover investigators and whistle-blowers. The organization locates the problem it suggests for cure at an imaginary place elsewhere, somewhere impenetrable by the lay patrons of the cause who open the solicitation mailings at home.[5] The newsletter is filled with allusions to readers' impossible relations to the ailments they desire to cure and the daring of PETA's undercover agents, which is the only resource that makes the cure possible. "You could be killed there if people find out [about your identity]," intimidates one of PETA's ex-undercover investigators.

The organization's newsletters in general strive toward effects of immediacy and coevalness, as much as such a letter can achieve. Many narratives start or end with a chilling reminder: "By the time you finish reading this paragraph, over 25 animals will be tortured here. Every second that passes costs three more animals their lives. Remember, procrastination is exactly what has allowed painful animal experiments to continue for so long" (solicitation mail, 1995). Immediacy is also effected by a dramatized intimacy. Featuring a diary kept by an undercover investigator is one way. Alongside the covertly taken photographs of a cruelty den, we see page after page of hastily scribbled-down depictions of atrocity, ripped from a yellow-pad notebook, with date entry and all. Cruelty here is ongoing and imminent, at the expense of the helplessly distanced reader.

However, it is not the undercover investigator him- or herself who voices the above-quoted warning; a diary is supposed to be only self-addressed. The surrogate witness of cruelty does not talk directly to readers but is merely being *presented*, not as a provider of the interpretation, but as a kind of instrument of monitoring (cf. Meyrowitz 1985:89).

"An Undercover Exposé: Not a Leg to Stand On"

Our undercover investigator's diary reveals what life is like for the "downer birds," the chickens who live with chronic leg pain, bent or bowed legs.

Day 1: "He was just one of the thousands of chickens confined in the stifling 'grow out' shed. I watched him limp to the feed pan and take a few mouthfuls of food before falling down, his legs no longer able to support him. . . . "

Day 4: "The callousness is hard to take. I have to bite my tongue. . . . I photographed one chicken whose legs were bent out at an obscene angle. . . . "

Day 6: "Today one of the vets said that as long as the chickens make it to slaughter, the industry people don't care if the birds' feet rot off. . . . "

Day 7: "As I finish this entry I think back to the chickens I saw lying on the floor of the overcrowded broiler house this afternoon. . . . I think of the billions of chickens who are in the same situation. If only people in the supermarket would think the same thoughts and drop that plastic package that represents the pain of so many sad little birds." (*Animal Times* 1995:14–17)

By being made visible mutely, in the first person, the body of the surrogate witness invokes an abstracted place of danger that is distant and yet under constant surveillance by PETA's undercover agents. The anonymity of the undercover investigator and the whistle-blower combined with the danger's temporal immanence hint at the ubiquity of both the menace and the watchful eyes of PETA's agents simultaneously. For, as a non-person, a whistle-blower-cum-undercover agent could be anywhere and everywhere.[6] The newsletter locates the organization on a par with the imminent threat.

However, the inaccessibility of the crime scene suggested by the newsletter does not keep dangers at a comfortable distance from readers. The ubiquitous menace is kept away from the patrons only in the sense that PETA presents itself as the exclusive route to it. All exposures of cruelty seem like PETA's solitary work, carried out in a vacuum of possible help from government authorities and local people, not to speak of *other* animal rights organizations. Far from comforting those who find themselves lucky to stay away from the PETA agent's perilous journey, the newsletter terrorizes the reader by fusing the message of inaccessibility of danger with a relentless evocation of private fears. After telling of a gruesome animal experiment the newsletter warns: "As a matter of fact, your own dog or cat could easily become one of these victims . . . because each year 'pound seizure' laws force unwilling animal shelters to turn over some 200,000 lost cats or dogs to experimentation. . . . [Also], people who steal companion animals for sale to laboratories often roam neighborhoods in the evening. Keep your pets safely indoors" (PETA 1994–95).

Being addressed to the audience at home, the newsletter showcases family drama. The figure of a pet animal under threat rubs against the open sores of the familial disintegration mentioned already. Most successful cases reported in the newsletter are some kind of "rescue" stories. Upon being rescued, the abused animals are reported to have been "reunited with their family members," returned to their "jungle homes," or are given new homes through adoption. No matter how many truck-loads of animals are rescued, the newsletter selectively reports on two or three specimen cases of adoption, with the animals' photographs, newly acquired names, follow-up stories, and so forth. The increase in the solicitation of the figures of recovery and reunion in the animal rights literature in general is telling, given the prevalent perception of the problem of familial disintegration in America in the 1990s.[7]

The figure of recuperation of the family through a common love of the pet animal is classic enough. But the noticeable thing about PETA's version is that the rescued animals are hardly ever adopted by so-and-so's household, which would be the classic scenario; instead, they are brought to places like "sanctuaries," or some kind of animal-equivalent of retirement homes that are surrounded by a mystical and paradisiacal ambiance. Again, PETA does not allow easy access to the level of its existence by everyday, ordinary patrons. Instead, from the abstracted place where its agents operate, PETA holds up to us the ideal picture of normalcy that the specificity of our actual family always betrays, and that we can covet only from afar.

In short, PETA wants to meet its supporters as isolated consumers with mass desires. The first issue of *Animal Times* was launched with an assuring exhortation on its cover: "Meet the growing community of animal activists around the world, of which you are a part." But the "community" turns out to be an assortment of Hollywood celebrities. Thus, only alone, guilt-ridden and engulfed in personal and domestic problems, is a patron allowed to relate to PETA. The organization never asks readers to come and visit its offices, meet its agents, or participate in its demonstrations. Readers can only send it checks or at most "write to [their] congressmen." When PETA asks readers to picket, it asks them to form their own localized demonstration. Neither do the readers of PETA's newsletter constitute a reading public. Instead, each individual reader or subscriber is approached as an isolated individual with a fragmented attention. An indication of this can be found in the way PETA puts together the newsletter: there is no continuity from one issue to another. The literature is designed in such a way that anyone can tap into it at random points without feeling that he or she is missing anything. Regardless of whether readers are veteran subscribers or casual browsers, PETA addresses everyone as though they were potential new recruits.

People for the Ethical Treatment of Animals interpellates its readers as insulated, private selves of vulnerable intimacy, helpless vis-à-vis the externally permeable threat that is "cruelty to animals." The organization inserts itself as an exclusive intermediary between readers and this frightening yet enticing estrangement. Such a technique of PETA not only exploited photographs rigorously for the first time in the history of the animal protection movement but also turned the mass-mailing effect itself "photographic." For, as I will show presently, animal photography in PETA's newsletters is not a text-artifact "readable" in its own right,[8] but a complex effect that can be decoded between the intersecting significations of the domesticity-intended direct mailing as the medium, photography, and the use of celebrity icons.

Animal Photography, Animal Celebrity

The animal photographs used in PETA's newsletters themselves do not reveal any extraordinary tricks. Rather, PETA's (animal) "photo effect" must be understood as a whole gamut of devices deployed to uphold a regime of investigative representation for the purpose of justifying the existence of a social movement organization and drawing donations. Such a mechanism, as I will show below, mimics the ways in which the mainstream mass publicity machines "authenticate" their representational authority. The authenticating mechanism of PETA, I believe, is deeply related to what one might call "celebrity effect." I will borrow from theories of stardom to explain the workings of such a mechanism, and in the following section will demonstrate its enactment by the example of PETA's newsletter coverage of the campaign "I'd Rather Go Naked Than Wear Fur."

The star phenomenon is widely viewed as an outgrowth of the photo effect (de Cordova 1990, Dyer 1979, Ellis 1982, Gamson 1994, Gledhill 1991). John Ellis defines the photo effect as a paradoxical presentation of what is absent as present or vice versa, in the impossible mode of "this is was" (1982:93–97). That is, a cinema presentation of the star, as an instance of photographic presentation, promises the existence of an authentic, flesh-and-blood person behind the "mere image" and yet defers the fulfillment of it. Stardom, therefore, is a self-perpetuating mechanism in which the possibility of discovering the "truth" behind a star's staged image is incessantly promised and deferred between "subsidiary circulation of star images" and the staged

presentation of the star (Ellis 1982:93–97). Following Richard Dyer, Christine Gledhill observes that stardom arose when the off-stage or off-screen
life of the actor became as important as the performed role (1991:213). Thus,
in Dyer's words, "features on stars which tell us that the star is *not* like he or
she appears to be on screen," rather than undermining the star image, "serve
to reinforce the authenticity of the star image as a whole" (1991:136). This is
a regime of truth quite distinct from a make-believe illusion. It is a regime
that convinces us that there is more to a star image than mere hype or illusion, that there exists a personal, "real" human being behind the star image.
From this, a new ideology of truth emerges: "the basic paradigm is . . . that
what is behind or below the surface is, unquestionably and virtually by definition, the truth" (Dyer 1991:136). Dyer continues, "*The star phenomenon is
defined by an in-built means of authentication.* . . . The question of the star's
authenticity can be referred back to her/his existence in the real world. This
referral-back is tied up with the fact that stars exist in photographic media.
Stars are a particular instance of the supposed relation between a photograph and its referent" (135, emphasis added).

Gledhill adds that this interest in the referral back to the "authentic"
referent, the desire to anchor back to the personal and the everyday "truth"
of the star behind the screen, came about when images were subjected to
mass circulation in vehicles of modern journalism (1991:213). Stars served a
specific role in the newly emerging experience of the world of mass circulation, since as John Ellis argues, stars possessed a kind of "soldering function": "they hold the news (the realm of publicity) and the personal together
by being both public and intimate, by being news only in so far as they are
persons" (1982:96).

I have no intention of suggesting that the photographed animals in
PETA's newsletter are stars in Ellis's sense—the autonomous performing
self is unthinkable with animals. However, mass-circulated images of animals, narrowly in PETA's newsletters and more generally in the mass media,
appeal to the "truth" of the intimate and the personal: they too possess a
"soldering function" between the realms of the public and the intimate.
Animals are prone to this because of what one might call the genus-, or at
times, species-anonymity (or ambiguity). For example, a black Labrador in
my household is hardly distinguishable from someone else's black Labrador or a black Labrador on television—whereas I can always distinguish my
own child or spouse at a flash of their images. Despite the contemporary
urbanites' professed hyper-individuality of their pets as family members,

Alan Beck and Aaron Katcher observe, humans possess an extremely poor ability to distinguish individualities of animals (1983:205). This is why so much "educational" value for rehearsing the experience of death and other sensitive emotions is heaped upon the practice of keeping pets: the death of a black Labrador can be remedied with another black Labrador, which is unthinkable with human family members.

In this sense, animals are semi-individuals, at once personal yet incarnates of an anonymous mass. In explaining why animals commanded poetic imagination in the premodern past, John Berger wrote that "an animal's blood flowed like human blood, but its species was undying and each lion was Lion, each ox was Ox" (1980:4–5). He sang this line as a kind of requiem to the death of animal metaphor in modern societies. He claims that this inherent "duality" in the human perception of an animal—that is, both as an individual entity and a member of its genus or species group—is forever lost to our reified individualist approach to our animals today. Now, "animals and populace became synonymous," he claims (17). But I would argue that animals' power of stimulating our imagination is still alive: now, animal-as-metaphor allows us to grasp the experience of the "unique," intimate, individual(list) existence *amid the mass*. Hundreds of thousands of people own black Labradors, but alone. By the power of recognizability they allow, animals easily transgress the spheres of intimacy and mass publicity. Their images circulate freely, unhampered by specificity. They are intimate yet "faceless" mass bodies (Warner 1994:381). The animal as celebrity, or "star,"[9] is not only a frequent *object* of mass circulation; it also validates the *medium* that carries it because of its personal-public "soldering function."[10] Such is the animal photo/celebrity effect.

Celebrity Effect as a Mode of Investigation:
The "I'd Rather Go Naked" Campaign

The People for the Ethical Treatment of Animal's conflation of the human celebrity and the animal victims is nowhere more palpable than in the campaign "I'd Rather Go Naked Than Wear Fur." There are a whole range of activities and advertisements that fall under this campaign title, but the nakedness of female "supermodels" remains constant—although popular adaptation by lay bodies has been growing recently, nationally and internationally. The core material of the campaigns that are circulated in PETA's newsletters consists of photographic images of supermodels, either completely or partially naked, wearing real fur with bloodstains or clean fake fur or T-shirts with the PETA logo. What is often censored out from the mass-media representation of the campaign is the picture of a bloody fox, "naked" of its fur, frequently juxtaposed with the supermodel images during PETA's demonstrations. The supermodel Christy Turlington succinctly confirms the unstated association always suspected: "If I save one animal's skin by showing some of mine, I'll be satisfied" (PETA 1994–95:24). Animals are supermodels, or vice versa.

The persuasiveness of the "I'd Rather Go Naked Than Wear Fur" campaign can be understood from the mutually reinforcing, multiple layers of paralleling figures: the models' undressing, the consecrated model of PETA's signature exposé-style, and the photo effect of the animal icon (see Olson and Goodnight 1994). An unraveling of this interlocked rhetorical structure should first of all pay attention to how PETA positions itself vis-à-vis this publicity stunt. It positions itself as a promoter (not an initiator) of the event, which partially fulfills the role of press agency that represents the models. It schedules and arranges photo sessions and press conferences between the celebrities and the mass media, provides the models with costumes (for example, a garment of fake fur or a PETA T-shirt), and, infrequently, has a carefully selected top PETA executive pose with the models (see Ferguson 1994). Namely, PETA stays in the background as the one that oversees and frames the event.

The campaign is projected as some kind of scandal. The mood of the models is unmistakably prankish and frolicsome—strange dispositions considering the gory seriousness of the campaign's message. Professional fashion models appear not in designer clothes but in imitation furs, expensive garments inflicted with the practical joke of blood staining, or mundane T-shirts. But more than anything else, a fashion model rejects her clothes. The campaign is scandalous in the sense of seemingly rejecting a public persona, prestige, and power and revealing what it claims to be the hidden and unglamorous side of the personal, "real" self.[11] So even when the model in question had not been in any way linked to the fur industry in the past, her participation in the campaign is portrayed as though it were a major "change of heart." And PETA poses itself as a witness to that authentic moment of "conversion." It enunciates a triumph of the mundane over the glamour industry embodied in fur. The campaign is perceived as so effective that the participating celebrities themselves (some are not fashion models by profession) seem to regard the occasion as a chance for secondary publicity. There emerges a notion that one is not quite "super" until joining the ranks of the

PETA-endorsed (not just PETA-endorsing) celebrities. In turn, the newsletter (as a medium of the campaign) fulfills the role of the tabloid magazine or fanzine, a vehicle of "subsidiary circulation of star images" (Ellis 1982:93).

By arranging and partaking in such a moment of subsidiary circulation of celebrity images, PETA authenticates itself. It poses to be seen together with celebrities in the scandalous backstage moment of "undermining" public persona and the authority of publicity industries. It borrows celebrities whose fame had been created and maintained by the mass publicity apparatus in the first place and momentarily steals the publicity industry's own authenticating technique of revealing "backstage real life existence" or how things are "really" done in the mechanics of manipulation. It is a tactic of riding on the star-text that someone else has authored. Just as network television implicitly makes a self-validating statement, "TV was there," vis-à-vis a scene of catastrophe (Doane 1990:233), the scandalous revelation of a model's naked self, witnessed and overseen by PETA, accompanies the message "PETA was there."[12] What is validated for PETA, through this trick of authenticating one's representational authority, is its trademark status as an effective conveyor of exposés; the one that probes "beneath the surface" to reveal how "things are really done" backstage. The message is this: whether it is "truth" about science establishments or the glamour industry, PETA bares the veneer of the status quo authority just as it shows the "true beauty" in the naked bodies of the celebrities that is at once truthful and intimately graspable.[13]

Through its traffic with celebrities, PETA effectively courts the newsletter readers who are positioned at home, now aligning itself with the power and prestige of mass publicity, now tapping into the mundane existence of the reader, abstracted and removed at one moment and yet privately relevant at another—just as threats in the newsletter were seen to be dually situated. Thus, PETA finds a perfect spokesperson in a celebrity because, according to Dyer (1979), the power of a star-text depends on the tension between hype and the everyday tangibility. And this is the image of the animal too, since, like melodramatic characters, animals are so intimately familiar and yet so emblematically anonymous. Making full use of the recognizability of the emblematic, the newsletter penetrates the domestic sphere through linking the animal victim out there with the potential one within. The reverse of that is that *the reader discovers the public that is transparently knowable* in terms of the intimate. The organization claims to expose the below-the-surface "truth" about public institutions, the status quo of science, and fashion establishments with the trickster-like figure of the "intimately graspable" (yet public) images of celebrities and animals.

Animal Fetish and Human Otherness

John Ellis draws a direct parallel between the claims of "the delegated look" in television and in right-wing "vigilantism," the ideology of guarding wholesome interiority (the family) against troublesome and obscene exteriority (1982:163–70). He argues that in order to prolong the pact of "delegation," the delegate strives toward building "complicity" with the audience and thus processes the message in the way that conforms to the familiar/familial environment of the latter (cf. Brunsdon and Morley 1978). As the result, in a televisual representation, for example, what is removed and distanced presents itself in a familiar guise. At the same time, he continues, such a vantage point pushes the world being presented "beyond the familiar/familiar" in the mode of the "third person," or "they," since the "complicity" establishes a sense of "first and second person togetherness" between the delegate and the viewer (Ellis 1982:139). This kind of relegation of the viewing power brings about a sense of domestic isolation in the viewers, inducing them to recognize "the outside" as the problem and problems as being on the outside, claims Ellis. Politically, he says, such an isolation impels "lack of involvement," rendering the viewer "powerless to do anything about events portrayed" (170). And vigilantism tunes into the attitude of "skeptical non-involvement" such a sense of domestic isolation brings about. In this sense, he says, a right-wing vigilante such as Mary Whitehouse (of the United Kingdom) succinctly expresses and exploits the effects carved out by the mass media.[14]

To paraphrase Ellis's idea, an apparatus of the "delegated look" would be potent as a medium for exploring the exterior to the extent that it affirms the interior, domestically isolated self-image of the audience. Much is presumed in this proposition when a successful medium such as television is presented as its instance. For, whether it is an illusory feeling created by television or not, Ellis seems to regard the "normality and safety of the viewer's presumed domestic situation" as a *fact* rather than an aspiration (1982:167). This is particularly problematic when extended as a theory of vigilantism. Seen from the recent surge of conservative activism that merits the rubric vigilantism in the United States, the opposite is true: it is precisely through invoking domestic vulnerability and affliction that a vigilante establishes his or her status as a potent apparatus of a delegated look. American "vigilantisms" in the 1980s and 1990s seem to have flourished with an anxious realization that "what is closest and most sacrosanct is also the location of the most terrible violence and horrors" (Acland 1995:149). When there have been waves of panic over the disintegration of the American family since the early 1980s, with concerns of child abuse, incest, juvenile crimes, and so forth, there have followed frenzied efforts to identify the sources of the evil outside and away from the family (Acland 1995:149; Ivy 1993:229–30)—the fact that the overwhelming majority of abusers were family members themselves and that 98 percent of kidnapped children were taken by their fathers did not prevent the "crisis" from being used to "defend the family" (Massumi 1993:26). One might imagine a close relationship between the impulse for "outward" surveillance and the "inward" lack: it was the anxiety over the presence of the Other within the familial realm that turned the figures of the familiar into a productive form of knowledge for exploring the exterior.

The heightened awareness of the familial disintegration in the early 1980s is instructive regarding the advent of the animal rights movement in general and PETA in particular during the same period (see Ehrenreich 1989:247; Hacking 1991).[15] It was also the period when mail solicitation made an explosive debut, including the aggressive advertisements of missing children on milk cartons and in mass mailings (Ivy 1993, Massumi 1993). The roaring success of PETA, it seems to me, was due greatly to its successful direct-mail courting of the anxiety over familial disintegration during the time.

Speaking of the American professional middle class of roughly the same period—which provided the majority of animal-rights sympathizers (see Jasper and Nelkin 1992:38–41)—Barbara Ehrenreich observed that the experience of counterculture and anti-war movements in the preceding decades had forced them to discover the hedonistic Other in their midst, among their own children. This stirred a panic over "growing soft" or over failing to replicate their class and the family—since this was the class whose economic and social status had been based on self-discipline and education rather than on the ownership of capital or property (1989:12–15, 262; cf. Acland 1995:29). This panic over the failing interior drove the professional middle class to project the perceived Otherness (in their midst) "outward," to the other classes and impelled them to pitch a vehement campaign against the "hedonistic" poor and the "undisciplined" consumerism of the blue-collar working class (Ehrenreich 1989:15). At the height of such a shift toward an alternate moment in the discourse of the Other, the professional middle class—who were favorably disposed or committed to liberalism—made a massive exodus toward the issues of the environment, New Age, the animal, and so forth. It is widely known that most founders of the major animal rights organizations in the United States were veterans in human rights causes of one kind or another; most made a complete transition to the cause of the animal (Jasper and Nelkin 1992; *Newsweek* 1984; Perez 1990).

In the animal rights rendition of liberal ideals, the idea of "victim" became abstractly all-encompassing and foundational to a visionary degree. In an epochal statement for the turn to modern animal rights, Peter Singer declared that "the pattern of prejudice in humans' treatment of animals is identical to that of racism and sexism" (1990[1975]:6)—and he called the former "speciesism."[16] This manifesto spawned a myriad of household catchwords around which the movement rallied—for example, "animals are the exploited proletariat" (Nash 1989:10), and "stray animals are the homeless" (PETA solicitation mail, 1992). But for Singer and those who followed suit, speciesism was not only commensurate with racism and sexism in urgency and importance but subsumed them (see Sperling 1988). The argument went that animals were the most helpless among all the vulnerables, and hence their plight was indicative of the basest of all human vices and the alleviation of their suffering the ultimate test of our altruism and of the advancement of our expanding democratic ideals (Nash 1989; Perez 1990:125; Singer 1990[1975]). Such a perspective re-reads human history as a history of the victimization of animals and upholds the animal as the primordial prey to the inherent violent nature of humans. Having thus enshrined the animal victim at the origin of the society, such a track of thinking bestows on the alleviation of animal suffering more than the significance of "liberation" for animals: it represents human redemption itself (Regan 1983: passim). Measured against the greater urgency and profundity of animal suffering, therefore, it was argued that "humanism must now be protected against its own excess" (Nash 1989:84). The purity of the plight of animals vis-à-vis that of humans is well captured in the following remark by an activist: "I think what moves me so much as the animals are concerned is that like children, they are very very natural. They are really innocent. They are totally victimized. [But] with adults there is always some element of responsibility" (quoted in Sperling 1988:122).

The totalizing notion of all adult humans as belonging to the responsible party alludes to the fact that every one of them is an accomplice and a beneficiary in a society of egalitarian power sharing. Underneath such a broad stroke of argument inheres a narcissistic dream of a societal oneness that is purged and relieved of differences. Human Otherness displaced, disavowed, and encapsulated with the figure of the animal victim answers to such a narcissistic longing. Animals' universality, their genus- or species-anonymity, serves as a symbol of innocence that humans have lost; they are naked and their needs are transparent, constant, predictable, and unanimous among themselves. In this sense, animals constitute an instant "we," a "we" of natural consensus. Their "non-specific" appearances are hieroglyphs of a social unity that is unattainable amid human differences. They are unique individuals, but at the same time they carry a utopian image of human harmony, a socially and politically tamed image of difference—for they are *naturally* differentiated into genuses and species (Lévi-Strauss 1963).

As the sign of (non-specific) "recognizability," animal victims call up, condense, and render intelligible, with an utmost clarity and drama, "victimizations" of all kinds; they furnish a familiar perspectival ground from the point of view of which myriad victims and criminalities all join in a narcissistically and transparently knowable oneness. In this sense, the delegated look of the animal rights vigilante inscribes a different cast of footing, a different kind of "complicity" or narcissistic reflexivity, from what John Ellis has elaborated. Such a delegated look warrants a certain confidence in the altruistic potential of embracing all the "theys" in the knowable oneness, that is, in the familiar and normalizing terms of animal innocence and victimization. Hence, instead of being grounded on domestic security and resulting in "non-involvement," this sort of narcissistic reflexivity immanently references domestic lack, and optimistically and aggressively appropriates the "outside" as utterly intelligible.

The power of intelligibility in the figure of animal victim recalls Homi Bhabha's notion of fetishism as a productive form of knowledge. A fetish tames and normalizes a perceived difference by affixing the fetish-object as a mask of that difference (Bhabha 1990:79). Hence, fetishism is fundamentally based on the desire for pure, undifferentiated sameness (1983:33). Racism as a fetishism, Bhabha observes, is based upon the desire for a pure origin that is threatened by the opaque differences of race and culture (1983:27). However, the regime of representation that ensconces the articulation of difference within a narcissistic affirmation of undifferentiated oneness sanctions such a recognition of difference as "natural," as obtained in a spontaneous and innocent discovery (Bhabha 1990:82). In other words, the fetish as a (metaphoric) substitution for the missing sameness gives an illusion of presence, but by the same token it (metonymically) registers absence (Bhabha 1986:xviii). Likewise, human difference—made intelligible in terms of genus or species difference of the animal, while it is invested in the dream of transparent harmony unachievable in the actual experience of the human society—reifies such differences as natural and spontaneously perceivable. The case of the nineteenth-century economy of animality clearly demonstrated how a fetish-object with which common humanity had been avowed became the very means with which to think and reify differences. The salience of the issue of human otherness at the Labor Day Shoot is a moot point to repeat. So I turn to an important predecessor to the contemporary animal rights newsletter. The text I will analyze in some detail here is a home-delivered magazine or newsletter called *Our Dumb Animals* (*ODA*), issues from 1888 to 1900, published by the Massachusetts Society for the Prevention of Cruelty to Animals (MSPCA).

The Mise-en-scène of Self-Possession:
The Problem of Public Order

Our Dumb Animals was the main publication of the Massachusetts Society for the Prevention of Cruelty to Animals. It came into being two years after the birth of the first anti-cruelty organization, the American Society for the Prevention of Cruelty to Animals (ASPCA), in 1868. *Our Dumb Animals*, a monthly magazine or newsletter, was launched in the same year and managed to last until 1970. The MSPCA tried to distinguish itself from the ASPCA as an organization whose principal focus was on the education of humane sensibilities, and *ODA* was the primary mouthpiece toward that goal. The instant success the magazine enjoyed was unmatched by the ASPCA's similar attempts or any other like publications of the time (see Coleman 1924:41). The exact number of copies printed is hard to come by, but given that all members of the society received free copies, the number must have easily reached tens of thousands by 1890. The MSPCA published the magazine as a charity and hence kept the price relatively low, 50 cents *per annum*, to allow it to reach even the "humble segments" of the population. However, the general tone was elitist and patronizing, despite the organization's intention. *Our Dumb Animals* rode on the power of the status quo so much that briefly Boston police hand delivered the magazine door-to-door (Coleman 1924:91).

Each issue of *ODA* was nine by twelve inches in size, twelve pages thick, and delivered by mail to subscribers. The magazine carried a mixture of general readings on "humane education" and news about the organization's activities and its members. By "humane education," *ODA* meant a pedagogy toward the betterment of humanity in general, not the alleviation of animal suffering for its own sake.[17] Thus, each issue began with parables, poems, quotes, and hearsay for general lessons on humanity, which bore little direct relation to animals per se. The animal-related reports came in the latter half in three formulaic segments: (1) an instance of ill-treatment of animals would be reported by a subscriber in the fashion of a "letter to the editor" addressed to the president of the society, George T. Angell; (2) the animals' intellect, faithfulness, sense of responsibility, et cetera, would be extolled and contrasted to the existing lamentable treatment; (3) George T. Angell would propose specific steps to remedy the reported case.

However, the general tone of the search for "humanity" teemed with optimism: signs of improvement were everywhere; the MSPCA was a quiet witness to what seemed to be inevitable progress—even the cruel people repented easily, or sinned only with apprehension. Each "report" sounded emblematic, lacking in specifics, a sort of manifestation of a preordained fate rather than news. The middle section was allotted to anecdotal tidbits on the organization's activities and the everyday lessons of humanity that ordinary subscribers sampled. Through the mode of a personalized correspondence with George T. Angell, as the embodiment of the society, the magazine proffered a sense of close-knit community with average readers.

Since the inception of the animal protection movement in England in 1824—at a coffee-house meeting, I might add (French 1975:26; see Habermas 1989)—its organizations' publications assumed the position of addressing delicate readers situated at home about the cruel, harsh world outside. From the first issues of their newsletters, the early humane societies in America put great emphasis on catching readers at home. *Our Dumb Animals* often wrote that it "ought to be a constant visitor to every home" (*ODA* 1890 May:63), not just as a solicitor and a propagator of domestic virtues but as a caring (and censoring) conveyor of harsh realities from the street. The pre-1900 humane movement in America is of particular interest for this study because of its charged engagement with the problems of public order. The pre-1900 era, for American humane organizations, was a period of charismatic patriarchal leadership with flamboyant personalities who encouraged their "gentlemen" members to confront cruelty out in the streets and to actively seek publicity for the maximum exposure of atrocities (Coleman 1924:104). This was the time when the organizations were greatly concerned with issues of "public cruelty" in open spaces, especially those concerning working animals. An important change occurred in the style of the American humane movement roughly around 1900. The turn of the century was characterized by an increasing number of women leaders around the nation who avoided the light of publicity, checked zeal for policing activities, and brought antivivisection issues to the fore (Coleman 1924:180).[18] In the newsletters they published, heroic vigilance stories were replaced by accounts of visionary experiences, and the tales concerning working animals by those about smaller domestic animals.

For late nineteenth-century animal protection advocates, the victimization of animals in "public" was, more than anything else, a terrible sight to behold. Along this line, *ODA* once declared its mission to be the protection of its readers from the "gory and impersonal newspaper coverage of the cruel scenes of abuses and accidents," which the motley crowd of urban masses gorged on (*ODA* 1888 April:26).[19] Hence the delicate task: "We could easily fill these columns with the terrible details of American cruelty . . . but nine-tenths of our readers would soon stop reading, and our influence upon them be lost. So we are seeking constantly for bright and happy stories and thoughts, determined to catch every gleam of sunshine, and then, with those, contrive to weave in the sad and solemn facts which it is our duty to tell. Kind readers, send us all the bright and happy thoughts and pictures you can . . . that we may spread them . . . into American homes" (*ODA* 1888 April:86).

Since the magazine's main objective was the uncovering of cruelties, this self-imposed mission bore Joe's aforementioned paradoxical task of fighting heinous exposures with another kind of exposure (the camera). *Our Dumb Animals* posed itself as a direct antidote to such a mass-consumed indulgence in cruel sights. Through a controlled exposure of its readers to disagreeable scenes, as it were, the magazine promised to help readers transcend the impersonal and anonymous public of the mass press and become a member of the circle of refinement and humanity. *Our Dumb Animals'* contemplation of the street displays of cruelty, therefore, was more than just exposé; it was an exercise in negotiating the position of its readers relative to the mass public onlookers present at or implied by such a street spectacle. This positioning required the figure of an on-the-scene humane witness/narrator as the conscience incarnate and the embodiment of the readership—that is, a vigilante.

Naturally, the on-scene humane observer was a figure diametrically opposed to the perpetrator of cruelty. As has been mentioned, *ODA* and other newsletters of the nineteenth century reported almost exclusively on the areas of working animals, that is, where animals were found in close proximity to working-class men. Cruelty abounded in places where animals coexisted with economic interests. The cruel subject was most frequently portrayed as "greedy."[20] In contrast, *disinterestedness* was the mark of the (predominantly male) humane observer, who could "speak for those who cannot speak for themselves," as the mission statement of the MSPCA read. Here are a typical opening and a typical ending of cruelty narratives from two different episodes—the convention was so fixed you could paste different episodes together to make one story. The first episode tells of a man taking a walk when it suddenly began to rain: "He came out of the Boston and Albany station, expecting to find a carriage. By some mistake, however, the coachman had failed to be on hand, and he stood under the roof sheltering the sidewalk before the station, waiting for him. As he stood there, a drunken teamster, who had overloaded his horse, attempted to cross the horse-car track and got stuck. The street resounded with his oaths, and the blows he began to give the horse" (*ODA* 1893:9).

At this moment a Quaker stopped and pushed his way among the crowd. Unable to endure this scene for a moment, the Quaker approached and took the arm of the carter, who turned with a menacing look. "Friend," said the Quaker in a calm tone, showing the carter fifteen *louis d'or*, which he held in his hand, "will thou sell me thy horse for this gold?" "What do ye say?" enquired the carter; "will ye give me that sum for the brute? . . . But why should ye buy the horse? . . . *I cannot tell why you bought* [sic] *the old brute*," said the carter. "I can tell thee; it was to free him from thy cruelty that I bought him," replied the Quaker (*ODA* 1889:119, emphasis mine).

The humane observer was supposed to have nothing at all at stake in the place he discovered an offense. Appropriately, it was usually during his leisurely hours of strolling that the discoveries were made, or else some unforeseen event, such as rain, drove him to the scene of the crime. Only accidentally and unexpectedly did he stumble onto an atrocious display, freed of the burden of private interests—a state that is utterly beyond the comprehension of the above cruel carter. Here is another passage that shows how the humane impulse shines through suspended worldly interests. In this episode, a lawyer had witnessed a white horse cruelly driven in the earlier hours of the day. Returning to his office, "he dropped the white horse completely out of his mind and took up the papers of a great railroad case, and after that the contested will of a millionaire, and after that a disputed water right, and so on, through the day. But when night came, and he *set his face homeward*, he went out of his way to look for the horse" (*ODA* 1888:21, emphasis mine).

The humane observer discovered more abuses at places where a "gentleman's" presence was unseemly. The members of humane organizations must have known exactly in what quarters of the city cruel practices were perpetrated daily—today, one has only to take a glimpse at the recurring place names throughout the pages of their newsletters. But this tale of accidental discovery and surprise dominated the witnessing narrative. Moreover, recall that gentlemen members of the society were asked to be active vigilantes out in the streets. But when they actually located a case of cruelty, they turned into unsuspecting strollers. It was supposed to be a vigilantism without a preconceived design.[21]

The trope of accidental discovery had an effect of mitigating the appearance of apparent class differences, for the vigilante was turned into an innocent bystander who commonly populated the street. In actuality, class differences, or clashes, to be more exact, must have been glaring at these scenes. Humane organizations boasted of the number of "raids" they had made on the barbaric spectacles of working-class blood sport and exploitation each year in their annual reports—they were in the hundreds (see ASPCA 1873–76). But only the statistics were provided: the elaborate stories of witnessing that filled the pages of the newsletters hardly ever re-created the scene of gentlemen in top hats cane-swinging their way, escorted by constables, through the rowdy throng of harsh and wretched countenances, when practically every case must have been confrontational. Class contrast did serve as a major figure in these narratives, but only after inscribing the humane observer as an unmarked citizen, the bearer of a spontaneous and unassuming witnessing. The central narrative strategy for the figure of the compassionate witness relied on the tension between the moments of being seen among the street crowd and the abstracting/distancing gaze toward them; the figure at once positioned the reader as part of the urban public and yet inscribed an unmistakable distinction and distance. The newsletter shrouded the distancing move with a halo of self-reflexive gazes for its readers to generously feel for a moment as part of the urban masses. That is, the position of the reader was contrived by sublimating the sphere of the mass public through negotiating participation and abstraction, exposure and protection, or proximity and distance.

The desire for simultaneous participation in and abstraction from the cruel scene and its spectators found a poetic relief in the oft-used guardian-angel-like figure in the witness narratives. The story usually goes that the angelic figure mysteriously emerges *out of the crowd* that is helplessly watching an animal being abused. He then masterfully overpowers the culprit, helps the animal, and disappears just as mysteriously without a trace, leaving every bystander wondering "who that might have been." Anonymity, or social unmarkedness, was the driving narrative force of this character, but no such episode failed to reveal the respectable status of the savior with ever so subtle clues such as "the soft white hand" that "stopped the rough, brown hand of the teamster" (*ODA* 1890:21).

As I have tried to show so far, the humanitarian reaction toward open displays of cruelty was neither impelled by an unambivalent indictment of the other classes nor by an unfaltering conviction of radical difference from the crowd at such harrowing spectacles. This finding calls for a reassessment of a well-accepted view on the politics of public order implied by the visions of the late nineteenth-century American "preventive societies," which included all kinds of societies advocating for the causes of animals and children and against prostitution, vice, and so forth, pioneered by the American Society for the Prevention of Cruelty to Animals. Timothy Gilfoyle has argued that the preventive societies' vigilance and besieging of the working class and immigrant districts, especially their entertainment sectors, was an effort to contain and prevent the coarse elements from spreading into respectable areas (1986:643), for the societies regarded the city as "frontiers to be conquered and tamed" (642). Such "morality-based tactics," he further argued, had "furnished ideological sustenance for later methods of modern political surveillance" (649).[22] It is true that the ASPCA and the MSPCA did generally associate cruelties with certain "places"—for example, industrial ghettos and red-light districts where they were most likely to face anonymous multitudes of dubious origins—and made efforts to police the growing urban masses at such places in the name of keeping a vigil for animals. However, as I have tried to show, the discourses of anti-cruelty vigilantism expressed in the newsletters were far more ambivalent than simply hypocritical. The zeal for reform was not just a veneer for conservative calculations but was a conservatism of a particular kind, one that anxiously courted a progressive aspiration, namely, that of the reformers *seeing themselves as part of the common public.* Thus seeing themselves seeing, the *genre* realized what we have established (in the Introduction) as the matrix of *perversion* to the latter.

As Timothy Gilfoyle has observed, the first anti-cruelty societies in America did indeed react to the emerging "popular culture" among the displaced, rootless, and promiscuously mixed underclass masses that increasingly flooded urban streets. But the politics of safeguarding "respectable areas" was never secure: one should remember that the readership imagined and addressed by the then also newly emerging mass distribution system of a newsletter like *ODA* was no less a part of an "anonymous" mass. It was only that this segment of the masses shared a distinguishing anxiety to distance themselves from the rest of the growing urban public. The sentiment that *ODA* catered to, therefore, was *a yearning for the absent or disappearing public*, the exclusive circle of humanity and refinement that had been threatened by the encroaching mass society. Contemplating animals victimized on the streets had a special persuasiveness in achieving the effect of what one might call "sublimation," since, in the Western humanist-humanitarian tradition, discourses on animals were inseparably intertwined with ideas of human Otherness. The bourgeois economy of animality shared with the humanitarian politics of public order the paradigm of sublimation.

Just as in the case of "science" inscribed by gloved love, the reform rhetoric firmly situated the rationale for discrimination within the narcissistic affirmation of common humanity (or animality) and universal kinship, or the disavowal of (class) differences. Such a move self-absolved the privileged status of the humane observer and inscribed a perception of difference as natural, freed of social biases (cf. Shell 1993). This double-faced anxiety, which is distinctly that of the "middle class," seemed more intense in the American humane movement, which, having been in the shadow of its British and aristocratic (in the dual sense of class and nation) parent, had more drive to forge a popular movement.[23]

Animal as Fetish

In short, the late nineteenth-century humanitarians in America deployed the relation-to-animals as a key signifier, as a kind of "fetish," in understanding and containing the newly surging urban masses. Once again, fetishism, in Homi Bhabha's construal, is a mode of knowledge that appropriates and controls singularities of the unfamiliar by affixing them to something established, and thus normalizes them as versions of previously known things (1983, 1990). Fetishism, Bhabha continues, disavows a recognition of difference by displacing the alterity with a fetish-object that masks that difference and narcissistically restores an undifferentiated oneness and similarity, within which only a limited and stunted version of Otherness is allowed in a palatable and digestible way (1983:27).[24] The relation-to-animals was a sign that simultaneously articulated human differences and yet avowed universal humanity (or animality)—that is, as that which signified differences as long as the universal sameness and similarity is narcissistically affirmed first.

In *ODA*, the stereotypes of the growing underclass masses were constituted *in relation to* animals. The image of the working class's proximity to animals was imprisoned within the humanitarian contemplations on the extremes of either/or, as signifiers of redemption or the fall. *Our Dumb Animals'* contemplation of the animals' well-being was always about the contiguous human others' animality, about their redeemability or degeneracy, never about animals per se. For while working-class existence seemed to have been inalienably linked to that class's animals, no animal depicted in *ODA* explicitly recalled the animals within the readers' own proximity; their pets were hardly ever implicated in the magazine's speculation of human animality. The gentlemen observers in the *ODA* narratives, to my knowledge, never rendered their own household pets the objects of didactic contemplations. It was precisely one's detachment from animals that permitted one to claim to be the representative who could speak for those who could not speak for themselves. I called this earlier the "human" consolidation of human/animal boundary, that is, our increasing self-possession vis-à-vis animality.

The humane observer, when he embarked upon the mission-filled stroll, was supposed to have shed all traces of private interests at home, among his pet animals, so to speak. Through abstraction from his personal interests and attachments, the gentlemen delegate of conscience inhabited a public subject who transcended himself. By identifying with him, in turn, the readers could commune with the publicity of pure humanity, which transcended the promiscuously mixed urban masses either by sublimation or allegorical distancing. In Chapter 6, I link this axiomatic "pure humanity" to the rise of biopolitics.

CHAPTER THREE

Hooliganism

In retrospect, it was no accident that I found myself in the middle of the memorable skirmish between the protester and the boy on that unlucky afternoon. It was the first (and last) time that I equipped myself with a camera at the shoot—and a brand-new photographer's vest to go with it.[1] Call it an identity crisis of some sort: having already had two fruitless visits to the shoot, I was anxious to display myself as occupied and vainly sought to blend in with dependably industrious reporters. Because I had been recognized by participants and protestors as a media person of the most alien kind, the incident could have sought me out. For I have seen countless times, since that incident, how disturbances and media personnel, especially television cameras, travel together inside the park. "Scenes" followed media crews and cameras, rather than vice versa. There was always a flock of rowdies surrounding the television camera—turning each deployment into a procession. Most fights, confrontations, and ostentatious cruel acts broke out in the path of this pact. Away from the television camera, even protesters were left in peace.

But then, in turn, television cameras deliberately followed falling wounded pigeons, because "that's where the action is," one television producer told his novice cameraman. Hence, at the shoot, the dominant crowd activity is materially dictated mainly by the television camera and the uncontrollable, untamed flights of frantic birds.

According to the figures provided by the Fund for Animals, nearly 70 percent of pigeons released at the shoot escape instant death by shotgun.[2] Of them, only a fraction seek freedom and the majority, mostly wounded but quite alive, return to the park ground. This, I was to learn later, was due to the birds' tragic impulse to examine their wounds at the first available landing. Plus, as "displaced" birds, as will be detailed below, they flocked together out of alarm and panic in an unfamiliar environment. This tendency provides rowdy spectators with a chance for ruffianism, and the animal rights protesters with a heroic action to "document."

The notoriety of the Labor Day Shoot was earned primarily by the free-for-all manner of impulsive, hands-on killing by the general public, not by the organized shooting game itself.[3] It is the image of this kind of atrocity among the spectators that both animal rights organizations and the media are eager to capture. And copious images do they collect, thanks partially to the just-mentioned collusion on the part of the killers themselves, who seek out cameras. Exactly what portion of killing is perpetrated actually "on camera" is impossible to establish, but it can be readily argued that the mediated "outside" attention frames the impulse to maim and mutilate at the Labor Day Shoot.

Putting a face on violent elements at the shoot was an intimidating task. It was a face of petty criminality—unwilling to be identified and hostile to inquirers. Studying them, I was lucky if I did not become a target. But, in retrospect, I did become their target repeatedly—if not in explicit violence, then in numerous episodes of not-so-subtle jeers, taunts, and threats. All along, the protagonists of rowdyism at the shoot had been so introducing themselves to me—one by one and year after year. And one day, I suddenly realized my well-honed ability to recognize repeat offenders from the rowdy pack that usually surrounded the television cameras: they were the very ones I had been working hard to avoid. Let me call this group of men "hooligans."[4] They cannot number more than thirty at each Labor Day Shoot, but nonetheless they are the determining factors in the physical "volume" of the event: their bigotry is the flashiest, their support of the shoot seemingly the most unconditional, and their cruelty the most bloodthirsty and willing. But notwithstanding the recognition, finding out who they were was an entirely different matter.

The police chief of Hegins suggested going through the list of those arrested each year but was too unnerved to produce any further material himself. Newspaper lists gave only offenders' names and their places of residence—most of them were from once heavily mining-dependent and now fast-decaying company towns, such as Minersville or Joliet. After some stagnation in my timid investigation, a small breakthrough presented itself by chance. Animal rights groups trumpeted one year, through well-coordinated press releases, their sponsoring of court costs for offenders on their side. Soon, pressure began to build from the other side—that the Labor

Day Committee express the same monetary gesture of patronage toward its jailed foot soldiers. Hence a list of those "patriotic sons" was drawn up, and it was sitting on Bob Shade's desk one day. Its deliverer, Warner Klinger, was still in Bob's insurance agency office when I walked in.

Warner was a natural choice for this job of unwelcome delivery. This virile man in his early seventies was an "ex" of every possible blue-collar job available in the area: an ex-miner, ex-bus-driver, ex-machinist, ex-carpenter, et cetera. At the same time, he was a self-educated man, armed with articulate speech, quick wittedness, and immovable opinions. Besides, he had an army of equally virile sons—seven altogether—who were regarded by the entire "West End" region (the southwest of the county) as a family to be reckoned with for their solidarity and machismo. No serious community activity that required volunteer time and sweat could proceed without soliciting Warner's approval. Thus, he was an important member of the Labor Day Committee, side-by-side with business owners, a banker, an insurance agent, and a lawyer. Warner was a perfect fit for the job of mediating between the "rougher" segment of the shoot's supporters and the elite leadership.

Such mediation can often be a very delicate job. For, when stepping out of the blinding sensationalism of the "us" and "them" of the Labor Day battle, even the reputations of the leaders of the shoot—the unquestioned chief commanders during Labor Day—are vulnerable. Solidarity cannot be guaranteed when the leadership is gossiped about in accordance with the everyday standards of conformity among everyday acquaintances: when the topic of the shoot finds its place back in the web of everyday twists and turns of other fields of meaning and other relations of power, local identities and local quarrels, scores to be settled and debts to be paid, and so forth. In addition, beneath the prescriptive conservative rhetoric on Labor Day, if not beyond that, there simmered frustrations—at the rhetoricians' unfulfilled promises of equality, communalism, self-sufficiency, and so forth—all inflected through and enmeshed with everyday local scenes of power asymmetry.[5] In this context, the media attention and the officially sanctioned staging of malice toward the "common enemy" provides the disenchanted an opportune moment to momentarily take hostage the official script, the leadership, and the reputation of the powerful. Riding along on the authority of the officially sanctioned aggression, subordinate groups such as the hooligans bring in their own "projects" of intimidation—clearing the ground on which their future violence, stalling, and vandalism can be anticipated.[6]

Such "projects" are never explicitly articulated but inhere in loaded insinuations, nuanced gestures, and delicate shifts of footing strewn through diverse contexts, space, and time. Rendering them visible is the work of the anthropologist bent on outlining hardly legible traces with a particular angle of interest, compelled by certain unshakable impressions and premonitions. I was struck by such an impression after witnessing a cryptically worded "deal" between the leadership and one of the most notorious hooligans from Hegins.

> There were about seven of us still lingering inside Hegins park in the late night hours of one Labor Day, drinking beer and chatting about the day's scandalous scenes. The two main leaders of the event, Bob Shade and Jim Schaeffer, were there along with some volunteers. Among them was a regular thug of a youth who belonged to the local fire company. An oxymoronic role of "security" was annually awarded to this hooligan by the leadership, his savage unruliness having a better chance of being harnessed toward a useful end that way. That night, the hooligan interminably rambled on about his hell-raising ventures during the day, getting louder with each crushing of a beer can. And when sensing that the herd was breaking up, he increased the volume yet another notch and concluded by vowing what unprecedented meanness he will show everyone (perhaps to protesters, but tactfully unspecified) next year. As the group dispersed, calling it a day, I began to walk next to the hooligan hoping to borrow a lighter, and from behind us I heard the two organizers asking him out of nowhere about his long-suspended driver's license. Then, the insurance agent [Bob Shade] turned to the attorney [Jim Schaeffer] and said: "We should do something to get him back on the road." I sensed the hooligan's chest broadening in the darkness. (revised field note, 1995)

My emphasis here is not so much on the possibility that actual deals might be made behind the contrived stage as on the fact that hooligans can inspire anxiety even in the most powerful. Judging from their appearance on Labor Day—and as it is shrewdly sensationalized by television—hooligans must be the most unsparing yeomanly vanguards of the causes that the shoot's organizers champion: their roars are the loudest, their gestures the most grandiloquent, and their physiques the most overwhelmingly expressive of violence when confronting, to use their favorite term, the "outsider intruders." But their volatile energy always borders on indiscriminate rampage and disquiets even fellow partisans.

There, too, was a certain forwardness about Warner's address to the elites like Bob Shade or Jim Schaeffer, despite their social consequence, and it showed in the matter of the "patriotic sons" list that day in Bob's office. Warner was not a man of many words, but when he talked, his opinions thundered to the point of unintelligibility. Generally, I had a hard time comprehending him, though he was widely known for persuasion. The reason I felt him to be louder that day was because, I came to surmise from his exchange with Bob, his youngest son was among the listed. The son's name was Tom. Tom Klinger—it occurred to me at this revelation that the name had been by no means a stranger to the past offender lists that I had studied. (This was the same Tom Klinger who commented on the "glassy eyes.") Though it was a common enough name in the area, I could not resist hoping for an acquaintance with such a "hard core" case. For I knew that Warner's sons were active in the shoot preparation, and over the years I, too, became a fixture in the kitchen on the days preceding Labor Day. The problem was that we—the "Tom" I fancied and I—belonged to different domains: there was an insurmountable barrier between the kitchen work, performed only by women and elderly men, and the virile labor of "field" preparation to which the Klinger brothers, along with other area toughs, applied themselves. Having been introduced to the community through Bob Shade, I was naturally first adopted by the population at ease with elites, women and the elderly, that is, people of the kitchen. Giving my teary eyes a rest from the onions under my charge, how I used to watch—with a mixture of dread and yearning—those guys toiling with hammers, wires, and tractors in a distant background! But once thus introduced, I was expected at the kitchen, and as the years passed, the laborers seemed ever more remote and impenetrably self-sufficient. Approaching an imaginary Tom among the latter was not going to be easy.

One day, I declared dramatically at the kitchen that I had had it with the olfactory trauma of my job and that I would employ myself only at a man's job from then on. The effect of this rather lame jestful fuss with an "older-generation flavor" of gender transgression was commendable—perhaps because of my perceived uncertain social status to begin with.

"Report to Mike, he'll give ya job," chuckled Shorty, the elderly man in charge of the soup. I headed to Mike, with a crowd of amused mothers and grandmothers looking on behind me.

A step into the blazing sun was the first change the transition to manly work entailed. A group of men were huddled together on a field of traps some distance away. At my uncertain approach, the heads poked up one by one in curiosity like a pack of hounds, but hurried back down in an attempt to ignore. As I intruded within earshot, I inquired for Mike, Warner's second son, with a determined aggression. And as it so frequently happened, Mike, with whom I had no personal acquaintance, answered with a certain presumed but guarded familiarity, as if intimating my being studied by everyone and all the time. Feeling my approach thus checked, I tried a desperate and drooping version of my recently successful quaint line from the kitchen, only to see it fall flat on the quietly spreading mockery among the huddled men. Foreseeing that the conventional order of introduction, such as "Do you need help?" as a next step, would only invite a distantly polite rejection, I helped myself to the first opportunity made available and gruffly grabbed onto a pole another man was trying to hammer into the ground without ceremony. And so began my career as an uneasy fellow laborer in the populace of hooliganism.

Coordinated manual labor is such that a tacit fellowship may grow on it. This is especially true with working-class men. Mike, as the leader of this small bunch, willy-nilly became my "host" partner in sharing hands. We hardly ever spoke, but after hours of synchronizing movements, he offered me a can of beer during a break. While the men were thus idle with beer, Bob Shade came over looking for me. He wanted to take a couple of boxes of beer home from the park's freezer and asked me to join in the task.

Turning to a slender, bearded man near the freezer, Bob said, "Give a couple of boxes to Hoon." The man very slowly turned his downward slanted gaze at me, raised his index finger, and muttered while pointing, "You mean *this* one?"

Bob did not hear him, or pretended not to. During our walk through the expanse of the parking lot with our heavy loads, I asked Bob who the slender bearded man was. His name was Tom Klinger.

I was haunted by Tom and his index finger all through that sleepless night, between alternating feelings of anger, fear, and curiosity. There was something familiar about his sour expression. Toward morning, I decided that he was the very man who had thrown the headless pigeon at me the previous year—now made hardly recognizable by the addition of a beard. It was strange: despite the overnight torment, by morning I was teeming with excitement at the idea of sharing this intelligence with none other than Tom himself. Suffering the researcher's fancy in the most acute form, I found myself, as it were, taking delight in reflecting on a situation with my own abuse as the subject.

The next day was Labor Day, and I easily located Tom hanging out in his usual company of area toughs around the fire engine proudly displayed at the entrance. I wasted no time in marching up to him and jovially announced my discovery of our prior acquaintance—as in the drama of paying homage to one's secret benefactor after a long search.

He smiled oafishly and groaned, "I did?"

The effect of waving my status as a victim was propitious. I felt I was entitled to more familiarity, and Tom seemed to comply without further ado. By the death of that luckless pigeon a small sacrifice had been made and a barrier torn down.

There were fewer protesters that year and the shooting game proceeded without interruption to end well before dusk. Bob Shade suggested that we celebrate this smooth run of business by having a game among ourselves with leftover pigeons. About thirty men mirthfully gathered with their shotguns at the southern end of the park. The group mostly consisted of labor volunteers, including the Klingers, and the members of the Labor Day Committee. The improvised game was simple: whoever was the shooter at a turn, anyone could bet one to five dollars on "kill" or "no kill." There were four traps and a shooter got two shots in each turn. Tom was selected as the puller-referee.

The evening was warm and breezy, there was a sense of triumph over the protesters, and beer was flowing liberally. No one cared about winning or losing, or killing pigeons for that matter. Given the darkening evening and drunken unsteady hands, most pigeons got away anyway. We indulged in jests and giggles instead. I felt happy in Hegins for the first time, though I did not participate in the game for lack of a gun. I was intoxicated by the thought of how marvelously my fieldwork was unfolding when someone called out my name. I turned around to face the awkward silence of the whole group.

"Let me see Hoon kill them pigeon," a stranger was shouting—again, the feeling of everyone knowing me already. Encouraging shouts broke out here and there.

I turned to Bob and saw a shade of worry. It was a trial, a trial of my allegiance, so to speak. They were demanding that I demonstrate once and for all that I was not an animal rights sympathizer—about which there were constant innuendoes and presumptions despite my steady performance as an omnivore. Seeing me frozen, Bob's youngest son, Chip, came up to me with his gun and caring words of encouragement. I teetered to the shooting line, with regrets over having drunk too much and feeling the weight of the deadly weapon I was a total stranger to. Once I was next to Tom, who was squatting, I did practice sightings just the way I saw the others do, doing my best to make them credible. The expanse of the south side of the field felt unusually large, and the ground stiflingly close, as though I could fall on it, nose first, at any moment, with that heavy gun. But once I was "ready," a violent curiosity welled up in me: I wondered what it would be like to blast a pigeon; I wondered how disappointed my detractors would be if I nailed one with that aesthetically pleasing shot that turns a frantic flutter motionless and limp instantly in midair. So I aimed to kill.

But, as usual, drunken fancies were not to be rewarded in reality. Both pigeons got away unharmed into the lush green of the mountains at dusk. I wanted to try again—already feeling that I was getting hooked—and stood there motionless, not able to give up. The familiar voice shouted again behind me, "He missed 'em on purpose!"

There was no immediate seconding to this serious accusation. But, then, a feeble but authoritative voice spread for all to hear, "He brushed 'em alright. I saw them feathers flying."

I turned around again and there was Tom Klinger, still in the squatting position, rope in hands, looking out into the field as if disowning what he had just said.

Hooliganism

It turned out that Tom was regarded as a weakling of sorts among his burly brothers. He was slender where the others, including his father, were stout; his voice was feminine like his narrow face, where the others had broad, square heads and voices that rumbled; and he was analytical while the others were pushy. With the recent addition of a beard, he now looked like a hermit among the Goths of his brothers. He was the only man in the family who had not tried his hand at "independent mining"; being only in his late twenties, he was too young to catch the disappearing occupation's last hope of being a viable source of income.[7] So he had gotten by, since graduating from high school, as a handyman (with a wife and a child).[8] Nonetheless, Tom was the one who was the most knowledgeable and glorifying of the mining trade and its tradition among the brothers, and the only one deep in the cult of the more traditional form of miners' pigeon shooting (more on this in Chapter 6). It surprised no one but those who assessed him only by his looks that he turned out to be the most pugnacious of the shoot's supporters.

What impressed me the most about those like Tom at the Labor Day Shoot was a certain unflinching confident carriage of their bodies and their opinions. A hooligan descends on Hegins Community Park on Labor Day as if to confront his debtor: scandalized yet filled with conceited smugness, even a little bemused (as if by his own outrage). Unless charged with official duties of the event, such as security, as many of his fellows are, the hooligan is an embodiment of the superfluousness of the onlooker: he aimlessly paces up and down the park grounds, eyes wandering rapaciously, shoulders swaggering, and untied soiled boots dragging. At the sight of animal rights activists, state troopers, or reporters, he stops and simply gawks from an uncomfortable proximity, imposing his presence and pressing his simmering threat. When there is some attraction—an animal rights activist being interviewed—he lingers at the very center of the action, looking up at talking animal rights activists or reporters with a conceited grin and derisive incredulity. But he quickly shifts gears at the slightest provocation—for example, a wounded pigeon is spotted, screaming and shoving matches break out, media crews begin to move swiftly, et cetera. At the drop of a hat, the hooligan shoves and wrestles with anyone mercilessly, claws and snatches blindly at anything, any living being, as if for no reason other than the sake of being at the center of the action itself. It seems that a certain gratuitous and nonsensical assertion of bodily presence preoccupies a hooligan. Between idle desires to see and to be seen, his existence drifts restlessly and with an utter frivolity.

But when asked about his reason for attending the shoot, a hooligan's answer is unequivocal: it is to confront the "outsider intruders." For example, besides his hatred of the animal rights protesters, Tom's hostility toward the media and the state police knows no bounds. He, like many other supporters of the shoot, called animal rights protesters "media people" (with a frequently added phrase, "they aren't workers"), and often did not bother to distinguish them. In rare moments of drunken camaraderie extended to me—usually after late-night clean-up work following a shoot—some of Tom's articulate friends would place the media-protesters in the elaborate scheme of "New World Order" conspiracy, which is said to be an alliance between the federal government and Zionists to destroy "white civilization" through media distortion, trashy popular culture, the spread of drug addiction, abortion, and the protection and breeding of "disease-carrying" pigeons. Some even suggested that pigeons could carry AIDS—Tom laughed at this—and that controversies like the anti-shoot protest were small steps toward ultimately disarming whites, and so forth.

However, I was always unsure how seriously these drunken sessions of bragging and camaraderie should be taken. Although hooligans were always rallying around the recruiting tables of radical right-wing groups at the shoot—some allegedly had parents who belonged to extreme groups like Save America Gun Club or the Covenant (see Maclean 1994)—I had no means of proving or disproving their claims,[9] nor could I express too much interest out of fear for my security and of giving too predictable an impression (as a "minority," an outsider, and an academic). Hints were strewn out here and there, perhaps willfully or perhaps carelessly, but commitments were withdrawn in alarm at the first signs that I was paying full attention. Some bore such an ephemeral commitment to bigotry with pride and as a clear threat intended for me.

All in all, whether seriously or half in jest, area residents in general, not just hooligans, are prone to abandoning themselves to all kinds of conspiracy theories around the time of the Labor Day Shoot—theories that are partially fanned by the alarmist leafleting of the participating organizations such as the Ku Klux Klan or the National Rifle Association. The theories are more often than not variations on the theme of media distortion (about the shoot and the Hegins community), with occasional excursions into riffs on the federal government, pro-abortion liberals, homosexuals, the Federal Reserve, and, infrequently, ZOG (Zionist Occupation Government). Signs of besiegement are detected everywhere, but not without elation on the part of the chosen victim. The tone is only rarely apocalyptic, but more often merges with the complacent lament-cum-fascination over the exceptional state of being caught in the intense outside heedfulness—not as an instigator of programs for action but more like a pastime. The air is saturated with a vague premonition that "anything could happen," "the whole world is watching." Under the exceptionally intense media limelight in 1996, a group of excitable area teenagers even reported a UFO sighting over the mountain behind Hegins Community Park the night before Labor Day.

The social function of a conspiracy theory, as I will elaborate in Chapter 5, does not lie in its truth-value. Rather, one indulges in conspiracy theory with an eye toward freeing oneself from the burden of truth by way of imputing to the protean manifestations of the "powerful evil other" the possession of culpable "knowledge" (Barkun 1994, 1998; Campbell 1972). In the agency of the big Other, then, an exchangeability between knowledge and power consummates. Such an Other is viewed not only as the cause of the conspiratorial subject's current impoverished lot, but also as the one blocking his or her representation of the situation. In this way, the theorists' "theory" is rendered invincible, since it contains, within its explanatory power, its own referential fallibility. What is effected thereby—that is, by bestowing the existence of the knowledgeable and knowledge-robbing big Other—is an inverse of tethered agency: a precipitous affirmation of an autonomous agency, transcendent of the oppression that overwhelms him or her. Within the "space" of such a paradoxical freedom, one is temporarily imbued with a license to experiment with all kinds of opinions, however *frivolous* they may be.

"Frivolity" and "hooliganism" are precisely the terms Jean-Paul Sartre used to characterize anti-Semitism in his classic *Anti-Semite and Jew* (1986[1948]).[10] The contemporary value of this brief monograph lies not in its sociological rigor (of empirically identifying anti-Semitic populations) but in being a prophetic and poetic account of a prevalent form of modern ideology generally. It is for the latter benefit that the work is invoked here, not toward labeling "anti-Semites." Sartre's foremost observation is that anti-Semitism is not an idea but a passion (10–33). By "passion" he conjures up a certain attitude of immunity to contradiction, scoffing adherence to irrationality, or the immovable carriage of whimsical opinions. Thus, he observes, anti-Semitism precedes the facts that are supposed to call it forth; it seeks them out to nourish itself upon them, all the while it is fully cognizant of the contradiction: "Anti-Semites know that their remarks are frivolous, open to challenge. But they are amusing themselves. . . . [They are] hooligans" (20–33). This is because, he continues, what an anti-Semite longs for is a certain "impenetrability"—"he chooses for his personality the permanence of rock" (28). Sartre contrasts such a thing-like self-assurance in the subject of an anti-Semite to that of the "man of reason," which is characterized by existential contingency, or "openness." What is foregrounded in the former thereby is the quality of reflexivity over reflectivity; there is an element of self-reflexive conceit in the complacent smugness of an anti-Semite's thing-like self-certainty. Hence, Sartre ends up rephrasing his opening statement: what anti-Semites amuse themselves with is not passion but instead the "state of passion." In other words, what Sartre saw behind "frivolity" and "hooliganism" is none other than the disposition of self-doubling or self-othering. From this, consider the following.

Mass Media Coverage

Media coverage of the shoot has been extensive each year. The shoot is a field day for most central Pennsylvania television stations (for example, WBRE, WYOU) and some state-wide television stations (for example, WNEP, WGAL), whose media vans and buses descend upon the town with a great air of importance. National media have joined the frenzy.[11] Local television stations provide almost hourly newsbreaks throughout Labor Day, in addition to weeks of pre- and post-shoot coverage of the controversy's developments—lawsuits, arrests, injuries, sentencings, et cetera. Some stations even set up hotlines for the more anxiously curious. Normal life in the county halts on Labor Day, as a majority of eyes and ears turn to the unfolding day-long clash on television. Even in the towns remote from Hegins, signs of homage are ubiquitous: in support of the shoot, men thump their chests and raise their fists in the air, and drivers honk their horns when they spot those who look like outsiders.

As has been mentioned, the media generally portray the commotion at the shoot as an eruption of the underlying culture conflict between the conservatives and the liberals, the rural population and urbanites. The early morning news on Labor Day typically brings an aerial shot of the caravan of vehicles the narrator claims to be those of the animal rights protesters branching away from the interstate highway and streaming into Hegins.[12] From the ground, footage shows the protesters gearing up with bull horns, placards, and armbands, taking up positions on the slope of the parking ground as if readying to storm the park; a few ferocious-looking supporters of the shoot—some literally clothed in anti-homosexual, anti-feminist messages, some swaggering with shouldered shotguns—graze by the assembling protesters while hurling menacing looks and jeers. As the confrontation unfolds, reporters interview the leaders of the protest and the shoot's officials for their respective "next moves," interjecting anticipations of what crisis might transpire: the shoot could be interrupted, people could get seriously hurt, or the number arrested could break the record. A television reporter dressed in a khaki vest assumes a warlike air—taking pains to time and position a pose with an unfolding brawl between protesters and supporters as the backdrop. Shots like these make up the archive of images television stations play and replay virtually all year round, piquing interest and beginning a restless countdown as early as May, with a promise of another dramatic showdown on Labor Day.

Another characteristic of the shoot coverage, which makes it stand out from other news segments, is its open-ended "liveness." Television concentrates its effort on publicizing the shoot as the place to be on Labor Day. A tradition with the appearance of impending doom—the powerful animal rights organizations' ceaseless lawsuits and legislative lobbying efforts perennially at its throat, and an explosive confrontation with suggestive gun blasts in the background—the Labor Day Shoot is suspenseful subject matter that "live"-hungry television cannot resist (see Doane 1990). Narrative function is attenuated and television strives to assume the role of a monitor, with long takes of sustained relaying of images, collapsing event-time and transmission-time. Instead of talking heads, the whole bodies of the reporters are shown almost constantly (see Brunette 1994), against the well-timed backdrop of hostile outbursts among the anonymous crowd, only to be interrupted by close-ups, lots of close-ups, of pigeons blown up in mid-air. The atmosphere is intense, the event imminently catastrophic, always with ominous gun blasts cracking in the background.

Speaking of the usefulness of catastrophe for the televisual medium, Mary Anne Doane suggested that a piece of information acquires its greatest referential power when threatened with imminent extinction (Doane 1990). Despite the heavy presence of the media, the television producers I spoke with expressed only lukewarm enthusiasm about the coverage: "There is not much going on on Labor Day, and people are at home all day." Some also pointed out that there is no statewide interest in the controversy. However, all added that they have to cover it anyway "because other stations do." I take their comments as an acknowledgment of a sort of baiting function the shoot coverage offers for a particular channel's entire programming on one of the year's most profitable days. Thankfully, particularly for the regional television stations, the Labor Day Shoot lasts virtually all day, from dawn to dusk, providing a raw spectacle of blood and feathers, of foaming fanatics, and of gun-brandishing rages. The imminent threat of all-out manslaughter, carefully edited and unmistakably intimated by the televised images, causes suspense intense enough to keep curious viewers close to television sets all day long, or to propel the impatient to Hegins.[13] With its day-long development, the shoot constitutes a temporally parallel world "out there," an accompaniment to the "flow" of Labor Day programming; updating it, television validates the referential authority of itself.

Mass Media and Hooliganish Frivolity

The emphasis on coevalness on the part of the mass media seems to intensify hooliganish frivolity. Hooliganism involves a circular trajectory through a lapse of time, between the moment of being seen and that of mediated seeing. An observation of this behavior thus requires a sustained stretch of attention in time: on the one hand, across the segregated realms of public performance, and on the other, private moments of media consumption. For a person bent on expressing offense and intimidation, such as a hooligan, a lot hinges on this segregation. Naturally, this circular trajectory was one of the last to come to my attention, I myself having been, I think, the most uncommon and exquisite target of shock and insult, rather than the mate and conspirer in the celebration of hooliganish work. Not that I did not aspire to what is called in media studies "audience research" from the beginning (for example, Ang 1985, Morley 1986, Moores 1993). But "participant observation" of the audience—whose availability is taken for granted in this discipline as a superior method—seemed like a remote luxury from my lot. It would have been like asking someone who had just hurled insulting gestures toward me whether he would let me watch television by his side that evening (including the program that would replay that very insult).

But early one Labor Day morning, at my fourth Labor Day undertaking, something dawned on me after I walked passed a file of security personnel at the entrance of Hegins Community Park, timidly waving my "staff" pass.[14] By then, most of the entrance personnel recognized me. Such an early morning encounter with the rougher segment of the shoot's personnel was by far the most pleasant and amiable, compared to the rest of the day. For nerves were fresh, and the security personnel clearly seemed to find it a little comical to see me timidly show up for another wild showdown of a shoot without fail. So, little by little, a simple nod became a smile one year, a smile into a real greeting another year, and this time, some of them were willing to risk the potential stigma of talking to me. One man asked if I had caught the early morning Fox News on television. I had not. He jumped in anyway without waiting for my answer: "They say the entrance fee is a new thing this year; obviously, they've never been here before."[15] Feeling bashful at the honor of being spoken to by one of those men, I simply exclaimed an impressed "Aha!" and moved on, but only to run into another eager talker. This interaction was about newspapers: "It'll be fun, the protesters will be in full force this year!" (or something to this effect). So it went on, four different men altogether, all bringing up the media coverage of the shoot.

This brief encounter was hardly impressive at the time, although it was memorable from the point of view of improved sociality. For most people confused me for a reporter anyway; I thought that the mass media was brought up that morning just to make conversation. It was not until my better acquaintance with Tom that these early morning references to mass media gained a retrospective significance.

Tom was free of duties during the Labor Day Shoot itself, his charge being the setting up of traps the night before. So his presence at the shoot was only for his own pleasure (and pleased he was at the shoot!). I began to notice that mid-shoot he frequently went home, which was across the street from the northern end of the park. When I inquired about the reason, he said it was "because of the kid." But when I had a chance to accompany him once, his child was not home. Instead, Tom did not waste a second in turning on the television set as he walked into the living room. Frantically, he flipped channels through local stations and exclaimed "No news!" with obvious disappointment. Only then did he look around for the garden hose that Bob Shade had asked us to fetch.

So, it turned out, through numerous circuitous follow-up inquiries on my part, that Tom was going back and forth between his home and the park—between the television coverage of the shoot and the actual shoot. I also ascertained that Jon Lubold, Tom's fellow hooligan, was doing the same thing whenever he could afford a break from his entrance security duties. Those other hooligans who lived farther did not exactly straddle like that, but nonetheless all were eager to catch the evening news before and after the shoot. Some of them were constantly tuning in on pocket transistor radios throughout Labor Day.

"Media Event"

Recall that our issue in this book is a certain vaticinal spatiotemporality I have provisionally called "whiteness." Having thus subtracted the authorship of such a spatiotemporality out of the ownership of the "white" subject, we turned to the gaze of the Other that organizes it. How can we make sense of the role of mass media in such an instance?

There are theories of "media events" that are centrally concerned with the modern media's influence on public events.[16] Most prominently, Daniel Dayan and Elihu Katz proclaimed that such theory's goal is to "bring the anthropology of ceremony to bear on the process of mass communication" (Dayan and Katz 1992b:2; also see Dayan and Katz 1985, 1992a, 1992b; Katz 1980; Katz and Dayan 1985). They celebrate the mass media's potential to bring together individuals dispersed over vast areas. A live television broadcast of an extraordinary public event has the power to "integrate societies in a collective heartbeat" (Dayan and Katz 1992b:9). For such media events interrupt the routine course of life, the normal flow of television programming, and bring together anonymous mass viewers in front of television sets at the same time. On such occasions, microcosmic public spheres simultaneously form in front of the scattered home television sets vis-à-vis the electronically delivered ritual center. Partaking together in ritual symbols, Dayan and Katz continue, and being confident in the knowledge of the simultaneous similar activities engaged in by millions of others, anonymous viewers all converge in the communion of a nationwide (at times, global) "imagined community" (1992b:305).

For the adherents of the notion of media event, the difference between media events and ordinary news events is crucial. In Dayan and Katz's words, media events must be "live, remote, interrupted (from the routine), and preplanned" (1992b:5). Their flow and coherence are dependent upon the "real" event that occurs regardless of television's attention (1992b:64). Not in sound bites but in its "entirety" is a media event relayed in "real time." Minimized here is self-reference to the medium's interpretive authority, and maximally dramatized instead is the medium's *spatiotemporal continuity* with the event in progress. Dayan and Katz argue that much more important for the purpose of spatiotemporal continuity than the narrative guidance (for symbolic meanings of the broadcast ritual) is the display of responses of "primary spectators" at the site of the actual event—their in-person and on-site cheers and rapt attention (1985:65). For it is "through the eyes of those directly involved . . . who cannot perceive the whole" that television restores the senses of "distance" and "depth" of an event (Dayan and Katz 1985:64). The interest taken by these attendants becomes the camera's subjective justification for shot selection. Their complicity with the camera's gaze is supposed in this way to restore the "aura of being there"—validating and transcribing the inhabitable space believed to exist outside and independent of the medium.

The Labor Day Shoot as a televised event differs in some superficial aspects from the definition of media events. The shoot coverage appears merely as a series of news items on local channels and as an occasional national evening news item—falling short of nonstop broadcasting for the entire duration of the event (seen above as one of the important characteristics of media events). However, although mere news items, the coverage of the shoot includes hourly "newsbreaks" that stay with the event throughout the course of Labor Day, the media's heavy emphasis on "liveness" accordingly striving to collapse event-time and transmission-time. And to elicit such an effect, the coverage of the shoot places much emphasis on the presentation of anonymous, in-person crowds in attendance. Moreover, the shoot coverage's "interruption" of the everyday lives of the county is indisputable, and so is its "preplannedness," with Labor Day inexorably returning every year (the issue of "remoteness" is addressed below).

According to the theory of media events, on-site participants' complicity with the television camera constitutes the central figure for the "singularity" of an event. The theory's emphasis on singularity by definition requires that, as has been already mentioned, all participants present themselves to the event simultaneously. This is possible, claim Dayan and Katz, because with electronic communication a televised event can be "simultaneous within a temporal frame shared by all protagonists and by the audience" (1992b:210). It is in this sense that media events appear evenly "remote" to all participants. Hence, the potential perspectival difference between the television (on-screen) audience and on-site participants poses a problem for the theory. Dayan and Katz avoid the conflict by drawing participants at these two positions temporally parallel and as mirror images of each other. They claim that "in-person audience attend the broadcast event as . . . actors," as a prop to add depth and distance to the on-screen image's ironed-out flatness (1992b:96–97). Dayan and Katz claim that this holds equally true for nonconformist, disruptive outbursts such as football hooliganism; football hooligans only carry the ecstasy of communitas further. In their words, hooliganism at a broadcast sports game is a result of too much "sociability"—too much rapt enthusiasm "exploding" beyond the boundary of the game (1992b:206). Here, we see a certain perspectival isomorphism fundamental to the theory of media event: a certain identification between the gazes of the television camera, on-site participants, and television viewers. We identified the same matrix as a perversion earlier. Such is the theory's condition for conceptualizing the "embrace" of sender-addressee-referent in communication, in a media event's "single" inhabitable space-time envelope. The theory's heavy emphasis on the "single spectacle" of spatiotemporal concurrence, as constitutive of a mediated "imagined community," owes almost exclusively to Benedict Anderson's (1991[1983]) famed concept of the same name (esp. see Tsaliki 1995:346). Hence, a criticism of this can be done most fruitfully through that of Anderson's notion of imagined community.

"Imagined Communities"

Benedict Anderson argued in *Imagined Communities* that the genesis of nationalism had been partially paved by the changing consciousness of time, specifically that of simultaneity (1991[1983]:22–26). The newly arrived idea of simultaneity, in place of the medieval temporal notions saturated by the imminence of Divine Providence, was conceived as a horizontal temporal coincidence in "homogeneous, empty time," mensurable by clock and calendar and authorized by the developing secular science. With such a notion of simultaneity, Anderson claims, people for the first time could imagine the steady existence of a bounded group of mutually unknown, unrelated individuals sharing the same temporal plane.

Anderson saw a direct reflection of such an emerging concept of simultaneity in the discourse genres that were centrally formative of the collective consciousness of "nationality": the print languages of the novel and the newspaper. In the passage that hardly needs reproduction, Anderson demonstrated how, for example, literary devices of the novel conjured up the feelings of "simultaneous" belonging in a community (1991[1983]:26–36). He argued that novels mapped text-internal time to the "exterior" time of the reader's everyday life, thereby temporally embracing author, characters, and readers in the solidity of a "single community" (27). The literary techniques he identified were familiar ones: the inscribing of the setting in the time, space, and socioscape recognizable from the reader's everyday life; the emplottment of simultaneously occurring but unconnected activities that were relatable only in the reader's consciousness of clock/calendrical time; the usage of pronominal forms such as "our" or "we" that were supposed to effect fraternizing bonding between the author, the reader, and characters. The "social organism" so figured by the novel, claims Anderson, has served as an "analog" for the idea of the nation. It was an "imagined community" likened to the indexical co-positioning of author-readers-characters—or sender-addressee-referent in communication—in a *single* inhabitable space-time "envelope" that moved calendrically through homogeneous, empty time (26).

In "Whorfianism and the Linguistic Imagination of Nationality" (1994), Michael Silverstein takes issue with Anderson's direct mapping of time in language to an "objective" temporality mensurable by clock and calendar. Silverstein concedes that Anderson follows Benjamin Lee Whorf's fundamental tenet of the cultural relativity of linguistically constituted thought-worlds (in Anderson's case, the print-language-constituted nationalities) (for example, Whorf 1956[1939]:134–59). But he accuses Anderson of falling into the trap of assuming a "fit" between linguistic structure and the "habitual thought-world of Newtonian space-time," which was precisely the kind of native speaker's trap that Whorf was at pains to show. For one of Whorf's contributions lay in demonstrating a disjuncture between our linguistic categories and what we consider to be the objective, empirical space-time reality on the one hand, and on the other hand, how native speakers (especially those of the languages belonging to what he called the Standard Average European) are wont to assume an unproblematic "fit" between the two. For example, the grammatical category of tense has nothing to do with "time" as clock-mensurable continuity, but the native speakers of the Standard Average European habitually presume a transparent coding of the former by the latter.[17] In thinking that literary devices—such as references to "a particular month of a particular date" or the pronominals of "intimacy" such as "our"—directly and denotationally indexed the text-external and scientifically verifiable "objective" space-time reality, Anderson has committed precisely the mistake Whorf had expected (Silverstein 1994:41).

Silverstein then moves on to Anderson's formulation of the linguistically constituted experience of inhabiting a social group. A sense of group membership for Anderson obtains from the sharing of "objective realist" discursive linguistic forms, argues Silverstein. For such a sense in Anderson's exegesis is an inhabitable trope (inspired by discourse genres such as the novel) that is also coterminous with "objective," homogeneous, and empty space-time. In this, an analogy is drawn between the sense of belonging in a group and occupancy in a spatiotemporal field, between the sense of homogeneous membership—the sense of self and other's being "no one in particular" from anywhere within the confines of the group—and an equitable and interchangeable (that is, homogeneous) placement of self and other in a spatiotemporal field. For Silverstein, such an idea of social membership as equivalent to free and homogeneous spatiotemporal occupancy is precisely a hegemonic ideology. Specifically, it is the hegemonic ideology of the Standard Language that was seen to be inculcated, in Anderson's rich documentation, in the web of nationalizing education systems and bureaucratic institutions (Anderson 1991[1983]: chaps. 5 and 7). For the Standard Language projects in our minds the sense of belonging in its linguistic community as an "inhabitable objectivity" (Silverstein 1994:44–45). The kind of "standardized" identity Anderson deems a prerequisite for nationalism thus radically differs from the sociolinguistic sense of "voicing" of identity: being an "inhabitable objectivity," the Andersonian idea renders irrelevant all those sociolinguistic factors essential in voicing, that is, who one is, and to whom one communicates in what contextualizing frameworks, et cetera (Silverstein 1994:44–45).

In short, Anderson presumes an uncontested appeal of the Standard Language qua "objective realist reportage" (Silverstein 1994:45). And this, for Silverstein, is counterintuitive to our understanding of the hegemonic order of a linguistic community, where standardization is often a fragile sociopolitical order demanding continual reaffirmation. Silverstein proposes the following correction: even when identifying with the Standard Language, "forms of *diversity* must be at least effectively ordered to cultural consciousness" (46). That is what we learn from Mikhail Bakhtin's study of the "realist" novels as the nationalist literary imagination's privileged genre, and how objective and commonplace societal observation and judgment were figured in them (Silverstein 1994:49). There, the "objective authorial voice" with which the reader was called upon to identify could be "voiced" only in opposition to the polyphony of *other* voices existent in the society, which were first realistically portrayed and emplotted as characters. In other words, even the plenitude of an unmarked objective authorial voice requires a moment in Othering. With perversion contrastively in mind, I want to emphasize this "Othering," which necessarily presupposes self-othering.

The Ideology of Homogeneous Space-Time

We can now see clearly how Anderson's idea of "community" as a *single* inhabitable space-time envelope has taken an even more literal turn in the theory of media events, which sought to incorporate the role of "live" television. From television's capacity to broadcast live, the theorists of media events ascertained the ultimate cultural technology of space-time synchronization. By doing so, Anderson's shortcomings are uncritically reproduced: just as Anderson's objectivist commitment led him to reproduce the hegemonic discourse of the Standard Language, a media event's literal construal of television's liveness replicates mass media's rhetoric because a media event stakes its popularity, its "ratings," precisely on the assertion of a spatiotemporal continuity and immediacy with the "real event," that is, by presupposing and conjuring into existence an imagined community of those who tune in "simultaneously."

For this reason, when the notion of media event is put to use in the search for nationalism, it smacks of a self-fulfilling prophecy in both temporal and spatial senses. For instance, such a study strives to show how a national regime successfully maneuvered symbols of a nationalizing importance in a bygone prominent media event—for example, the Greek state television's broadcast of Melina Mercouri's funeral (Tsaliki 1995). Temporally, the regime's current healthy existence would be a testimonial to the concerned media event's beneficial influence in the past. Spatially, the present boundary of the regime would retrospectively confirm the circumscribing efficaciousness of that past media event. The boundary of the communal entity is construed therein: as far as the television signal was tuned in. The effectiveness of a nationalizing media event presupposes the existence of a national boundary, its reach of influence self-evident in the way the broadcast range is isomorphically superimposed upon the spatiotemporal field of the national community.[18]

Is this not precisely the way a national regime and a "sensationalistic" media go about their business: circumscribing millions by the rhetoric "millions tuned in"; generating popularity by circulating images of popularity (Rogin 1987); manufacturing the importance of an event by portraying it as melodramatically and breathtakingly "live" and immediate? In short, Anderson, Dayan, and Katz reproduce the *ideology* of community membership rather than explaining it.[19] For what is ideology, if not that which creates and acts in a social world while masquerading as mere description of that world (see Woolard 1998)?

Dayan and Katz, in theorizing the role of mass media in the problematics of identifications, are at pains to exclude any suggestion of self-othering. This is evident, again, in their anxious handling of "primary spectators." They arbitrarily acknowledge only the constructive role of primary spectators to a media event. For example, they make an unsubstantiated argument that on-site participants-as-props are wont to comply willingly and dutifully with a media event's implicit interdiction against looking directly toward the camera (1992b:96–97). What of looking into the camera? And how does its prohibition redeem Dayan and Katz's idea of spatiotemporal continuity and depth? Such an interdiction is one against returning the television audience's gaze, against its doubling. Recall that, for Dayan and Katz, the non-imitating gaze of on-site participants, in an obliging complicity with that of the camera, is supposed in this way to restore the "aura of being there." How? Following the non-imitating, corporealized gaze, they argue, the television audience is supposed to momentarily bracket the medium's usual constructivist "flatness," to forget its status as a champion apparatus of mimicry (1992b:64). In short, for the theory of media events, on-site participants constitute the central figures of the non-citationality of a media event (Derrida 1988:7–12).[20] They guarantee the aforementioned perspectival isomorphism or "identification" between the gazes of the television camera and television viewers.

Media-Directed Frivolity

Then, what is the significance of media-directed frivolity in understanding media event? A media-directed frivolity, first of all, requires the ability to imagine both sides of the camera lens: to anticipate disembodied others as the audience, or to imagine oneself beyond the situated passivity of being filmed. That such an ability—for what one might call abstraction—is only a literacy proper to the media-saturated modern world is testified by numerous counterexamples from the non-West. For the sake of comparison, take the most dramatic tale of "first contact," in *Nanook of the North*.

Michael Taussig dwells much on Robert Flaherty's classic image of *Nanook of the North*: Nanook's fascinated engrossment in the sound coming out of the phonograph (1993). Taussig's attention turns on the established genre of the frontierist photographic/filmic representations of the primitive Other's look of shock and enchantment at the white man's apparatus of mechanical reproduction. Why the enduring fascination with this image in the West? The problematic in this image, says Taussig, is not in Nanook's fascination, but in our (white men's) fascination at his fascination; it is not in the primitive man as a perceiving subject but in how his perception constitutes an object of our fascinated perception (1993:200–203). He says that taking the talking machine to the frontier was an attempt to recapture the genuine "magic" and accomplishment of mechanical reproduction in an age in which the (phonographic) technology was seen not as mysterious but as routine. The Otherness of primitive men accomplished that recapturing of the magic, which was viewed as no longer articulable in the daily lives of westerners. For it was none other than the natives' extraordinary capacity for mimesis—so richly documented in colonial travelogues and ethnographies—that validated such a mimetically capacious machine as the phonograph: their fondness for mimicking and stealing the westerner's demeanors and possessions; their indifference to the decorum of bodily distance; their lack of concept of private property; and so forth. In short, it was their supposed inability to distinguish between self and other, subject and object, and their uncontrollable conflation of the two—so dramatically testified by Nanook's attempt to eat the record from the phonograph. The mis-en-scène of first contact mimes that primitive Others' mime, their spontaneous, visceral attempt to "merge" with the machine, thereby authenticating the modernist claim of the new filmic technology's enabling of "mythical participation" between subject and object.[21]

But there is more to be said here than what Taussig allows. His narrative is silent on Nanook's relation to that other inevitable apparatus of mechanical reproduction at the prototypical scene of first contact—the camera. This is a curious omission given that the point Taussig tries to prove, that is, Benjamin's theory of a "tactile" mass medium, is largely about visual experiences. Then we can ask: If Nanook's enraptured sensuous "merger" with the phonograph validates the machine's mimetic prowess, what does his total ignoring of the camera's presence prove? It seems that the pristine quality of this scene greatly hangs on our faith in the primitive man's innocent relationship to the camera; the assurance that he is not imagining both sides of the lens, conflating the subject and object positions of the camera gaze; in short, that he is not *miming* the role of primitive Other. The pristine quality of the scene requires that the viewer "steal a look" at someone else's losing of the subject in the object; the viewer's aloofness warrants the Other's subject-object conflation. And to that precise extent of "stealing," the primitive man is deprived of the possibility of self-possession. In other words, the camera remains here a transparent and voyeuristic apparatus that desires and objectifies the primitive subject-object conflation from a distance—celebrating contact but not itself sensuously implicated in the mis-en-scène—incidentally, the point exactly opposite of Benjamin's.

Taussig himself has to stop citationality qua mimesis in order to theorize this scene of pristine, authentic, homogeneous space-time of first contact.

The same applies to my own attempt to describe the vaticinal spatiotempo-rality as whiteness. Am I not thereby looking for an authentic, homogeneous moment of whiteness without becoming implicated? The same applies to the problematic of "conspiracy theory."

"Media Distortion"

The intense preoccupation with news coverage was far from being confined to hooligans. Before getting acquainted with the media-directed enthusiasm of hooligans, I was already very familiar with what went on after a shoot at Bob Shade's house. The post-shoot cleanup took some time—garbage needed to be collected, dead pigeons had to be disposed of or sold, dishes had to be washed, et cetera. By the time the park's gate was locked, it was, more often than not, well into the night. Then, we—usually Bob's wife, Jenny; their two grown-up sons; Palmer the accountant; Jim the attorney; Warner Klinger; and I—would walk or drive over to the Shades' (across the parking lot from the park) and have an impromptu party with leftovers from the vendors, cheerfully sharing gossip of another Labor Day fracas. As the eleven o'clock news came on, the Shades' three television sets across the house would blare, each tuned to a different station. There, a collected "textual analysis" of the news was unthinkable. Besides the unfamiliar challenge of the triple sound-track, side remarks about the coverage unstoppably and simultaneously raged, and invariably, Warner tried to talk everyone down with his signature thunderous voice. I doubt anyone could actually catch what was said on the television in such a sonorous environment, but as I recall, ardent opinions about it were always abundant—opinions filled with sarcasm and censure. It was a mode of engagement with the media, but surely one irrespective of its "content."

One year, I was allowed a calmer observation of media consumption at Tom's place—a rare chance for me to share such a private moment with the most militant hooligan of a man. The rare chance was occasioned by Tom's uncommon mood that Labor Day, which was the day of another center-stage hooliganish action on his part. Tom was certain of his appearance on the eleven o'clock news, and I exploited his hopeful excitement to get myself invited to witness Tom relive his glory. Tom's wife, Amanda, was home. I had known Amanda's face for some time, she being a regular at the kitchen operation of the shoot. A fast-talking, feisty woman, she had the habit of bluntly asking me to send her a copy of my book whenever we met, hand-ing me a piece of paper with the scribble of her address on it. Thereby, as I chanced upon her year after year, empty-handed, it felt as though she had my conscience doubly leashed: one for the slow progress of my book, and the other for the end result that was (somehow I knew) bound to displease her. Amanda made me uneasy.

As usual in the area, there was no awkward ceremony of the offering of seats or the excuse on the casual state of things; rather, I was allowed to blend in immediately and inconspicuously in Tom's private quarters. The interior was somewhat dusty, but it was arranged tidily—with lacy furniture covers, flower pots with colorful artificial birds, endless picture frames of nameless faces, a Latin American rendering of Jesus Christ, and a stack of photo albums on the coffee table. The eleven o'clock news was coming on then anyway, as I stood still awaiting the next move. The television set easily won over our willing attention. Tom was engrossed, Amanda was paying attention only half-heartedly amid her knitting. As had been well foreseen, the incident of Tom's passion was at the top of the news. Regrettably, I cannot reproduce the reportage, since Tom, again, channel-flipped from one report to another until he had sampled, piecemeal, from all three channels to his satisfaction. I don't recall anything remarkable about the reports, except the complete omission of the harassment of news crews themselves, which Tom triumphantly told me happened again. Tom's bony but staunch visage was all over the television screen, up close and far.

Tom's general reaction was a mixture of subdued pride and well-practiced outrage. He did not lose a beat as soon as the segment was over: "Them reporters are full of shiiiit," he declared. His eyes were still glued to the television set, as if merely talking to himself, but he was clearly waiting for my encouragement.

"How do you mean?" I asked dutifully.

Tom assumed an analytical air: "First of all, them kids was there from the beginning. They saw it all from the beginning . . . didn't arrive there later. It's a LIE. [inaudible] It was them reporters who came late, and the protesters too. Anyone from this area can see [from the news] that it happened around trap number six, which is farthest from the entrance [of the park]. You know how they [reporters and the protesters?] all hang around the entrance always? Scared to come in? And they say as if it happened right in front of their eyes!"

"I'll be damned," Amanda rewarded him, and added: "Some reporters don't seem to come in to the park at all. They sit in them air-conditioned media buses in the parking lot all day long, or somethin'. You know what they do, they just talk to people . . . especially protesters. It's all rumors they say on TV."

Tom resumed, much scandalized: "I was there from the beginning to the end, and nobody bothered to ask ME a question . . ."[22]

This was as close as I got, throughout the fieldwork, to the way the accusation "media distortion," which boils so many people's blood among the shoot's supporters, was substantiated. Instinctively, I knew that the moment of a reflexively richer native exegesis on the media stance would not become available to me, nor would such a session significantly improve my research. This was because, as it became clear to me from both sessions of television watching, at the Shades' and at Tom's, the target of censure is beyond the conceptual content of media representation. For example, there is nothing from the exchange between Tom and Amanda that suggests the media's imposition of viewpoints—except perhaps in Amanda's suggestion that they "just talk . . . to the protesters," or their neglect of Tom, the firsthand witness. Rather, their attacks touch on the failure of representation at the level of literal and physical presence; that is, failure to be at the appropriate spatiotemporal location, a mistake, it is presumed, that "anyone from this area" would not make.

Hypothetically speaking, a descriptive referencing can go on interminably; one can endlessly add an additional descriptive feature that a particular case of reference (for example, that by mass media) has missed. Then, a criticism that mobilizes descriptive failings in its argument has its eyes firmly set on prolonging the dispute for dispute's sake. For Tom and Amanda, it is clear that the media can never be "right"; its guilt is predetermined. It is guilty by virtue of setting its eyes on Hegins and its people. As has been said about conspiracy theory earlier, the accusation of "media distortion" is irrespective of truth-value. Criticism for its own sake, its meaning is in the form itself. Media watching and criticizing here, then, is an exercise in an already familiar attitude. Its "success" hinges not on what is being said but on *who they are*. What would be the aim of such an exercise?

Superficially, we can readily point to a collusion between the ideologically driven "media event" and hooliganism. Let me sum up this impression. The shoot-supporting local men frequently profess to have come to the shoot in order to confront the "outsider intruders," of which the media ranks as the most manipulative and sinister culprit. Like Tom, many of these men are the harshest critics of the mass media, and precisely for that reason they are the most vigilant and voracious consumers of the media coverage of the event. They tend to begin Labor Day by watching media reports before going to the actual shoot, and then return to the post-shoot coverage in the same evening or the next day. As a continuation from media consumption, the actual in-person participation at the shoot comes as an attempt to confront the inscribing moment of media (mis)representation, "on-site."

The most intriguing aspect of this media-related short-circuiting is this: upon returning to the consuming mode, many of the shoot's supporters, especially hooligans, are keen on following the media portrayals of *their own* on-site violent exploits, and passionately analyze and criticize them from the *authority of their in-person experience* of the "real" event. For the hooligans at the shoot, the rendering of themselves as a sensationalized object of media gaze directly results in further proof of the media's crime of misrepresentation; on camera hooliganism provides the very material with which further evidence of media distortion can be studied later. Temporally speaking, a hooligan *projects* his exploits on camera so that he can *retroactively* discover the discrepancy between his in-person experience at the shoot and the mediated version of it. In other words, a hooligan *first* bursts into camera-directed, on-site brutalities as a kind of projection into the future (because he will catch up with the broadcast only afterward) so that he *will be proven* justified for his outrageous deeds during later sessions of media watching and critiquing—where media distortion is confirmed through the very hooliganish behaviors now shown on television.

Hence the ironic collusion between media event and hooliganism. Through the process of circular trajectory, hooligans themselves provide the very ingredient for media sensationalism and distortion they so vehemently denounce. Their passion against the media is the very source of this media event's appeal and animation. Similarly, we can say that the hooligans' measures to "test" media distortion are already caught in the process of the reality they are testing. Even when it is condemned and censured, a media event has its "opponents'" participation written into its formula. The job of mass media is not to make people agree but merely to capture their desire, that is, their desire for inclusion in the "objective" status of a media event, from which they are presumed to have been excluded.

Having identified it, I came to dread such a collusive space of mediatized hysteria. We might once again call it the "vaticinal spatiotemporality" (see the Introduction), pried open (between the moments of seeing and the moments of being seen) by the media gaze. In it, I felt vulnerable, vulnerable as if anyone—even, say, an old man nearing his death bed—could turn into the like of Tom and throw a headless pigeon at me, so to speak. Just as in the vaticinal spatiotemporality of Bob Shade's making, there was something cruelly comic and unpredictably violent about this space-time of reflexive doubleness. Somehow, the louder the shoot's supporters' complaints (about "distortion"), the more culpable I felt; it was as if the complaint were meant for me, as if I myself were hiding or distorting something they wanted. As I must repeat, it was not the (white) people I came to dread so. Upon a closer inspection, the cause of my trouble seemed to be, once again, the "third gaze," whether that of the mass media or of the protesters. The more "objective," distanced, "documentary," and "national" such gaze's rhetoric—that is, the more "glassy-eyed" the gaze became—the more frenzied the supporters turned. And my feeling of vulnerability in it grew proportionally, as if the abstractly imagined communities of the national audience had lent their third gaze to directly encourage us, the supporters and me, to spiral down into "scansions of misunderstandings." But why, exactly? The protesters certainly seem to deem such a third gaze (of the national audience) a humiliating eyewitness presence, a deterrent security measure for themselves. But why does the same seem to have an opposite effect for me?

In the Introduction, I intimated two different kinds of relation to the gaze of the Other. It is time that I spell out the difference. One was "self-possession via a third party," which I aligned with so-called whiteness. The other I called "shame" after Agamben. Arguably, both are responses to what I am calling the gaze of the Other. Specifically, both are responses to what one might call the enigma of being—that is, how we become "riveted to our being" (Emanuel Levinas's term cited in Copjec 2006) precisely to the extent that we become alien to ourselves, come to find a creaturely "animal" in us, on account of exposure to the "injunctional impossibility" of the gaze of the Other. Lacan saw the first response as that of guilt, and the second, just as we have, that of shame. And just as we have, he deemed the latter the properly ethical posture, as Joan Copjec establishes (2006). Why?

As Copjec summarizes, shame, for Lacan, is a "flight into being" rather than a "flight from it" as in guilt (Copjec 2006:111). Shame "seeks comfort" in the said enigma of being. Guilt, in contrast, constitutes itself in relation to a supposed "external" agent who, presently in my place, is supposed to hold an answer to that enigma (of being). Hence, guilt, despite the presumed anguish, effectively relegates the burden of the creaturely enigma to some Other. In guilt, that is, the originary enigma/loss becomes a recoverable/

answerable loss, particularly through acquisition of a better "knowledge" (Copjec 2006:109). Thus, instead of embracing the enigma/loss as constitutive of our being—as in the posture of shame—guilt sends us searching for the "core of our being" in some knowable "identities" or properties. For example, the "enigmas" of our inherited, unchosen racial and ethnic identities would send a guilt-ridden one looking for an "actual past" that can be recovered via knowledge in an "ideal future" (109). What we have here is none other than a transition from the "ethics" of self-loss to the pursuit of self-possession.

In a short step, then, the guilty one turns an "enigma" into a certainty—hence the previously mentioned self-satisfied smugness—the certainty that the pursued "knowledge" is stolen (from me) and now resides in the possession of the Other (qua external agent). What is peculiar about this fantasy is its mirror-image inverse (dis)proportionalism: my loss *is* directly the Other's possession, no more or less. Its upshot, as Copjec elaborates, is the denial of the same extent of the "enigma of being" that shadows me, that is, my humanity, from the external agent so fabricated. Hence, for an anti-Semite, a Jew, unlike the anti-Semite himself, "*knows* what it is to be a Jew" (Copjec 2006:105, emphasis added).

My point is that such a fantasy horizon is opened up at the shoot by the "third gaze" and the imagined communities it abstractly implies. That kind of riveting Other Scene must be posited in order for us to make sense of the intensity of the passionate unveiling and short-circuiting on the part of the shoot's supporters. Under the third gaze, I am arguing, the constitutive enigma of being was momentarily rendered answerable, insofar as that answer is presupposed as stolen, residing in the Other. For thus having relegated the burden of Truth, the shoot supporter is, as Sartre puts, "amusing himself," even as he is scandalized. He is self-satisfied (and momentarily self-possessed) by the utter recognizability of the Other, all made same in the complicity of the Stolen Knowledge. "Well, well, what do we have here!" smirked one supporter spotting me entering the park. In the vaticinal spatiotemporality facilitated by the third gaze, I momentarily became so readable—so culpable. Such was the source of my sense of vulnerability.

CHAPTER FOUR

Pests and Outcasts

Pest, Exogenous

I was perched with a benchful of local elderly men under the shade of a tree one scorching Labor Day afternoon near the entrance of Hegins Community Park. "Pest control," blurted out an old man from one end of the bench. "Pigeons are rats with wings," he said. "They don't belong in the countryside; they live off grain yards and make hay go moldy."

When I moved to his side, he repeated his favorite singsong: "Rats with wings." "That's what they are, flying rats," he intoned with self-righteousness and a look of disgust at this imaginary monster with the body of a rat and the wings of a bird.

Herman Clemens—I remembered his name from the letter to the editor in the previous day's *Citizen Standard*, which I mentioned to him. Encouraged, he recited part of the letter, this time eyeing me with interest: "Pigeons are birds of fouls, not animals. Maybe Mr. Cave [the president of Trans-Species Unlimited Inc., the first national animal rights organization to protest the shoot] should read Genesis 1:28" (interview, 1993).

I was to hear this set course of abominations countless times from different informants, but none with the flair and authority of Herman Clemens. A retired miner who was frequently interviewed by the media as an authority on the Labor Day Shoot, he was especially compelling in making the case for pest control with an urgency and absoluteness of eternal truth. "Tradition" and pest control were inseparable for him. This twinkling-eyed elderly man was thus always ready to make a smooth loop from the singsongs of a pest-case to "tradition" and back in a well-rounded, impeccable logic, and he would triumphantly punctuate his lecture like this: "And so, the shoot is a time-honored tradition that helps get rid of pests that would otherwise be

poisoned for befouling property with their droppings and living off farmers'
grain yards" (interview, 1994).

For him, the "pest" was a threat to the very survival and continuation of
a community and tradition—narrowly that of the Labor Day Shoot but frequently in a more general sense. What is "traditional" is inherently hygienic
while the pestilential is rootless and delinquent. His battle cry of "rats with
wings" passionately merges two constitutional requirements for the survival
of a rural community: the vitality of tradition and agricultural utilitarianism. In this way, the sacredness of the pigeon shoot tradition took on the
exigency of subsistence, and vice versa. There lies the extraordinary persuasion of his rhetoric.

Herman's refrain was exceptionally coherent and mannered—adept at
sound bites and as catchy as a battle cry. But detail was not his strong point,
details the firsthand victims of pigeon pests would readily know: the particular vulnerability of row crops, newly planted seeds, just-sprouted plants, and
so forth. He often sounded too "studied" to be suffering from the problems he
so well articulated. The first question that welled in my mind, then, was this:
How long has the "traditional" and endemic pigeon, an agricultural pest,
been a threat to the region anyway?

Since coal's downturn as the nation's energy source after the end of the
Second World War, the region has been going through a steady deindustrialization and population loss. It is not agriculture but the garment industry
that has filled the vacuum left by the waning coal industry. The total number
of agricultural employees in Schuylkill County has never exceeded one hundred since 1953, while employees in the industry categorized under "apparel
and other textile products" reached twice that of mining by 1962, roughly
one-fourth of the county's total labor force—though the trend began to abate
a little in the 1980s (U.S. Department of Commerce, Bureau of the Census,
CBP-74-40 *County Business Patterns* 1995).

So, again and again, I brought up this point to other local residents, as
well as Herman Clemens. Responses roughly struck the same chord:

> *Hoon Song:* You said pigeon shooting started largely to protect
> farming, but there haven't been a whole lot of farms around
> here, right?
> *Herman Clemens:* You are from the city. You cannot imagine how
> badly farmers hate them disease-carrying pigeons in their
> barns.

HS: Have you farmed yourself?

HC: No, I am a retired miner. I got the black lung and still get
    pension for that. [Impatiently] You see, the shoot is a good
    alternative to getting rid of them disease-carrying pigeons that
    are a nuisance to farmers and cities.

Lloyd Smelt: And with where them pigeons come, the cities.
    [Inaudible] . . . and our historical places that are defaced . . .

HS: Disease?

HC: Yeeesss. In Pittsburgh, Washington, and Philadelphia, they
    spend hundreds of thousands of dollars to gas and poison
    them pigeons. This [the Labor Day Shoot] is a nice family
    affair. You don't see people who shoot pigeons shooting drugs.
    (interview, September 4, 1995)

Two years after our first encounter, we were sitting on the same bench where
this conversation took place and positively choking at the dust clouds kicked
up by the bustle of an agitated crowd nearby. I was thinking at that moment
that almost the same amount of time had passed with these informants, particularly Herman, proving utterly invincible with respect to my suggestion
of an apparent no-farm-but-farm-pest contradiction. No one on the bench
stirred even slightly at my polite but disputatious invoking of the absence of
farming worthy of a pest epidemic in the region; they seemed only puzzled
at my blinding ignorance. They neither contradicted nor acknowledged my
persistent question but just yielded. Yielded were the issue of farm pest to
that of city origin of the bird, the threat of crop stealing to that of contagious
disease, and the theme of disease to that of urban moral degradation (of
"drugs" and avian vandalism).

Moments of silence followed. I was thinking, "What a convenient change
of subject!" But they, carefully and innocently observing my agitation, were
clearly prepared to repeat themselves all over if necessary. My suspicion was
shaken by their determination; it seemed no use pursuing them anymore. At
that point, the new problem I was burdened with was this: "pest" defined not
in terms of endemic ecological parasitism but as that which included threats
from without; or the locally defined culpability of pigeon pests being utterly
conflatable with what was supposed as exogenous to the wholesome rural
community, that is, urban evils.

Could it be that the locally found pigeons are migrants from nearby metropolitan areas, say, Harrisburg? No informant was sure of this and did not

seem to care to know. Feral pigeons are known to regularly fly considerable distances beyond city limits to farms or ranches at which feeding is possible (Johnston and Janiga 1995:274). However, feral pigeons are not migrants but "commuters" between nesting (or breeding) sites and feeding sites (Goodwin 1983). The known maximum round-trip distance they would commute is forty-three miles, putting Harrisburg, which is roughly one hundred miles round-trip from Hegins, beyond the "striking distance" (see Goodwin 1983). Moreover, such a phenomenon is shown to be relatively infrequent in the United States (Glitz 1959, McDowell and Pillsbury 1959). In Schuylkill County, farms and ranches have been rarities in any case.[1] The "pest" connection is even more lacking as one looks back in time, into the active coal-mining eras. I have pored through microfilms of the *Citizen Standard* and the *Pottsville Republican* (the county's largest newspaper) for coverage of early pigeon shoots beginning in the 1920s, only to find not a single mention of pigeon pests—that is, until the start of the protests. The rather uneventful coverage of the first Labor Day Shoot in 1934 was no exception.

Pigeon as Food

When I set out to confirm this elusive "tradition" orally, I tried interviews outside and away from the Labor Day Shoot, and redirected my question as "Do you remember the early shoots?"—without positioning it in the context of the current controversy. The result was immediate and surprising: what was generally recalled was not the tradition of pest control but the sentimental memories of pigeon consumption. This drastic change in response was more thoroughgoing among women than men. For men tended to be miserly in allowing the nostalgic taste of pigeon to permeate their reminiscences and often self-consciously corrected themselves to revert back to the polemical stance. Elma Hatter seemed to feel particularly free to portray pigeons in an edible light. An elderly widow on the lowest economic rung, she had, as it were, neither men nor allegiance to the community leaders' publicized position to worry about. Her recollection enthusiastically mused upon the first Labor Day Shoot as some kind of big communal feast.

HS: Why did they start the Labor Day Shoot?
EH: They were awfully poor. That's why we started the shoot.
HS: You mean the shooters?

EH: Nooo. There were eight guys who started the shoot as a charity. We didn't have money to buy beef or pork. So they let us get them dead pigeons from the shoot and eat them. They stuck together very well then, during the Depression.

HS: How did you eat them?

EH: Pot pies and soups.

HS: How does it taste?

EH: As good as chicken.

HS: Do you still eat them?

EH: Nooo.

HS: Why not?

EH: They put lead in them pellets now.[2] (interview, 1995)

The recurring theme in Elma's and others' like narratives of the first shoot is the extraordinary ethos of charity and communal solidarity—how they all "stuck together very well"—whose memory today materializes as the nostalgic savor of pigeon meat. However, the way the event is remembered now must be by its spirit rather than its nutritional contribution, because despite the claim that the event was essential for the survival of the entire community during the harshest times, the Labor Day Shoot was precisely that—a once-a-year event. An exaggerated exaltation of the past always hides a criticism of the present; this is especially true of the nostalgic remembrance of the harshest times (such as the Great Depression)—a well-known tactic of the conservative. Elma was accusing, but of what I could not fathom. It was certainly not pigeons.

"Where is the pest discourse?" I thought to myself, then asked, "How about pigeons not shot with shotguns; can you eat them today?"

She said cryptically, "I don't know; I am too old to fight."

That was the last roughly comprehensible thing I could make her say that day. Her poignant image of savory meat that is now spoiled by lead poisoning stayed with me tenaciously. Who is she blaming for that? I regretted not having been more explicit. But she was elusive, and I too timid. When I caught up with her next, we were at another contentious rehash of the Labor Day Shoot.

I spotted Elma in the main outdoor dining area with Jon Lubold, her only remaining relation, with whom she now resided. We already met Jon in Chapter 3. He is a regular thug of a youth, who over the years had built a notoriety to be reckoned with at the shoot—for his hell-raising ventures against pigeons, protesters, and state troopers. One could not think of a more radical exemplar of a shoot supporter. Under Jon's suspicious eyes, I began to place my questions cautiously, with a tactful calculation that there would be no more benign way to break the ice than with some recollections of the old days. But I was not to hear a word on the blissful memory of pigeon consumption from Elma that day. She suddenly feigned disinterest in outmoded ways, which forced me to tempt her thus:

> HS: How is today's shoot different?
> EH: Every shoot is like the one used to be.
> HS: Is it still a charitable endeavor?
> EH: The birds are often donated by farmers. Pigeons are killed for the sake of charity to farmers.
> HS: Can't farmers dispose of them themselves? Perhaps eat them without shooting them with leaded pellets?
> EH: [Disgusted] Nooo. Them pigeons are no good for nothing!
> (interview, 1996)

At my paltry pursuit of pigeon minutiae, Elma grew cold, inexplicably repulsed, and finally, censuring. Only momentarily was I encouraged by her recalling of the theme of "charity," merely to find that this time it was compromised through the official rhetoric of pest control—the beneficiaries are now pest-plagued farmers. There was no use pursuing logic on the pigeon issue with her: lead or no lead, they were now declared inedible, however you looked at it. But what most bothered and mystified me at the same time was her sudden violent disgust with whatever had to do with pigeons. After her punctuating curse, I could not carry on; I was made to feel somehow impolite to mix the issues of pest and food. I had to wait until someone else confronted the forbidden mix.

As it turns out, Eddie Becker, the director and producer of the documentary on the Labor Day Shoot controversy, *Gunblast: Culture Clash* (1995), was after the same food/pest "incompatibility." Only after his film was released did everyone learn that Eddie's project had been secretly supported by the Fund for Animals. Eddie must have decided early on in his project that he had found a key rhetorical weapon in the shoot supporters' utterly inconsistent discourses on pigeons' "dirtiness"; his unedited twelve-hour-long footage contains some twenty-two different occasions in which he pursued the same question—but none made it into the final version. The following two exchanges are from the footage.

Clip #1:

Eddie Becker: Did you know about people's consumption of pigeons in this area?

Jenny Shade: Of course. Dead pigeons were sold for consumption after the shoots. My mother used to prepare pigeon pot pies at home on Saturday afternoons. I still remember the smell.

EB: When did they stop selling them?[3]

JS: People stopped selling them because cities where they got them started to use poison.

EB: But now people call pigeons "rats"!

JS: I don't think I've ever had a pigeon.

Clip #2:

EB: Pigeons must have been regarded as differently than they are now, because they ate them.

Patrick Canfield: Back then, all the pigeons shot were eaten by the poor people. The whole community survived like that. It was a way of life during hard times.

EB: Now they call them "flying rats."

PC: Those are not from here. They are outsiders. They are like the people protesting. They don't have the credibility. Protesters take the man who killed rats to court, and that tells the mentality of the protesters. We don't have very much use of [sic] protesters, not in this area.

Both conversations took place outside and away from the Labor Day Shoot. The exchange with Jenny Shade (who is in her sixties and hence too young to remember the first shoot) took place at the aforementioned dining area the night before Labor Day, while Patrick was interviewed in someone's garden (perhaps his sister's). I was present at the first conversation with Jenny, where there were about thirteen volunteers preparing ingredients for food vendors, idly joking, drinking, and munching at the same time. Eddie Becker had been pursuing the theme of pigeon consumption for some time that evening; filled with nostalgia, everyone cheerfully pitched in, before he suddenly decided to tape the conversation.

Eddie must have learned quickly, as I did, that he could make the senior shoot's supporters drop their guard down by initiating conversation with an invitation to discuss recollections of early shoots. And then, in both of the clips, he abruptly cuts his interlocutors' idle musings short and throws them back to the stakes of contemporary disputes on pests. The results are impressively reminiscent of the reaction my less explicit but similar "mixing" move (though stretched out in time) had provoked from Elma: a dramatic turn to a distressed but firm denunciation—a countenance met neither when pigeon consumption is discussed alone nor in the triumphant textbook recitations of "rats with wings" variety. Jenny's change of stance is breathtaking, from nostalgically lamenting the loss of a homespun past through reckless modernity (that is, poisoning) to shuddering over that very past. (Her sudden renouncement—"I don't think I've ever had a pigeon"—is particularly striking in light of the lengthy session of nostalgic recollections that had gone on that evening before the camera was turned on.) Patrick, in contrast, is set off into an incomprehensible harangue in which even his well-known pro-shoot fanaticism is obscured.[4] Let me examine Patrick's last comments in some detail.

Patrick's interactional strategy is aimed at offsetting and recovering from the already committed stance in order to affirm its seemingly opposite proposition, that is, pigeon-as-pest. For this, he begins by censuring the question itself, through discrediting Eddie's source of information, that is, the outsider. This scapegoat figure is a convenient mediator between pigeon-as-food and pigeon-as-pest that allows Patrick to have it both ways. Thus, instead of Patrick denying that pigeons are rat-like pests—a necessary move not to contradict his initial position—he blames the scapegoat outsider for having suggested that pigeons are pests. Then through logical sleight of hand, he switches "outsiders" with "protesters"—hence, ironically implying that it is protesters who hate pigeons (as pests)! Once the outsider-protesters are thus partitioned to one side, he can now reverse his initial stance and have it both ways, and suggest the equation between the rat and the pigeon—which had been made unmentionable by the initiating comment. By the reportedly shared plight suffered at the hands of the outsider-protesters, "rat-killers" and "pigeon-killers" find themselves in the same boat (of legal troubles)— and so pigeons are no different from rats.[5] Whether pigeons are pests or not is not his real interest, but blaming the outsider is. I will return to his usage of the outsider figure as a kind of guarantor that allows him to have it both ways—pigeon as food and pest.

Eddie was victorious over these and twenty other similar clips—though I can only haphazardly guess why none made it into the final cut. He has interpreted the seemingly confused reactions of Patrick and Jenny as embarrassment at being made aware of a stark contradiction in their attitude toward pigeons. But if "confusion" were the true state of their reaction, it is strange that in all twenty-two sessions captured by his camera the interviewees consistently came out at the end siding with the pest discourse. Patrick is no exception. Although he seems to be denying the suggested equation between pigeons and rats at the outset of the interaction, in the end he subtly reverses that by implying the shared plight of "rat-killers" and "pigeon-killers" at the hands of the protesters. What I see from these clips is not shamefaced, improvised mumbling but patterned repulsion.

Eddie's conclusion was instructive of my own bias. We both presumed that at the shoot everything was "about" pigeons. We presumed that in Hegins, by now, matters of pigeons consisted of a discrete area of discourse, which can be readily isolated and "read." And we were ready to read with the basic premise that the food and pest discourses were inherently opposing, or at least logically distinct—or even anthropologically "ambivalent" (see Chapter 6). Hence our shared curiosity in what may transpire when the issues of food and pest collided.

Eddie is further blinded by an exclusive either/or logic of food/pest dichotomy as a conceptual categorization that is supposed to *causally precede* behavioral responses such as poisoning or consumption. Thus, a possibly reversed poison-pest conceptualization, that is, pest *because* poisoned, escapes him completely, which is close to what Jenny is saying in the clip. For Jenny expounds a kind of theory of pest when she unassumingly explains how pigeons turned from being edible to being inedible, that is, how *in time* they became "pests" because cities began to poison them. It is as if, in such a discourse, the state of being "pest" consists not just in the animal's specific and positive present qualities, but also in its having crossed a certain (temporal) threshold. Pigeons are culprits but also victims of what is done to them in changing times; the nostalgic taste of pigeons is sumptuous but equally a scandalous reminder of what has gone rotten. This threshold event seems to be differently hinted at by each of the above informants. It seems to be implicit in Herman Clemens's turn to blaming the city origin of the bird, Elma Hatter's exasperation at lead in pellets, Patrick Canfield's outrage at outsiders, and Jenny's theory of poisoning. Despite differences, they all seem to be speaking of an irrevocable loss of wholesome past, spirit of charity, and communal solidarity through the image of the current inedibility of pigeons (though Herman's hyper-rationalized polemic is an exception). What is no more, what has been lost is condensed in the pigeon's "fall" to the status of pest.

I knew that such a "threshold" was not to materialize in front of my eyes as a discrete, well-defined event, or come to be evidenced by a fantastic informant. It was rather like a profound doubt that was always there, always suspicious of the present, vaguely looking backward, and aimlessly accusing. I could only feel it through its abstract proximity in muffled complaints here and masqueraded justifications there. Nonetheless, its forceful presence warped and distorted the logicality of pest discourses so much that there seemed to be no use in pursuing consistency in them. Whether it (the threshold event) is called the collisions of past and present, locals and outsiders, or rural and urban, from the permutating combinations of these larger issues pigeons could come out in any number of different ways: victims or victimizers, pests or the afflicted, and so forth, as is graphically illustrated in Patrick's harangue. In his shuffling, the lot of animal rights protesters, too, precariously oscillates, somewhere from misguided but well-meaning defenders of pigeons to outright abusers.

Meanwhile, when pigeons' dirtiness was affirmed, it was as if the regrettable state had been established already sometime in the past—when they were made inedible—and has since left the realm of the birds' current happenstance. Their status of being pests, as a kind of commentary on the general state of affairs, was no more contingent upon empirical specifics of where they came from (indigenous or urban-originated), how they were fed (parasitic or non-parasitic), how they were killed (poisoned, leaded?), and so forth: they were all dirty and inedible, or more correctly, they were all *made* to be dirty and inedible. Once we take the practice of pigeon killing in such a transphenomenal sense, it becomes clearer why the fact of their being poisoned elsewhere looms so much larger than their "inherent" quality. For the shoot's supporters often rant with even more gusto (than "rats with wings") that pigeons are poisoned in the city, that they are "drugged with all kinds of chemicals," on top of wallowing and breeding in the squalor of diseased inner-city streets. It is as if the act of poisoning itself is morally defiling, and the pigeon either a victim or an avian accomplice to some kind of reprehensible "drug exchange."[6] Only causally understanding such comments, I was often led to ask, "When should a pigeon shoot take place, before or after poisoning?" And I became utterly confused by answers that seemed to affirm both ways. At times, it was said that pigeons needed to be inter-cepted *before* they were exposed to the reckless poisoning of incompetent "city bureaucrats" (who do not know how to do pest control properly), but at other times, it was said that they had to be eliminated *because* they had been already poisoned and were found in the wholesome countryside. Either way, the conclusion was the same: pigeons have to be killed.

The Pigeons

Tracing the route of pigeons headed for the Labor Day Shoot—where do they actually come from?—is a laborious and frequently unrewarding process. Pigeon "dealers" responsible for the provisions of the event are justifiably secretive about their operations. They have been stalked and threatened, and their properties have been sabotaged by animal rights activists in the past. So only very reluctantly had Shally agreed to Bob Shade's exhortation to "show me around." For years Shally had been overseeing matters regarding pigeons for the Labor Day Shoot, contacting dealers, storing birds, and set-ting up traps for the game. His barn was set ablaze and the shoot-destined pigeons released one year, and a bomb threat dogged him the next. Though all but a few of the "freed" pigeons "homed" right back to the barn and the bomb threat proved empty, Shally was shaken. He was calling it quits the year I met him.

An owner of a plot of fruit trees and a part-time independent miner, Shally was a tough-looking, quick-witted guy in his late thirties, with a soiled pair of jeans, a checkered flannel shirt, and a grimy cap as his uni-form. Though he was a "honky" of Lithuanian ancestry, his speech was thick with the "Dutch language" (Pennsylvania German)—he often left me guess-ing. I had to gather courage before being introduced to Shally, because for years in my mind he had been ranked in the company of area toughs. I had seen Shally swear, shove, beat, decapitate, and get arrested.

In my memory, one Labor Day episode outshines the others in demon-strating his potential for vileness. A wounded pigeon had fallen in an area fenced in with bold, red "no trespassing" signs. Several animal rights activ-ists rushed up and desperately hung onto the fence, helplessly watching the suffering bird unavailingly flapping its broken wings. An activist came up with a device of connected sticks and a net, which was slowly lowered and inched toward the bird. From some distance away, a bemused Shally was watching this group of tear-jerking, melodramatic crusaders, his torso lazily leaning against a tree, his arms folded on his broad chest, and a restrained smirk on his face. And just as the improvised device had nearly reached the pigeon, Shally began a heavy, ominous walk toward the bird. When his dusty and sturdy boots stopped next to the bird, everyone held their breath. There was no telling what he was going to do next. Even the rescuers forgot their signature beseeching and demands. Amid dozens of such suspended stares, Shally eyed the rescuers as if in pity, then slowly picked up the bird. He tossed it lightly in the air a couple of times with one hand, and then in a flashing, mid-air, one-handed yank, he popped its head off. With his held-up, outstretched hands, like Jesus on the cross, he carried the bird, walking toward the stunned protesters as if granting their wish. Then he threw the quivering bloody messes over the fence, spitting out, "Now, fix it."

Regarding the bird-acquisition process that Shally was going to let me see, I was told that the birds would be delivered to a storage shack right outside Hegins Community Park two days before Labor Day in the middle of the night to avoid detection. That was as far up the pigeon transportation route as Shally was willing to tolerate my prying, no closer to the originating source than that. I was assured that the storage place itself was a tightly guarded secret. On the appointed night, a pickup truck pulled in without headlights, drawing a draped trailer. The license plate was from Lancaster County, the southernmost county of central Pennsylvania. The dealer, a heavy guy with piercing, suspicious eyes, was not at all happy to see me. In greeting, he gave a quick touch to the visor of his cap, but he did not go for my eagerly extended hand. Perhaps because of my presence, he demanded that the cargo be unloaded as quickly as possible. There were fifty wooden and plastic crates in all, with two hundred birds per crate; it was difficult to believe that ten thousand birds, all alive and having wills of their own, had submitted to becoming a mere wagonload of cargo. It was even more difficult to believe that they were so quiet, as if accomplices to the clandestine operation. Shally, three security guys for the shoot, and I began unloading the apprehensive creatures.

Awakened by the sudden light in the storage shack, the birds stirred a bit, some clamoring to keep their distance from our hands, some poking their heads out to examine their surroundings. The birds were undoubtedly normal ferals, "street pigeons" or "city pigeons" in common parlance, *Columba livia* by the scientific name—though a little smaller and gaunt at the neck, perhaps from the stress of traveling. The darker melanin blue in the checker and T-bar pattern dominated the plumage, with occasional ash red and brown, as supposedly is found among the North American urban population. Molting was apparent, with down smeared with droppings on the floor here and there—a sign of the birds' origin in the northern latitude (molting at this time being in preparation for winter). I showed off these observations to Shally to perk his interest and win some trust in me, and I was immediately rewarded with a crucial piece of information: about 90 percent of these birds were trapped in the train yards of Philadelphia and Pittsburgh, and the rest on the farms of Lancaster and Manheim Counties.[7] So much for the theory of "pest control," I thought, unless the tiny town of Hegins thinks in terms of a statewide-size passion for "charity."

After the other helpers were long gone, Shally busied himself with watering and feeding the exhausted birds into the wee hours, taking care not to miss any, despite the daily demands of his early morning chores. He even moved some visibly sickly ones to a roomier cage he had brought and gently hosed them for fear of hypothermia. Not a word was passed between us during almost the entire period of this long, tedious operation. Shally was totally absorbed and was not to be disturbed. The birds had to be fed and watered twice the next day and I made a point to be present there, but I found that Shally's trips were more frequent: the storage door was cracked and an electric fan was turned on already before I got there. That day Shally was as before around pigeons: focused, determined, and oblivious.

Early on Labor Day morning, I first spotted Shally standing on the cargo of crated pigeons being pulled by a tractor to the firing line. The engine-loud parade of pitiable pigeon prisoners, soon to be executed, drew a large curious crowd. Some cheered and taunted, as if the birds had just been caught, some pointed their camcorders. Shally stood on the moving crates of his captives with his legs wide apart, tall and stately with a grim face. As the tractor reached the farthest trap, it turned around and Shally began unloading crates, two per trap, even as the tractor was in constant motion. He positively threw them down on the ground by twos, as though nothing was alive in them anymore. Shally was back to the usual brute I used to know; another Labor Day Shoot had begun.

By the end of the day, two crates of pigeons were left unused, and Bob Shade, enterprising businessman that he is, made the best of the situation as usual.[8] He told the media that these pigeons were up for purchase, but otherwise destined for a private shooting the next day. And as usual, the animal rights protesters did not have any choice but to fall for his doubled-up price—seven dollars per bird—lest they should lose their humanitarian face.

The price was settled and money changed hands; the pigeons were prepared to be transported by the protesters. Shally directed this operation. Amid the strange scene of enemies—young, acrid, and slender protesters versus grungy, slack, and beer-bellied shoot officials—sitting or standing side by side, Shally once again patiently watered and fed his birds for the journey (back to the cities) with as much care and meticulousness as on the previous night.

As the crates were carried away, he mournfully grumbled: "Them kids don't know how to care for 'em; they will all be dead by tomorrow morning." And he shouted at the back of the disappearing protesters at the top of his lungs: "Don't forget to water them once more tonight!"

At this, the protesters turned around and roared into a chorus of exaggerated, jeering laughter. "You care about pigeons?" retorted a voice in contempt, followed by some inaudible insults.

Shally, looking puzzled, did not say anything.

For at least a week after the Labor Day Shoot, pigeons were visibly numerous in the Hegins Valley area, though I lack the benefit of a scientific census.[9] Besides the intuitive "feel" for the dramatic increase in number, there are other behavioral indications of the supposed surplus's transitory status. Most pigeons spotted after Labor Day came in small flocks (fifteen at most) or as individuals. They were extremely jumpy and moved about a great deal, though they never seemed to fly at great speed or distance. Low speed, especially, is an indication of their unfamiliarity with the territory. Pigeons are famous for their keen senses of direction and home territory. The fast flight of ferals indicates their confidence in their environment, which links the nesting and breeding sites with a stable feeding source.

The fact that the pigeon population after Labor Day lacks such a source is evident also in their flock formation, since a stable and lasting social formation of any size pigeon group depends on a predictable feeding site. For a better observation, I took a bagful of peas—feral pigeons' favorite diet—to Hegins Community Park one day and spread them underneath a shack. It took an unusually long time (by the standard of Chicago's Hyde Park) for a flock-worthy group to begin pecking on them simultaneously. All of them seemed to be on their own more or less, minding their own business of stuffing hungry stomachs. There was no apparent pecking dominance, no sign of heavier-looking birds occupying the central position of the feed spread. This meant an unstable and improvised social formation, perhaps a mere result of seeking the company of other pigeons out of alarm and fear. While this was going on, a child on a bicycle appeared and viciously darted toward the middle of the pecking congregation with a gurgling imitation of shotgun blasts. The birds jumped simultaneously but scattered in every capricious direction, without a hint of that famous patterned maneuver against a predator. There goes another sign of their unfamiliarity with each other, I thought to myself dismally (see Davis 1975). These were clearly displaced birds.

Pigeon as "Pet"

There is another way changes in pigeons indicate the "threshold event." This indication came to me one day in an unexpected form, charged with a bewildering complexity but with an almost pinpointing concreteness. For this, I have to situate the Labor Day Shoot in a wider context of pigeon-related practices in the area.

Had I not witnessed Shally's tender side in addition to his usual frenzied bouts at the Labor Day Shoot, I would not have been able to believe the rumor that he kept numerous prized pigeons at home. Of course, what was prized here was not a keepsake value but the ability not to perish in pigeon shoots. But still, it was difficult to imagine how he reconciled the "prizing" attitude with the idea of pigeon pests. The chance to see it came unexpectedly. Patrick Canfield had offered to take me to one of his main informants, a legendary pigeon handler who happened to be Shally's father, Pop. Pop was an ex-miner with many debilitating illnesses. He was in the mood for bragging about his colorful trade in the pigeon business of late, encouraged by a heroic treatment in Patrick's book (1993). Due to his indisposition, the unwelcome charge of showing me around fell on his reluctant youngest son, Shally.

Right behind Pop's house was a gun club—a very modest group-owned facility where Shally and Pop were core members. At the edge of the property, Shally and Pop kept a pigeon pen as large as a cottage. It was raised from the ground for dryness and had a large, wired window facing south for sunlight. Next to it was a hawk trap, a five-by-six-foot structure of a wired maze into which hawks were lured by the bait of a sickly pigeon and were trapped. As Shally and my secretly terror-stricken self entered the cottage, some two hundred pigeons peered at us indifferently from a sunny but slightly dingy room; all perched up orderly on the middle shelf. In the long feeder placed next to that large window was some unidentifiable mixture of grains. "Those grits," Shally explained, "is made of anise oil extracts, ground oyster shells, sand, and charcoal [pigeons' favorite flavor] for good digestion."

Next to the feeder was a top-covered water basin and on the floor was a bathing pan. Overall, the birds seemed well cared for. But I wondered in what sense those birds were "prized." To me, they were indistinguishable from normal ferals, except some almond, grizzle, and pied (normal color flecked with white feathers) plumage, which were slightly rarer among urban ferals. The majority of Pop's birds were the common "blue bar" pattern, and I asked the reason for the preference. They are dominant in defending nest sites and have a larger protected territory than other breeds, Shally explained.

"So they fly better?" I inquired.

"Right," he said, mildly enthused.

"Like homers?" I inquired again.

"Nooo, homers are useless in trap-and-handle," whined the exasperated Shally. And at my silenced gawking, he was already reaching for the bird-catching net for a demonstration.

The game of pigeon shooting comes in two forms in Schuylkill County: "straight shooting," the style practiced at the Labor Day Shoot, and "trap-and-handle" (or "matches"), regarded as more traditional in the region. In straight shootings, the birds used are "barn birds," ordinary, untrained pigeons. The birds are arbitrarily chosen and put in traps. When the shooter yells "pull," the trap of the puller's choice (among any number of traps set for the game) collapses and the bird takes flight. In trap-and-handle, the trapped birds are "brushed," meaning manipulated or trained to fly in particularly designed patterns unbeknownst to the shooter. Trappers, who are usually experts in the craft of breeding, nursing, and training pigeons, team up with a shooter, and each shooter has to shoot the bird trapped by the opponent's trapper.[10] Gamblers bet not only on the overall outcome of the shoot but on a particular trap, implying that a match is as much between the trapper and the shooter as between the two shooters. A skillful trapper is as much a celebrity in the pigeon shoot arena as a prized marksman.

With the selected birds, we drove a short distance to the middle of the club's firing range. Instead of a shotgun—to my relief—Shally pulled from his pickup truck a wooden trap like a shoe box, a bundle of strings with perforated bottle caps tied at the end, and a red mop-like object with little bells attached here and there called boogla-woogla.

"This is how we brush 'em," he said, and tied a stringed bottle cap on a tail feather of one bird after moistening it by spitting, then closed the trap after the bird.

"When I open this trap," Shally went on, "the bird will fly for about one second to the left, two seconds straight up, and then down."

He held the puller (a piece of string) of the trap with one hand and gave a quick, syncopated whistle with his lips while shaking the boogla-woogla vigorously right behind the trap. At the pull of the string (which made the trap collapse to the sides), the pigeon darted out. The bird dutifully performed a little air show, exactly in the pattern Shally had predicted, and obediently landed on the roof of the pigeon pen, as if calmly waiting for us. Henceforth, one after another of the remaining birds exhibited the tricks of their breed and training. And yes, blue bars flew most swiftly.

Bottle caps, when drawn through the air swiftly, simulate the sound of a hawk in pursuit, and so do a syncopated whistle and the boogla-woogla, I was told. The pattern of flight is manipulated largely by how the bottle cap is tied to the bird. When tied to the head, the bird will dip, thinking the hawk is above, when tied to the left of the tail feather, the bird will veer right, and so on. The duration of the veering move depends on how long the bottle cap hangs onto the designated area, which in turn is manipulated by the amount of moisture applied to the knot. The trapper in a match chooses the flight pattern of a bird first by acquiring information about the habit of the opponent shooter—for example, a "riser" if his gun is rumored to be heavy—and also by observing the shooter's mood at a particular juncture of the match—for example, a "hesitator" when the opponent shooter shows signs of impatience. Also, depending on the setting of the match, a darker bird will be used at dusk, an albino when the ground is covered with snow, and a "dipper" when the trap is placed at the edge of a culm bank.

It is all about knowing the territory, I was told, on our way back to Pop's. A territorially familiar pigeon is confident, aggressive, and engages in an evasive flight without hesitation. I chimed in that I had read that a flock of territorially well acquainted pigeons at times harass their predators (Johnston and Janiga 1995:189).

Speed is not the sole measure here, Shally said, but the cutting, erratic maneuver flying is. Homers possess the keenest sense of territory, and they are fast and high flying birds, but their acceleration is poor and their bigger bodies make larger targets.

It was clear that such a topic animated Shally a great deal. He used well-rehearsed, colorful vocabulary and seemed to give a spin of moralistic teaching to every aesthetic of avian virtue he elaborated: you might be weak and poorly endowed, but with alertness and weathered toughening you can turn the table on your predators.

Barn Bird, Brush Bird

Winter (November through February) is the high time for trap-and-handle matches, because molting ends in October and pigeons are better equipped to fly faster in winter. Ironically, since the post-protest enlargement in scale, the Labor Day Shoot provides the central meeting ground for enthusiasts of pigeon shoots, where winter matches are "tied" (i.e., arranged). Such a match, conceived in Hegins, was awaiting Pop and Shally in mid-November. Shally was to "trap" under Pop's supervision while his twenty-one-year-old cousin, Mike (a former champion at the Hegins shoot), came forward to shoot. The opposing team was made up of "West Enders," a derisive epithet loaded with ethnic and regional discrimination that goes back a century to the heyday of the brutally hierarchized mining work. West Enders were largely of Pennsylvania German and Welsh origin, the adversarial managerial classes in mining from the subordinate points of view of the Irish, Italians, and Lithuanians.[11] Bad blood still boils between them, if now only in the arena of the pigeon shoot. The purse at stake was three hundred dollars.

A match consists of a pair of games, one "away" and the other "home." This is to balance the advantage of home birds in their familiar territory. Even so, participants go through arduous haggling over the exact location of the match—for placing, I was told, is everything. Shally and Pop selected sixteen birds in all and began the preparation in earnest in mid-October.[12] First, the photoperiod was shortened inside the pen to hasten the termination of any lingering molting. Then, the birds were fed a high-protein diet with peas for better coats, and they were brushed everyday to balance the diet's fattening effect. And male blue bars were encouraged to enter breeding behavior, for they turned more aggressively territorial around nesting sites with the secretion of reproductive hormones.

As match day neared, Pop gave the selected birds an occasional tour to and of the "away" site to establish their navigational orientation. The purpose was to give them a chance to "place" the away site in an exact relation to the home territory. The reasoning was not different from that applied to homing pigeons: they needed an optimal calibration of geomagnetic and solar positionality plus olfactory information in order to fly confidently. There were numerous protocols for these "tours." The vehicle must be open topped, for example, and things that might hinder the birds' sense of smell, such as smoking, were strictly prohibited.[13] Birds poorly prepared navigationally for an away game get "sick" during the trip on match day, looking listless and intimidated. They are not only fated to lose but are also major embarrassments to the owners, Shally hinted. It seemed nothing is sweeter than winning an away game, and nothing more embarrassing than losing at home. The matches, in short, were all about staking and defending territories that were vicariously articulated by pigeons.

Among Pop's generation of trappers, especially, "knowing pigeons" is at times conflated with "knowing coals." Winning an away game in someone else's territory is not only a demonstration of "knowing" an opponent's territory but is also like making a statement about the winner's knowledge of the whereabouts of coal veins within the vanquished territory.

For example, when Pop won a game in the West End he taunted that "them West Enders don't know where their veins go"—meaning that they are poor miners. And he added that because of their stubborn refusal to consult him, they ended up "flattening a whole mountain for nothing when a shallow vein passed right under their women's outhouses."

The match day neared. I knew it. But neither Pop nor Shally was willing to tell me the exact time and place. Only once did I inquire in a feeble, defeated voice, as to my possible participation. I knew this request made them both uncomfortable. They did not want me to be around the match. So that was that. I could not raise the issue again. Shally and Pop won the match. But Shally lost five of his cherished birds (out of sixteen), a higher toll than usual for the masters. Brushed birds are not easily shot down. There was no celebration but only dejection for Shally. For days he got drunk, and I stayed away.

Referring to Shally's mood, Pop told me about a famous trapper long ago who died of a heart attack when his favorite bird was blasted at a match. And some trappers, he added, retire their favorite birds forever and never put them up for a match.

Perhaps this is an increasingly frequent phenomenon, I conjectured, since there are fewer matches year-round (with the passing of trap-and-handle as a sport) and thus more time to spend with individual birds. When Shally reemerged from grieving, with his usual machismo, he began speaking of his downed birds disparagingly. Perhaps in an attempt to repair his damaged sense of manliness, he spoke as if the birds' demise owed to their not having been "man enough" to handle the pressure—or something to that effect.[14]

With fewer men of the younger generation taking up trapping as a hobby today, matches are infrequent, and the birds essentially spend more time as keepsakes than risking their lives. Pop and Shally only had one more match the same year, but their year-round dedication to their pigeons was impressive. The maintenance of the pen required three daily visits and a total of four hours of work—or so I was told—seven days a week. The work was not divided sharply between them, but each willingly dropped by whenever he could. Besides the basic chores of watering, feeding, and cleaning, nocturnal predator-control consumed a great deal of work and nerve. The birds were let out twice a day to roam, but returned punctually as a flock before meal times. The extent of their roaming was unclear, but for hours they disappeared from sight. The daily roaming and a regular brushing (every three or four days) are necessary, I was told, to "keep the flying muscles in shape" and to keep them from fattening.

One afternoon, a few days after another Labor Day, their flock returned from the daily exercise with a couple of strangers. I suggested the possibility of the Labor Day Shoot's displaced pigeons tagging along with a flock flying swiftly and purposefully toward their awaiting feed, to which Shally was silent. But when I concluded with the possibility of cross-breeding with the wayward ones, Shally was scandalized. "Them barn birds are no good for brushing, can't teach 'em to fly," he protested, almost in disgust.

I did see him weed out freeloaders on a later similar occasion, but complete segregation was out of the question as long as he allowed his flocks to roam freely. Even if he killed the intruders, pigeons are known to engage in extra-pair copulation despite their reputation as a rare monogamous bird (Johnston and Janiga 1995:203). External breeding is apparent in the plumage of his flocks: isolated, domestic pigeons should show more rare varieties, while his flock is indistinguishable from a sample of normal street ferals—including the frequency of blue bars.[15] Taking Shally's prescriptive ideology as a moral imperative, however, I kept these thoughts to myself.

It is highly unlikely that these seasoned trappers, the keenest observers of pigeons you can imagine, are indeed unaware of the possibility of their flocks' extra-domestic breeding. They simply choose not to see it that way. Brushing, as I have been at pains to show, is a process of "claiming" a territory through habituation—and matches are a test of such a claim in the public arena—for which the free movement of birds in an extensive space is necessary. In time, the brushed birds embody the territory in their familiar recognition of the space, in their confident comportment, and, through some wishful thinking, by blood. The dilemma in such a "territorialism," of course, is that it can never be exclusive, never "purebred"; other flocks and the other's flocks fly through it, and nest and breed in it, someone else's property sits on it, construction may distort the terrain, and so forth; past/present, locals/outsiders, urban/rural constantly crisscross and pass through it, warping and distorting in their trajectories. This territorialism is merely a supplementary and an "ethereal" articulation of spaces already occupied by other, more real forces and other creatures—humans or otherwise. Then, the theater of the pigeon shoot arena is a space of suspended disbelief. Listening to the spirited conversation of trappers, one wonders if they have succeeded in dividing up the whole county among themselves; someone's birds took the west of Frakville Mountain, and another's the area between the Schuylkill River and Blue Mountain, and so on. But they "know" better. They know that the county is not a vacuum, and they know that brush birds are actually barn birds, pigeon-pets are indistinguishable from pigeon-pests, and pigeon-food is not far from pigeon-pest, et cetera. A momentary suspension of disbelief, trapping is a territorialism of the weak.

This suspended disbelief came to be shattered one day at that gun club. The newly elected president of the club after Pop, "Farmer" (see the Introduction) had brought a couple of crates of barn birds to the club shooting ground one Sunday afternoon and began a game of straight shooting with a few young men while we, the rest of the club members, drank and socialized inside the shack of a club house. And one by one, people inside were drawn to the game outside, until everyone was out, except Pop and his loyal friends. When Pop emerged pensive and withdrawn, the game was just running out of birds. And to Pop's grim face, Farmer audaciously requested Pop's birds from the pen, which was only across the field. Pop snapped. He gathered all the strength and contempt he could find and said, pointing to his pen, "These birds are not for you, you are wasting birds."

"Wasting birds" is a serious indictment in the pigeon shoot arena. It can mean anything from an accusation of excessive and unnecessary cruelty to that of sub-pigeon human status—it is said to someone who does not deserve to be shooting pigeons. Farmer, always an excitable fellow with rabid eyes, was not to be humiliated.

He declared that Pop was old-fashioned and that it was because of his old-fashioned policy that the club never grew. He foamed that no hardworking man ever had time and leisure for brushing birds any more, and that it was time for the club to promote straight shooting and earn some cash by tapping into the newly generated interest in straight shooting, thanks to the Labor Day Shoot.

Pop looked utterly disgusted but said nothing to Farmer. Turning to Mike (Shally's cousin), Pop shrilled at him to take all the "dirty barn birds" off the club's grounds.

Pop's tirade resumed back at home alongside Fats, a legendary marksman who is one of the heroes of Patrick Canfield's book, and me. Pop decried the vulgarity of people like Farmer: people who knew nothing but money, "outsiders" ignorant of the local tradition, whose kids all ran off to big cities. But more than anything else, Farmer was the worst shooter he had ever seen.

"Them Farmer always shoots in Hegins, you see," Pop continued. "He pays a couple of hundred just to shoot next to doctors and lawyers, and he can't even kill any of them slow barn birds."

My interest perked up at this point. I asked Pop who those participants at the Labor Day Shoot were—although I knew already from observing shooters' cars that the majority of them were out-of-state and from higher-income classes.[16] He said that those straight shooters were "doctors and lawyers" who shot "a hundred birds in a row just because they could afford them." I asked what was wrong with that, to which Pop repeated the "waste of bird" theme, but Fats intervened: "You don't even know whose birds they are, they don't belong to anyone." So, anonymity, materialism, rootlessness all contribute to the villainy of straight shooters and their birds, I thought. Fats continued: "Most of the shooters and protesters aren't even from here—until all this started, this was just a nice and quiet place." At the moment of this sudden appearance of shooter-protester alliance, Pop grinned significantly and made a stunning revelation:

Pop: Them Baumans only wanted straight shooting, so we gave 'em
    a hell.
HS: What hell?
Pop: (Amused) You sneak in a flock into a shirt factory overnight,
    and you can't catch 'em. It ruins them machines.
Fats: (Laughing) We sure did! We sure did!

Pests, Outcasts

If you could be moved in fieldwork as in reading a novel, intoxicated by the narrative frame of your own construction, this was such a moment for me.

The Baumans, whom Pop recalled alongside the straight-shooting, outsider doctors and lawyers, are the very family who initiated the protests of the Labor Day Shoot. They were one of the Jewish families from the eastern metropolitan areas who came to dominate the garment industry of the county, which has filled the vacuum left by the diminishing presence of mining since the 1960s.[17] As more men became unemployed in Schuylkill County, their wives and daughters were hired by the proliferating garment factories. From the beginning, intense hostility existed among the unemployed mine workers against the exogenous Jewish employers, who were perceived to "break up families" (by hiring women). From the point of view of the urban gentile employers, especially feared and detested were "pigeon gangs"—ex-miners turned coal bootleggers who were considered troublemakers, and the speakeasy owners who patronized them.[18] Both Pop and Fats were core members of such gangs. The Baumans, in an interview with me, confirmed the occurrence of the prank Pop mentioned at their Ashland Shirt Company (plus another factory unmentionable here as it bears the true name of the family) in the mid-1960s.

Contemplating the establishment of a new garment factory, in 1961 the Baumans moved to Hegins, a predominantly "Pennsylvania German" town.[19] No sooner had they arrived in Hegins than the patriarch of the family, Samuel, divorced his wife and married his housekeeper, a young, local woman of Pennsylvania German origin. This itself was scandalous, but to make matters worse, the new wife, Dorothy, conspicuously converted to Judaism. But the controversy that sparked the family's virtual expulsion from the community came, again, with the issue of pigeons. Samuel Bauman sparked a controversy surrounding pigeon shooting at a local gun club he had recently joined. It is this incident that Pop recalled. But the Baumans remember it differently.

According to Samuel and Dorothy, Samuel's first encounter with live-pigeon shooting (or flyer shooting) at the Hegins Trap Club was a case of aversion at first sight. Samuel immediately felt that "something was very wrong," but, in Dorothy's words, they "did not know about animal rights activism back then" (interview, 1993). But still, Samuel raised his voice against flyer shooting and unsuccessfully tried to organize a clay pigeon shoot in its place. He was immediately expelled from the membership. According to him, "living there after that became absolutely unbearable"—though he did not specify how. Soon after, in 1963, the family moved to Pottsville, taking with them the idea of a new factory in Hegins.

In contrast, according to Pop, who did not experience the incident first-hand, what Samuel opposed at the Hegins Trap Club was trap-and-handle shooting, not the flyer shoot altogether. Of course, opposing trap-and-handle was a class-specific statement; true to his class origin (of "doctors and lawyers"), Samuel refused the company of the likes of Pop and Fats. Documented evidence seems to lend credence to Pop's version. The Labor Day Pigeon Shoot's fiftieth anniversary booklet (published in 1985, the year of the first protest) lists all of the participants from the inaugural shoot in 1934 up to 1984. According to the list, Samuel Bauman participated in the Labor Day Shoot, a straight shooting, both before and after the reported incident (and did quite well), up until his move to Pottsville in 1963. From this, it seems that his renouncement of straight shooting was not as dramatic as his expressed aversion to trap-and-handle shooting.

To continue with the story of the Baumans' exodus, some two decades later, Dorothy became active in the animal rights cause, took up the issue of the pigeon shoot as her first mission, and with her children organized the first protest at the Labor Day Shoot in 1985. Since then, she has been successful in attracting the most powerful national animal rights organizations to the event. And to this day, Dorothy is a notorious figure throughout the county, especially in the Hegins area. A seductress, an animal lover, and a converted Jew, she still receives threats, according to her, in the form of dead opossums and pinned pigeons in her mailbox. Her effigy is hanged over a cauldron of witch's brew on a float arranged by a family of ex-miners and paraded down the Main Street of Hegins on every Halloween.[20]

The unexpected invocation of the Baumans by Pop on that memorable day of confrontation with Farmer was not an accident. That day, Farmer had transgressed Pop's most cherished "territories" at least three times: by bringing the "dirty" barn birds into the middle of the club's grounds; by ignoring the inviolable difference between Pop's birds and barn birds and regarding them all as mere targets; and by declaring that Pop's notions (or miners' notions) are obsolete. In the face of such a profound challenge, Pop resorted to the figure of outsiders. In a move very much reminiscent of Patrick Canfield's tirade in reaction to Eddie Becker's challenge above, Pop's accusation moves from the barn-bird shooter to the rootless outsider, and, with the help of Fats, from the outsider to the protesters, and from them to the hated "Jew." Just as the scapegoat figure of the outsider served as a convenient mediator that allowed Patrick to have it both ways in the pigeon-as-food and pigeon-as-pest debate, the barn-bird-outsider-protester-Jew alliance emerged on the very day Pop's sacred barn bird/brush bird distinction was unprecedentedly challenged. In both cases, the scapegoat figure of the outsider comes to the rescue the moment reality confronts the distinctions guarded in the pockets of suspended disbelief.

It is in this sense that the advent of the Baumans on the local scene marks the "threshold event." After the threshold, it was all topsy-turvy: pigeons were poisoned and became inedible, food and pest became confused, barn birds and brush birds became indistinguishable, et cetera. Do they really believe that the Baumans, or the likes of the Baumans, are responsible for all these changes? Of course not. They "know" better. They know that pigeon-food and the wonderful spirit of solidarity actually existed for a very short period of time during the Depression; they know that they actually import thousands of pigeons for the Labor Day Shoot; they know that brushed birds are actually barn birds. We must regard "knowing" here in the precise sense that Lacan established in association with guilt, contrastively to shame (see Chapter 3): one "knows better," but the burden of evincing the knowledge's validity has already left its owner, having been relegated to the Other who is supposed to hold its answer. In this sense, the Baumans exist as a *negative warrant* for a paradisiacal past they wished had existed. The Baumans are not the spoilers but the creators of backward-looking desires.

It would be a serious reduction of the problem at hand, though, to see this as a case of provincial anti-Semitism and pigeon killing as a vicarious execution of the "Jew" protester. The perceived primal "evil" alliance that scandalizes the shoot's supporters defies our customary pigeonholing of polemics; it warps and distorts our everyday logic. In it, for example, pigeons are pests *and* victims of pest control, protesters are pigeon killers *and* pigeons, et cetera. The figure of "the Jew" simply stops such a sliding logic as the most shadowy, and yet (or hence) as the most profound, warrant. It is in such an utterly transphenomenal sense that the advent of the Baumans to the local scene marks the aforementioned threshold event. I link this aspect to conspiracy theory in the following chapter.

CHAPTER FIVE
_____

Mimesis and Conspiracy Theory

The discussion of knowledge in the previous two chapters brings us to the issue of conspiracy theory. Around Labor Day, conspiracy theories were rampant among the residents. In hushed tones, as if wanting to shelter the bliss of my ignorance, they told me of the secret alliance between animal rights protesters and all other "outsiders"—particularly the "Jew-controlled" mass media and the state troopers. Accusations were grave, touching on nothing less than end-of-the-world scenarios and UFOs. But these sessions were fleeting and the imparted ideas merely suggestive; only one peep at a time is allowed into this unfathomably intricate and complex universe of conspiracies that led its sinister existence parallel to superficial normalcy. The punch line was in its aftereffect; the listener is meant to be abandoned, without the benefit of the details, to the mundanity of the everyday, which is now burdened and disjointed from itself with unknowable secrets.

For a long time, I did not think that my field site qualified as a candidate for conspiracy theory study. I took the coinage too literally and looked for theory in all its self-conscious investment in discursive coherence. Instead, what I had was nothing but performative exercises in the improvisational fluency of the dizzying array of fragmentary information and images. It was closer to the discourse of shamanic possession, with its famed improvisational eloquence in the hybrid idioms of the nether world (Tsing 1993: chap. 8).

And just as in the speech of the shaman, the aim was not the message but its illocutionary force. This force was felt everywhere around Labor Day—I mean everywhere! A certain righteous anger over some goodness robbed— be it by the Federal Reserve or the Jews—acrimoniously pressed against everything I observed and heard. If I still give that accusatory acrimony, that aimless Other-blaming consignment of responsibility the name con-

spiratorial, here, in Hegins, conspiratoriality—rather than conspiracy theory—boundlessly saturated everything. At least, that was the case from my
perspective; it was like a small patch of cloud that followed me around, cast-
ing shadow on everything I touched. As if on cue, people assumed a nearly
identical accusatory air upon my arrival at a conversation. It was as though I
was a walking reminder of the vocation of accusation they had temporarily
neglected before my arrival. I knew they were not blaming me directly, but I
was not completely exonerated of the present complaint either (see Chapter
3). My presence seemed to invite a certain sense of license, a license to exon-
erate themselves of responsibility for whatever bad had happened. Very importantly, this included the responsibility for narrative coherence. As if the
accused Other robbed them of the very reason to coherently tell their stories
(of victimization), they jumped around logic, dismissed details, and waved
away in disgust my invitations for clarification. And yet, they never stopped
talking, as if wanting to heap these ruins of speech before me as evidence of
the wrongs done to them. So, in the end, I have decided that these incoherences were indulged at my expense, as if the garbled logic was caused by an
unspoken proviso that "you, an outsider, must know very well what outsiders have done to this community." I was thus always already relationally
situated in some implied context to which my familiarity was presumed.

Paranoia

For me, talking to a conspiracy theorist was always accompanied by a vague
sense of reunion, as if talking to a begrudged long-lost brother who returns
an unwanted answer to a forgotten family secret. We academics are more
than implicated in the theater of conspiratorial imagining. Conspiracy theory's academe-mimicry has been (academically) commented upon frequently
enough: in terms of its virtuoso intellectualism, expertise emulation, reactionary anti-authoritarian occultism, and so on (see Barkun 2003).

Consider the following encounter I had after delivering a talk on conspiracy theory. When the talk was over, a man introduced himself with
gusto and animation as someone preparing a "big book" on the assassination of John F. Kennedy.[1] From that cheerful admittance of the self-mocking
term "big book," it was clear that he at present had deemed me an insider of
sorts—I must have said something right in my talk. A bearhug from him
seemed to be in order, perhaps set into motion by a vindication of his eso-
terica that my academic credentials granted. Then, he added roughly the

following snippet of logic, as if resuming an old conversation we had had: "That's right, academic historians had their chance, right? But the mystery of the JFK assassination is still unsolved, right? Why is that [as if I know the answer]? It's time that we think the whole thing differently? Like seeing it from the completely opposite direction?"

I was too tired to reciprocate his assumed familiarity and lethargically responded: "Hmmm ... What do you mean?"

The transformation of his air at this casual expression of skepticism on my part was breathtaking. A split-second silence quickly filled with suspicion. Then he blurted out with abandon as if reminding me of something of which I was currently only feigning ignorance: "Well, historians always tell *you* to consider multiple historical facts to explain one event. But you know ... you can see it the other way round: if you understand JFK, then you understand all the historical facts."

After this "reminder," he walked away triumphantly, as if having succeeded in exposing me. The quotes are not verbatim by any means, but his change of attitude I so distinctively remember.

Let us examine this interaction a little. Before my fateful utterance, "What do you mean?," markers of linguistic insecurity predominated the man's speech: repeated interrogative endings tested the possibility of laying claim to a supposed wealth of confidentially partaken memorative resources between us. I was thereby summoned to the demand of the present address authorized by a shared past, to some past commitment I was presently guilty of not remembering. So we found ourselves magically encapsulated as in a duel, set apart from standers-by—there were at least six. Once this exclusivity was achieved, my baffled muttering "What do you mean?" failed to prescribe an innocent inquiry: now it was nothing less than a betrayal. Once this betrayal was duly registered, a dramatic peripeteia ensued: the man exploded in disgust at this presumably all-too-familiar ploy on my part.

My reading here itself might sound given over to a little paranoia. It is jarring to step into an arena of interlocution where your role is already cut out for you—per conspiracy theory's aforesaid academe-mimicry—simulated and in wait, as if to entrap. It is guilt-inspiring to step into a persona whose status authority your interlocutor simultaneously courts, covets, despises, and dismisses. In the face of such a miming, you feel yourself splitting from yourself, becoming an Other to yourself, shall we say, feeling not only supplemented but also supplanted (see below for a discussion of mimesis). After all, mimesis is said to be contagious; I found myself answering the man's paranoia with my own. An encounter organized by paranoia is originarily excessive—as I wrote apropos bird phobia above—overdetermined by a mutually aggravated scansion of "misunderstandings." For this reason, as Jacques Lacan reminds us, an encounter configured by paranoia radicalizes with excess the very *materiality* of the speech. Sigmund Freud's famous joke serves as Lacan's eloquent example: "Why are you telling me you're going to Crakow? You are telling me that to make me believe that you are going somewhere else" (cited in Lacan 1993[1981]:37).

Here, the paranoid critique can never take a linguistic sign at its face value, as a mere messenger. Every sign is presumed to be an instrument of deception. Even a truthful statement—owing to the poor interlocutor's actual planned trip to Crakow—is taken to be a double deception that has already taken into account the hearer's suspicion. The hearer, in other words, *mimetically projects* his or her own deceptive deposition to the Other and then retrieves the message *inversely* as aimed at trapping the hearer him- or herself. On this account, Lacan writes, the speech of the paranoiac is never a "disinterested communication" (39), but always "bears witness" (41). The paranoid does not merely believe; he always *knows* (Flieger 1997:90).

What is to "bear witness," to "testify"? To bear witness is the opposite of laying claim to the lucidity of representational knowledge (see the Introduction). We instinctively expect a credible witness to be struck with a certain inability, an impossibility of clear vision and speech (Agamben 1999b:17). We also expect the credible witness to "embody" this impossibility directly and to speak in the first person—not as a medium that conveys in the third person. The witness voluntarily relinquishes the position of the autonomous master of the self-same speaking subject. And in exchange for this self-denying, self-othering move, the witness earns the right to speak on behalf of what-it-is-not (see Derrida 1995:77). Hence, witnessing involves a reversal: disempowerment and impossibility transform into empowerment and possibility. We see from the above Freudian joke a similar reversal, or as Lacan writes, inversion—of a sense of disempowerment and opacity inverting into an inflated sense of empowerment and clairvoyance. The trauma of a paranoid suspicion abruptly turns into an indubitable "knowing." The injury of displacement from the knowledge of the Other somehow earns the "testifier" a right to directly "touch" that Other.[2]

For now, I will say this much: what I call conspiracy theory is a relationally situated engagement actualized by projective identification and mimesis born of a communicative duel. This aspect brings out its "material" dimension, its ability to "touch." This is why conspiratorial reasoning is never meant to be a self-standing, disinterested "theory." It is originarily a counterdiscourse, a reactionary reversal, always already an answer to an anticipated discrediting, persecution, and censure. The probing gaze of the brokers of institutionalized academic knowledge, especially, are already given an interlocutor's role fully taken into account. This aspect, which is marked by the impasse of enigma of being as I have established in Chapter 3, has been neglected in the theories of conspiracy theory.

The Anthropology of Conspiracy Theory

Recent scholarship on conspiracy theory by anthropologists has already begun to move the discussion away from the rationalist topos to which the epithet "theory" had customarily installed the phenomenon. Dominic Boyer, for example, had this to say about a genre of conspiracy theory sampled in a (former East) Berlin *Stammtisch* (regular's table): there, "conspiratorial knowledge sought not only to reveal, to assert intellectual agency, but equivalently to disrupt knowledge, to cultivate doubt and uncertainty" (2006:332). Rather than clarity qua the matching of the logos to being, according to Boyer, post-unification Eastern conspiratorializing tends to operate under the sign of the "power to mask, dull, and distract attention" (332). The aim, Boyer reminds us, is the "displacement" (336) of the doxically inherited burden of its authoritarian past via a ceaseless probing of possible alternative scenarios. Boyer likens the practice to the technique of *therapy*, being a subjective measure—rather than a program of historical revisionism—aimed at subtracting individual agency from the neurosis of responsibility injunctioned by the superego of an official history. For "the temporary interruption of association, rather than the revelation of association . . . is the key to the therapeutic practice" (336).

Boyer filiates this turn away from the rationalist topos via the conceptual apparatus of the therapeutic to Susan Harding and Kathleen Stewart's groundbreaking piece, "Anxieties of Influence: Conspiracy Theory and Therapeutic Culture in Millennial America" (2003). Their anti-rationalist exegesis abides in the figure of the body. The pervasion of conspiracy theory in the postwar United States, they argue, took the form of an embodied mirroring of permeating social influences, which came to threaten autonomous, individual agency (264). Likening the trend to the turn-of-the-century psychosomatic symptom "nerve weakness," Harding and Stewart render the contemporary conspiratorial disposition configured within the horizon of the "nervous system" or "structure of feeling" (264).[3] For them, the transposing of the phenomenon to the elements of the culture of therapy is a credible prescription here as the latter also rose in response to the fragmentation and diffusion of selfhood attested to by the advent of modernity (263).

With a prophetic reach and a sagely erudition, Harding and Stewart enumerate the wealth of predicative traits proper to the ontico-empirical determinations of the epoch, to which belonged the culture of therapy(-cum-conspiracy theory). Abundantly detailed thus is the *culture* of the "talking cure"—but not the "talk" itself. What of the compulsion to talk, to insatiably interpret every sign, to passionately project or mimic as in a duel, and to engage in relationally situated contests? These are not activities confined to charged confrontations, such as with the "big book's" author. In psychoanalytic literature, at least, such activities make up the staple horizon of the curing technique. Clearly, the culture of the therapeutic is larger than that of psychoanalysis. But if we grant that psychoanalysis is at least coextensive with the proverbial culture of the therapeutic, we cannot ignore the most foundational Freudian wisdom: without the subject splitting from oneself for being relationally situated vis-à-vis the Other subject, there is no unconscious (Karatani 2003:33). Put otherwise, to speak of the therapeutic, we need an interactionally situated subject that resists, disavows, mimes, and projects in an answer to what I called earlier the enigma of being. To speak of conspiracy theory, that is, we need the hystericized subject-modality that is caught in the impasse of being.

Garbled Logic

Back to Hegins. I was discussing that certain incoherences were indulged at the expense of my presence. This "excess" of the always already—excess in the sense of indexing a presumed yet unspecified context—attests to the fact that by "relationally situated" we do not mean discursive localization. Neither does Lacan when he points out the paranoiac's overdetermined investment in the flesh of language. For the paranoiac, every sign trembles with animated materiality. As in heaping the ruins of language as material evidence, the paranoiac always *testifies*—but does not describe or theorize (Lacan 1993[1981]:40). There, speech not only references but (materially) exemplifies what it talks about. Thereby, the speaker directly embodies, or bears witness to, the impossibility of a truthful referencing. It is an event in the precise sense of self-designation, whereby one becomes what one declares. An event—if I follow the notion's most devoted contemporary student, Alain Badiou—is necessarily an auto-founding transformational procedure whereby the subject becomes other to itself (qua both "subject" and "object") by giving itself a new designation (2003:45). Hence, its meaning necessarily exceeds a "theory" that (pre-)informs it. That is precisely what I mean when I said that conspiratoriality saturates everything in Hegins around Labor Day. Now I turn to what I mean by "garbled logic."

As I said in the previous chapter, the discourse on the pest is confusing because the state of being a "pest" consists not just in the animal's specific and positive present qualities, but also in its having crossed a certain (temporal) threshold. To repeat, pigeons are culprits but also victims of what is done to them in changing times; the nostalgic taste of pigeons is sumptuous but equally a scandalous reminder of what has gone rotten. The fact of the pigeon's being a pest is a commentary on the general state of affairs; this is not contingent upon empirical specifics: where they came from (indigenous or urban-originated), how they were fed (parasitic or non-parasitic), how they were killed (poisoned, leaded?), and so forth. They were all dirty and inedible; or more correctly, they were all *made* to be dirty and inedible. The verdict is unanimous: pigeons must be killed now. In the previous chapter, I attributed the cause of this garbled logic to the "negative warrant" of the Baumans. I want to complicate that picture here and show that there is a dimension that is more than knowledge as associated with guilt.

The "Prick" of History

The official brochure for the Labor Day Shoot presents the current version as a positive continuation of the original event, which was held in 1934. Allegedly continued also is the wholesome spirit of charity and community, which is the version repeated by Elma in the previous chapter. But even Elma's testimony reproduces the official rhetoric only partially. What is dominant instead in the everyday representation is the rupture that separates the past and the present, which is condensed in the pigeon's fall to the status of the pest. On account of the rupture, the present and the past do not belong in the same moral universe: on the one hand, there is the wholesome past of solidarity and charity; on the other, the grim task of "pest control." A threshold has been crossed. There is no talk of recovering what is lost; historical discontinuation is a given fact. Nonetheless, instead of discrediting, the separated past seems paradoxically to strengthen the imperative of the present task. Crudely put, the reasoning goes something like this: "There was a loss of the past . . . and so pigeons must be killed now."

There is a certain correlation between the *indecipherability* of the traversed past and the *clarity* of the present task. Like trauma, the past is said to animate the present precisely in its *unrepresentable* absence. How exactly this conjunction of indecipherability and clarity operates is enigmatic.

For this, I turn, somewhat unimaginatively, to Roland Barthes's copiously cited work *Camera Lucida* (1981). I called this section "the prick of history" because his insight touches on how the weight of what-is-no-more, what is dead, comes to puncture and disquiet the photographic present. An example he discussed at some length is the photograph of a certain death-row inmate taken in 1885: "The *punctum* [or prick] is: *he is going to die.* I read at the same time: *This will be and this has been*; I observe with horror an anterior future of which death is the stake. By giving me the absolute past of the pose, the photograph tells me death in the future. What *pricks* me is the discovery of this equivalence [between this will be and this has been] . . . I shudder . . . *over a catastrophe which has already occurred*" (1981:96, original emphasis). The "catastrophic" effect is caused by an illicit coalescing of two different times: (1) the contingent moment of picture-taking; (2) the already completed death that is now in the realm of the inevitable and the necessary. The reason for this confusion is simple: every photograph vaguely prophesizes what is "likely but not certain to happen"—to quote a dictionary definition of the word "contingency." But from the time of viewing that contingent indecision had already been decided. In this "confusion" lies the catastrophe. Confused is the "has been" of the death note with a "will be." An enthralling suspense is effected thereby. The suspense obtains not by the uncertain fate of the referent but by the photographic present's scandalously fragile "innocence." The already known death of the referent leaves the photographic present without due. Historical reckoning is meaningless. But— this is what Barthes is arguing—precisely to the extent of the indecipherable loss that catastrophe renders the present tense of the photo gripping. He may as well moan: "How awful, the model is already dead and the photograph does not know it!"

I wonder if I could use this temporality to speak of why the present shoot in Hegins is gripping despite the ruptured past. I wonder if I could say, "How awful, the tradition is already dead and the Hegins shoot does not know it!" Let me explain.

The idea of historical filiation in this Barthesian sense is counterintuitive. When we normally speak of a historical legitimization of the present task, we think of an "invention of tradition," of discursive emplottment, of causal cohering across time. In other words, we speak of the causal rehabilitation of the present contingency by the closed past, which is now in the realm of the necessary. Contingency and necessity here are articulated in the measured tempo of exegetical chronicling.

Not so in the Barthesian prick of history. There, the gripping clarity of the present magically materializes out of the catastrophic muteness of the past. Between past and present, there is neither causal reckoning nor proportionalism. Nonetheless, the past authorizes the present ever more powerfully with a vengeful injunction: "There was a loss of the past . . . and so pigeons must be killed now."

The Excess of the Present

In both the Barthesian photograph and at Hegins, legitimization is instituted not through a positive historical filiation but through victimology. As a "victim" of a ruptured history, the present shoot in Hegins *self-legitimizes*—or, eventually self-makes—precisely on account of its unreckonable separation from the past. This kind of "evental" time-reckoning is consistent with widely accepted observations on the conspiratorial knowledge to an extent. According to the observations, conspiracy theory explains the world and itself at once. A conspiracy theory not only reveals a truth but preemptively explains why it cannot access the whole truth; its own referential fallibility is already taken into account (Barkun 2003, Hofstadter 1967). Here, ignorance is a mark of the victim's innocence, more evidence of stifled information. That way, even failed explanations glow with indignant righteousness.

I hear a similar indignant self-legitimization and evental self-making in the talks about the threshold event. They not only announce the past dead and pigeons turned pests, but explain why the past remains inaccessible to the present recovery effort, that is, the shoot at Hegins. The present shoot is not just a failed replica of the original; its failure *materially* and eventually bears the scar of the reasons why it had to fail. Hence the *prick* of the present shoot's enthralling innocence: "How awful, the tradition is already dead and the Hegins shoot does not know it!"

It is safe to say then, that in Hegins, it is as if conspiracy theory's aim is not so much to describe the Enemy referentially, but to directly bear the material inscription of the Enemy's sinister power. The aim is as much passivity as it is activity. Or, to be more precise, it is an active assumption of passivity. The "theory" does not so much mediate but im-mediately *touches*. A "theory" understood in its material force, as that which immediately bears inscription, as in touching, collapses the ideational immateriality with the materiality of the sign—furthermore, universality with particularity, multiplicity with singularity.

This aspect of conspiratorial knowledge is different from knowledge Lacan associates with guilt as I have established in Chapter 3. Guilt, as we have seen, converts a fundamental impasse (of being) into a recoverable loss that can be potentially appropriated from the Other in the future tense. Hence, it is intensely invested in the unveiling of what may lie beneath the "surface"—of, say, media distortion. Contrarily, Joan Copjec writes: "our relationship to the surface change[s] in shame" (2006:111). The knowledge apropos shame is "fascinated with (the surface's) intricacies" (111). This fascination with the surface is precisely what I am trying to grapple with here in the notion of "material force" (of the conspiratorial knowledge). I will variously refer to this aspect below as conspiratorial knowledge's "disproportionalism" (per the conflation of multiplicity and singularity) and mimesis.

Mimetic Doubt

How do we theorize a "theory" whose vocation is to "touch," to materially bear the imprint of that which it tries to theorize? Such an aspect of mimesis is the difficulty the social science of conspiracy theory faces. Put otherwise, how do we theorize a "theory" whose vocation is doubt for its own sake, the kind of doubt that has constitutively given itself over to irresolvability by any epistemic authority?[4] Just as in a child's impossible query—"Why is the sky blue?"—conspiracy theory's unappeasable doubt mimes academic inquiry to the point of its authority's derailment. This may occasion a rare glimpse into academic inquiry's silently presupposed imperatives as it hysterically reacts to its mimicking cousin, which is the task of what follows. As such, my aim is not to subscribe an alternative univocal theory on conspiracy theory of my own. It is meaningless to criticize other social scientific theories of conspiracy theory as inadequate representations of the phenomenon. Instead, the aim here is to show what conspiracy theory (as we have just established) *does* to social science.

Among the presupposed imperatives that may come into view vis-à-vis conspiracy theory is representationalism. Representationalism purchases academic monopoly on doubt. From its vantage, vernacular instances of doubt are instruments of so many competing epistemological regimes of representational truth-claims, whose differing degrees of (approximating, hence imitative) validity await the test of (non-imitating) academic doubt. Elided in this representational view is the ontological dimension of doubt, its existence—what does the child of mimetic doubt want if not the referential knowledge about celestial blueness? But what exactly is the ontological dimension of doubt—its existence? It will be my contention below that the suppression of the question of the ontological dimension of doubt prescribes one of the conditions of possibility for contemporary academic social science. The reception of conspiracy theory is symptomatic of this broader trend. One only needs to recall the currency of the infamous term "Cartesianism" in social science today. What is it in doubt that cannot be admitted to the normative register of contemporary social science? A contemplation on the phenomenon of conspiratorial doubt delivers us over to a direct confrontation with this unnameable normative horizon. This enlivening of the question of doubt has a broader aim: it is to reclaim "anthropological cogito" as a true vocation for anthropology (Clifford 1988). Michel Foucault arguably reserved the name "ethnology" to this vocation (Foucault 1970:376–80), to which I now turn in order to gauge the import of posing the question about doubt to contemporary social science at this juncture.

Cogito's Disproportionalism

The question of the ontological dimension of doubt has come to the fore in Western social theory of late, with a renewed interest in cogito as first formulated by René Descartes (see Mandarini and Toscano 2006:22–24). Cartesian cogito came to be appreciated anew as an unprecedented feat of experimentation with suspended representationality. What came into view thus for the first time through the Cartesian experiment was a "meeting-point between representation and being" (Foucault 1970:309). For thinking, vacated of all its representational content through unrelenting doubt, was made to confront its own existence. Doubt, here, is not just the name of a momentary shelter for the methodological checkup of representation's health. A reflexive doubling procedure, it draws our attention to thought's own "density" (336)—its drive toward circling around itself without representational telos. Specifically, the circling is between the doubter simultaneously "as an object knowledge and as a subject that knows" (312). Disrupted and exceeded thus is the complacent relation of a subject to an object, as the subject of knowing itself appears among the known objects. Now, the "account" between the two (subject and object) cannot be balanced, as it were. Instead, the awareness of a certain "dissymmetry" or "disproportion" (Foucault's terms) emerges precisely as thinking seeks a "balanced" self-possession from both ends of thinking. If we liken it to the "corporealized gaze" (312), cogito awakens to the fact that "my gaze, *precisely as regards me*, is no long the measure of all things" (Derrida 1995[1992]:27, emphasis added). Thought comes to "experience" its own existence as an excess, beyond and disproportional to its own grasp. More "passively" than "actively" does it experience its existence. This betrays Descartes' own famous conclusion: "'I think' does not . . . lead to the evident truth of 'I am'" (Foucault 1970:324). The overall outcome is ironic: precisely as thinking attempts to master its provenance, a dimension of "unthought" comes to hound (331). Cogito's thirst for empirical certainty only lets loose paranoia over what might lie beyond the empirical, even over the possible existence of a conspiratorial "Evil Genius." The more "material"-groundedness cogito seeks, the more "immaterial" and excessive that sought after materiality itself becomes (331). Foucault assigns to the task of ethnology this transcendental dimension of "unthought," which is ceaselessly generated by none other than thought's attempt to grasp the world. He assigns a parallel task to "psychoanalysis," to which I will return below separately.

Why is doubt, or, even better, conspiratorial doubt, important in this Foucauldian reform? And what might its implication be for a study of conspiracy theory? What must strike as most alien from the vantage of contemporary social science is how Foucault rendered ethnology beholden to *singular individual* experience, which doubt irreducibly is—and the concomitant celebratory pairing of psychoanalysis with ethnology. The measure of "disproportion" or "dissymmetry" owes to this investment in the singular-individual: the procedure of cogito counterintuitively coheres, on the one hand, the paranoid myopia of a singular-individual self-introspection with, on the other, a traversal into the unnameable, transcendental horizon of the "unthought." The strictest of affirmations of finitude somehow end in the discovery of a dimension of infinity. "Minuscule and yet invincible," Foucault thus diagnoses cogito's disposition (1970:340)—precisely the disposition I highlight from conspiracy theory.

Seen this way, Cartesianism's well-rehearsed infamy among us today

misses the point: we disdain critical cogito insofar as it is a privative enterprise indulgent in bourgeois interiority. This complaint re-institutes the
very conceptual dichotomies that critical cogito sought to problematize (if
not fully by Descartes himself) in the first place, that is, subjective/objective
or representation/being. Cogito, as the site where the very "material" being
of "immaterial" thinking is actualized, was meant to directly embody, by
its own existence as evidence, the very *impossibility* of these dichotomies
as fixed terms. It held itself up—that is, the indubitability of the fact that a
thinking "something" exists—as an evidentiary protest against the stable
parsing of thinking from being. In this sense, cogito is not a hypothetically
imagined "cognitive" laboratory from which a theorem is announced in the
third person.[5] Its ontological existence creates its own condition for this an-
nouncement in the first person. It is a testimony.[6]

Given the affinity between conspiracy theory and cogito, no social science of conspiracy theory can afford to overlook the fact that the idea of
doubt occupies a special place in the contemporary social scientific imaginary. Its compelling evidence is in the requisite denunciation of Cartesianism as an obligatory course of social scientific argumentation today. There
seems to be a pressing need to recall cogito again and again precisely as an
errancy. As will be explained shortly, this complex of libidinally charged
response—whereby what is supposedly "outside" renders what is "inside"
operative—I will name "sacrificial" after Jean-Luc Nancy (2003). It is my
contention that scholarly commentaries on the phenomenon of conspiracy
theory are already rehearsed in this sacrificial complex in which the ontology of doubt is caught; cogito and conspiracy theory are assigned a common
fate in this regime of thought.

Mimetic Doubt as a Critique

How do we respond to a "mimicking cousin"? Imagine the child of mimetic
doubt again—why is the sky blue? And imagine yourself falling into silence
at the end of an uncomfortable length of time in such a silly pursuit, irritated
and incomprehensibly embarrassed. Yes, such an embarrassment is likely to
be incomprehensible. It would be as though you are embarrassed by the fact
that you are embarrassed, as if you are embarrassed for someone else who
is embarrassed. Where does this *doubling* effect come from, as though you
are *both the subject of embarrassment and an object being observed in that
state*? And doesn't this doubling smack of the Cartesian splitting of thought

from itself? Such a mimetic doubt cruelly lays bare something that must be silently presupposed for us to speak meaningfully (as adults). Call it a place holder of our speech. Call it, say, authority. The problem (for the adults) is that the mimetic doubt in question does not bother to confront us at the level of an opposing authority, another Master. Accountability is irrelevant here. Instead, simple repetition (which is also self-miming and self-othering) effortlessly unhinges our speech from its place holder. Its evidence is in how, in those moments, right before silence falls, we would catch ourselves becoming hyperconscious about the very materiality of our speech's flesh, or as Foucault would say, density—as though we had become detached from it. And so the doubling effect: we are embarrassed by our embarrassment.

Welcome (in)to the play frame, Gregory Bateson might say. If I may paraphrase him: play frame, when it is linguistically constructed, is all about deliberately confounding the referential function of our language with its "material" dimension, that is, its indexical situatedness at the moment of utterance (2000[1972]:184). Or, in the language of cogito, it is about the confounding of representationality with being. Just as in cogito, a play directly embodies and testifies to the very impossibility of the dichotomy. There, language not only references but becomes an "example" of what it talks about— as in the statement "I am lying."[7] The messenger becomes the message, as it were, becoming both the subject of speech and the object talked about. What is more significant for us is that such a self-othering easily turns "contagious," allowing the joker and the object of the joke (the butt) to switch places just as easily. Likewise, to return to our example at hand, the mimetic doubter produces a like mimetic effect in the (adult) hearer: both the imitator and the imitated self-split into two, the subject and the object.

What does the child of mimetic doubt want? There is a surprising similarity with the desire that configures the critical cogito. Very likely, the child is pointing out the absurdity of our speech act (and of the authority that abides in it). Very likely, the child wants us to self-write the condition of our own enunciation, expropriated of all externally transposed authorities. If we are brave enough, our confrontation with the very limit of speech in such a moment can magically open up the condition for new possibilities. Isn't that what every child of mimetic doubt demands of us? My aim in this imaginary exercise is not to infantalize the phenomenon of conspiracy theory, nor to reduce it to face-to-face interactional engagements. It is rather to dramatize the unaccountable nature of mimetic practice, and by extension of critical cogito, and its power to effortlessly unsettle and lay bare the conditions of

possibility for every academic or representational attempt to "take it into account." By maximally operationalizing the mimetic impetus in conspiracy
theory the hope here is that we could explore new ethnographic possibilities,
the ones that self-write the condition of their own enunciation, which Foucault arguably saw in "ethnology."[8]

Enlisting a mimetic gesture in the service of a critique—my aim here—is
a well-established apparatus of criticism. Let's look at this technique more
closely. As others have observed, that which imitates is the *par excellence*
figure of non-identity, non-substance, or the non-proper (Lacoue-Labarthe
1989:116)—hence my questioning of conspiracy theory's referential unity.
Speaking of Thoth, the Greek god of mimesis, Jacques Derrida writes:
"Thoth is never present. Nowhere does he appear in person. No being-there
can properly be *his own*" (Derrida 1981:93, original emphasis).[9] Instead,
Thoth "takes its shape from the very thing it resists and substitutes for"; "In
distinguishing himself from his opposite, Thoth also imitates it" (93). He is,
Derrida concludes, the "god of nonidentity" (93).

That which imitates at once "resists" *and* "substitutes" (the imitated),
Derrida tells us. Here, the imitator not only supplements—as an auxiliary
"addition"—but supplants the imitated. Confounded by this operator of
"non-identity," then, is not only the distinction between the copy and the
original, between the imitator and the imitated. The imitator itself becomes
other to itself in the process.

Moreover, being "only" a parasitic imitation, that which imitates is more
often than not held in contempt as "poor imitation." However, being a sup-
plement that also substitutes, an auxiliary "addition" that is at once interchangeable with the original, that which imitates attests to the constitutive
lack in the imitated. As such, Derrida continues, mimesis configures all at
once the technique of the magician, the remedial "pharmacological" potion
of the shaman, and the poison of the witch; that is, wherever boundaries
are re-determined in a simultaneous gesture of dissolution and rebuilding
(1981:93–97). In this sense, mimesis is a contemptible "poor imitation" that
is also the necessary condition of possibility for any supposed identity to be
"identical with itself."

In short, to dwell on that which imitates is to interrogate the "health"
of identity and the rhetorical unity that is prescribed to a phenomenon. To
dwell on conspiracy theory is to tarry with academic discourse's uncertain
boundaries, its outlying threshold configured by deeply ambivalent, libidinally charged contempt toward that which imitates it (such as conspiracy

theory). My aim here is to deploy the mimetic magic/remedy/poison of con-spiracy theory as a measure for the "health" of social scientific knowledge, that is, the latter's ideological operation required to maintain the boundaries of the univocal topos for academic authority.

Necessarily an idiom of "mutuality," then, under the sign of the notion of mimesis, both the imitator and the imitated suppose the persistence of the other. Nancy deems such a complex necessarily sacrificial. For him, so-called sacrifice is the privileged figure of non-identity against whose supposed "poorly imitated" religiosity the spiritual religiosity of the West is conceived as a (non-imitating, hence imitated) plenitude. His assertion is ascribed by the peculiar way sacrifice is inaugurated in the Western episteme: what is supposed to be sacrifice proper, that is, the early or non-Western sacrifice, is foundationally rejected in the West as failing to live up to the "true" spirit of sacrifice (2003:55). (Instead, self-sacrifice became the West's ideal—more anon on this.) Put paradoxically, sacrifice was something that inspired reli-giosity's "true spirit," from whose vantage the actual sacrifice is disqualified from being an instance of its own supposed inner truth. In short, sacrifice at once *inaugurated* and *imitated* the religiosity proper. And in imitating, it became a poor imitator not only of the proper religiosity but of itself.

And this ambivalent installment caused a like ambivalent reaction. As the inaugurator, sacrifice was the West's obsession; as the poor and violent imitator of the "true" sacrifice (that is, self-sacrifice), it was an object of con-tempt and violence. On the latter account, we can announce that the "conta-gious" role reversal proper to mimeticism is accomplished: it was as though the Western appropriation of sacrifice was compelled to mimic its referent and repeat the violence (that is, sacrificial violence) it repudiated—the vio-lence that the former sought to "sublimate" and "spiritualize" in its own ide-alized version, self-sacrifice. Nancy calls this ironic procedure "sacrifice of sacrifice" (2003:58). We see a similar procedure in social science's appropria-tion of conspiracy theory, to which I now turn.

"Sacrifice of Sacrifice" in the Study of Conspiracy Theory

There is a curious consistency to be noted in the social scientific com-mentaries on conspiracy theory. It seems almost axiomatic that the sub-ject is broached with a rejection of the famed thesis advanced by Richard Hofstadter (for example, Bratich 2002; Fenster 2008[1999]: chap. 1; Husting and Orr 2007:139–40; Willman 2000). Hofstadter foundationally consigned the phenomenon to the pathology of "paranoia" (1967). It is as though the general analytical space for conspiracy theory requires a sacrificial cleansing of sorts, of which the "bloodletting" of his thesis is an obligatory course of action. A privileged symptomal place to which his offense is thus negatively assigned should not escape our attention. What rhetorical function does his thesis—precisely as a misrepresentation—purchase as the articulator of what I submitted as academics' contempt for conspiracy theory?

"Libidinally charged" was the expression I used to refer to contemporary social sciences' contempt in which cogito is generally beholden. Such a contempt applies here too. The psychoanalytic-sounding descriptor is meant to capture the operative presence of ambivalences proper to the mimetic proximity between the academic and the conspiratorial. This is to say that what is at issue is far from a manifest contempt, but one disavowed under the auspice of the protocols of academic neutrality and "disinterest." To name what is thus disavowed is to interrogate the libidinal function of the contempt in facilitating the very possibility of a "disinterested" academic inquiry on conspiracy theory, the ideological operation required to secure such a space.[10]

Slavoj Žižek argues that whenever an impossible horizon of (disinterested) universality is prescribed, there abides its symptom. Symptom, as he defines it, is "a certain fissure, an asymmetry, a certain pathological impulse which belies (any claim to) universalism" (1989:21). More specifically, "symptom is a particular element which subverts its own universal foundation, a *species subverting its own genus*" (21, emphasis added). In this sense, Žižek continues, the symptom is "a point of breakdown heterogeneous to a given ideological field and at the same time necessary for that field to achieve its closure, its accomplished form" (21). If we take the protocol of academic disinterest as an aspiring universalist foundation, then its symptom would be an element that straddles both academic universalism and the particularity of its object of inquiry—in our case, the academic theories on conspiracy theory and conspiracy theory itself. The symptom of contemporary social scientific commentaries on conspiracy theory is, I would argue, Richard Hofstadter. Let me elaborate.

We tend to identify Hofstadter's kind of reduction as "psychologism," and obligatorily call for more attention to the society, culture, political economy, historical forces, and so on. The label psychologism we inherited from one of the most well-rehearsed and familiar dialectics in social sciences: the individual versus society. Psychologism is said to privilege the individual at the expense of the social. I emphasize this familiarity. Put this way, Hofstadter's evidently useful "crime" seems not so much a reduction than too much likeness to the object of his inquiry. For psychologism easily recalls conspiracy theory in our minds because of its ready assigning of a conceptual unity to willful and autonomous psychosomatic individual agency (and "paranoia" as its pathological moment). From this view, Hofstadter not only theorized conspiracy theory, but (despite himself) mimed its logic: psychologism is a kind of conspiracy theory. By this operation, conspiracy theory itself is in turn seen to approximate academic mediocrity. From the normative register of the traditional site of social science, what psychologism nourishes itself in is a certain "disproportionality" between the particular and the universal—psychologism privileging the former.

I have just stated that psychologism and conspiracy theory partake in a certain disproportionalism. Given what I called psychologism's familiarity, we may conjecture about its role as an accessible "translator": psychologism translates conspiracy theory's disproportionalism in the simplest and the most graspable terms of the particular/universal dialectic: the individual versus society dualism. Put otherwise, Hofstadter's kind of psychologism functions as a proxy, which opens up the condition of possibility for the theoretical enterprise on conspiracy theory. Recall that it is a necessary proxy, which has to be rejected as lacking again and again—as none other than a "poor imitation." Then, this proxy does what any good talismanic apparatus does: pressing close to what it studies, as it were, it renders conspiracy theory—its disproportionalism—reduced and appropriable in a familiar language, all the while absorbing the "crime" of pathologization and reductionism away from us. In short, the analytical space for commentary on conspiracy theory is opened up in a double negation: by "slaughtering" the proxy, which itself supposedly "slaughtered" conspiracy theory. Hence, the sacrificial logic is completed: "In the evil of the [scapegoat] [the sacrificer]expels what is the vilest in itself" (Derrida 1981:131).[11] This paradoxical gesture (of drawing proximate and imitating the "crime" of that which is supposed to be purged as Other to the proper theorization of conspiracy theory) attests to the presence of a profound ambivalence. The cause of that ambivalence I have called disproportionalism in conspiracy theory.

Beyond Mediation

A word is in order regarding the broader intellectual configuration that renders my intervention here theoretically legible. In his recent work Kojin

Karatani diagnoses the contemporary vilification of the Cartesian philosophy of subjectivity born of doubt (2003:81–92). Lévi-Strauss's criticism of Descartes exemplifies Karatani's point paradigmatically: "Descartes believes that he proceeds *directly* from man's interiority to the exteriority of the world without seeing that societies, civilizations . . . place themselves *between* these two terms" (Lévi-Strauss 1976:36; emphases added). Karatani's diagnosis centers on this figure of the "between." He consigns the root of the figure of the "between" to German romanticism. The trend, for him, was responsible for the wealth of social science's foundational "middling" in-between categories such as language, culture, and the nation. Not that he rejects these categories; the emphasis is on how these became expedient conceptual currencies. But "middling" in what sense? Let us unpack Lévi-Strauss's paradigmatic statement a little further.

Consider his well-known attempt to rehabilitate the thesis of Hubert and Mauss on reciprocity in the same work. Hubert and Mauss observed that Papuans and Melanesians use one word for buying and selling, lending and borrowing (1981[1964]). In their characteristic manner, Hubert and Mauss divined, without fully explaining, a deeper wisdom in this im-mediate collapsing of what they called "antithetical operations" in the same word (in Lévi-Strauss 1976:49). To this, Lévi-Strauss responded, "Antithesis does not exist"; buying and selling are "just two modes of a selfsame reality" (49). Lévi-Strauss swiftly glosses what falls in between subjects of reciprocity with a "selfsame" semantic value in the grammar of culture. So he elides that inherent "gap" of imbalance qua "antithesis," which someone like Pierre Bourdieu might say can be traversed only by performative practices in time (Bourdieu 1997). Lévi-Strauss continues: "Exchange is not a complex edifice built on the obligation of giving, receiving and returning. . . . It is a synthesis immediately given to . . . symbolic thought" (1976:49). The "symbolic thought," here as something "immediately given," is a "selfsame" edifice that is potentially available to the seller and the buyer, the lender and the borrower alike. It is by definition a reproducible experience in the domains of empathy, sympathy, or common sense. For Karatani, such mediating categories were precisely what the romantic intervention needed to bypass the inherent disproportional "deficit" (my term) that burdened the critical philosophy built on the subjective doubt. For the doubting subject could not be easily "added up" to form the organic society predicated on common sense. Why?

Allow me to philosophize a bit further. Such a "deficit" was first properly articulated by Immanuel Kant, who tried to complete the radical potential of the Cartesian philosophy of doubt unrealized in Descartes himself. For Kant, just as has been stated by Foucault above, "I am" cannot be deduced from "I think" (Karatani 2003:87). A thought cannot properly think its own topos of existence. There is an irreducible gap or "antinomy" between our being the subject of knowledge and the object known. In other words, we, as subjects of thought, cannot representationally "situate" ourselves among the objects grasped in our own thoughts à la "God's Great Chain of Being." Between the fact of our being the subject of knowledge and at the same time being an object of knowable things the "account" can never be settled—there is excess in our being. Such is Kant's amended version of subjective doubt (which is reproduced by Foucault without due acknowledgment).

The consequence of Kant's antinomic deficit is that any universalizing category, such as society, requires a "leap of faith" (Karatani 2003:100; Kant 1970:55–56). For we cannot acquire a coherent, "organic" sense of unity for such a universalizing entity as society—no matter how much we generalize our empirical experience and its representation. We have no choice but to "passively" inhabit society as given to us without due. Paradoxically, Kant's idea of sociality draws its resource precisely from the "sufferer" of this antinomic deficit, beset by doubt and singularly-individually solitary in his or her passivity. "Minuscule and yet invincible," we might once again describe his solitary individual agent with a potential toward a socializing "leap." The foregoing has been an attempt to rethink conspiracy theory under the imperatives of this critical legacy, specifically, its disproportional measure born of the requisition of doubt and the ontological dimension of thinking it has brought our attention to.

An Ethnography of Doubt

I have embarked upon an examination of the ethnographic challenge posed by the conspiratorial doubt by comparing it to the child's game of mimetic doubt. By so doing, I let a proper ethnographic response to the challenge be unveiled in the intuitively familiar demand of the child's play. I take the resource for ethnography from the kind of "sociality" demanded of us in the child's play. And what kind of sociality is that? The child's play surely does not invite us to share in universally and "immediately given" idioms of commonality. Its "message," rather, is duplicitous and duplicative—as in "I am lying." Does not its approach to language rather resemble the "antithesis"-bearing language of gift giving as per Hubert and Mauss's noting? Both language usages "embody" certain "impossibilities": in the case of play, the impossibility of artificially distinguishing language's referential function from its being; in the case of gifting, the impossibility of the bookkeeper's kind of differential counting between giving and receiving. In both cases, language is employed only to reveal its inadequacy. In both cases, language is employed to index what cannot be linguistically represented. Surely, such is the wisdom bequeathed to us by the compendium of canonical texts on gifting: the role of the "thing" of the gift is precisely to flaunt its inadequacy, that is, to point to and summon what is unrepresentable and inaccessible (Mauss 1967).

Unaccountable and unrepresentable, such a sociality does not prescribe proper measures of response for us, either linguistically or materially. It inhibits our response and, in turn, remains unresponsive to our demands, which is precisely how I felt when confronted with the "ruins of speech" heaped before me "as evidence of the wrongs done to them." Such a linguistic ruin, such a flaunting of the inadequacy of language, is somehow more silent than silence itself. Similarly, a child's mimetic play with language is strangely more maddening than a total refusal to speak—is it not? Prolonged enough, such clowning can provoke in us an almost violent desire to punish this unresponsiveness, this unaccountability. And we would do so in the name of "responsibility." I suspect such a temptation to champion supposedly neglected responsibility is as strong in the social science of doubt. It is a helpless ethnographic cause—I am thinking here of my own field site—trying to write about people who neither embellish their cause in the patrimonial language of a worthy culture nor vaunt a cogent victimary exegesis but only doubt and doubt. The problem I see is that the commentators on this kind of conspiracy theorizing, as in Hegins, tend to *masculinize* the phenomenon, whether to celebrate or to criticize. Psychoanalytically speaking, such a bottomless doubting is close to the "feminine complaint":

> Melodrama dwells on figures of *innocence* [as in "the tradition is dead and the Hegins shoot does not know it!"] not to provide testimony for the need to install a law, but rather to indict existing laws and standards as unfounded. . . . The melodramatic world is one in which *masks proliferate as masks*, as disguises that flaunt their thinness. . . . The many copies or simulacra circulating through it refer not to an ideal lodged elsewhere . . . but rather flout the complaint that no such ideal exists . . . this sense of inauthenticity . . . is what

determines melodrama as a "feminine complaint." (Copjec 2004:117–18, emphasis added)

I want to emphasize the expression "feminine complaint" for this seemingly most virile of practices.

A bottomless doubt is likely to set into motion an academic defense against it, one that would restore accountability and responsibility. In such a defense, practices that supposedly "sacrificed" accountability themselves would be sacrificed, so Nancy predicted. This is why, for Nancy, the West had to replace (as its ideal) the disproportional and imitative non-Western sacrifices with the accountably balanced (that is, "selfsame," to use Lévi-Strauss's expression) self-sacrifice.[12] Indeed, although I lack space to elaborate, "ethically responsible" analytics abound in both the defenses of and the attacks on the "culture" of the Labor Day Shoot. Such analytics deliver us over to the Master tropes of liberalism's imperatives: the glorious culture of labor unionism (for example, Bodnar 1983, Dublin 1998, Dublin and Licht 2005, Kozura 1996), the patrimony of the agricultural-sacrificial tradition (Bronner 2005), and anti-Semitism, to name just a few. Only under the suspension of such ventriloquist regimes of "sacrifice of sacrifice" can the ethnography of doubt in its full ontological dimension be attempted.

Given what has been said about silence qua unaccountability, it seems significant that the paradigmatic site of play delimited by Bateson is not human children with language but wolf cubs, wolf cubs at play: "The playful nip denotes the bite, but it does not denote what would be denoted by the bite" (2000[1972]:180). Wolf cubs deliberately show their false "selves" (that is, bites) in order to point to something hidden, that is, a sociality that is absent and unrepresentable here and now. All of the central notions that supported my narrative heretofore—cogito, witnessing, touch, event—show the same technique of becoming other to oneself as a way of opening up an Other dimension or possibility. What we learn from the wolf cubs is that this potentially lethal play can continue only as long as this Other remains unnamed; only in the absence of the name of a guaranteeing Master can this risky experimentation with suspended subjectivity go on. The solitude and ceaseless doubt the player in such a play has to endure I called, in this chapter, "cogito."

By giving a narrative unity to the infamous dispositif called cogito, I do not mean to flatten the societal and political criteria that customarily name the ethnographic case considered here; I prescribe neither a revisionism for the unheard-of wealth of labor legacy nor an apologism for the presence of anti-Semitism surrounding the Labor Day Shoot. What I tried to shelter here is a glimpse of some new possibilities—even freedom—that came to rehearse themselves in the suspended lacuna of thinking pried open amid the "ruins" of what seem like nothing more than aimless complaints. Call it a sociality that remains undecided between taking place and non-place, whose meaning arises only through reference to the event of discourse. I have nothing to say as to where this sociality to come is headed in "ethically responsible" terms—say, in the terms of language, culture, and the nation in Karatani's senses. But I do know that this ethnographer is a co-player in this experimentation in suspended subjectivity; it is in the name of my outsider Other presence that such a doubt-cum-possibility paranoiacally and relationally realizes itself. As a co-worker in this enterprise of suspension, I must also remain beholden to this unnameable dimension granted "playfully." I owe fidelity to my own uncertain vocation of cogito. I am duty bound to a more radical kind of responsibility. It is said that the most radical form of responsibility "exposes me dissymmetrically to the gaze of the other; where my gaze, precisely as regards me, is no longer the measure of all things" (Derrida 1995:27). The last time I used this quote, it was to designate Cartesian cogito. Even earlier, I called the same "shame."

CHAPTER SIX

Representationalism's Animal Other

> Representation is what determines itself by its own limit. . . . [It
> represents] for itself, both itself and its outside, the outside of its
> limit. . . . [Representation] designates itself as limit, as demarcation.
> [It] appears as what has as its planetary, galactic, universal vocation
> limitlessly to extend its own delimitation. It opens the world to the
> closure that it is.
>
> —Jean-Luc Nancy, *The Birth of Presence*[1]

The "garbled logic" we saw in the previous chapter can be summarized as this:
There was a loss of the past . . . and so pigeons must be killed. I am positive
that this abrupt logic invokes "sacrifice" in the readers' minds. The invocation
would be a small proof that there is an almost instinctive comprehension in
us of the fundamental unreason of this ritual, of its senseless bloody repetition, of its notoriously mindless mechanical "economism"—"Here is the butter, where is the offering?" Also instinctively comprehended is the fact that we
often come across non-human animals at these sites—of unreason, excesses,
abrupt logics, and unrepresentables. The next two chapters are devoted to
dwelling on the reason for this encounter with the animal Other. The current
chapter examines the dominant intellectual trend that has been usurping the
proper questioning of such an "unreason": representationalism.

Representationalism

It is a banal truism that no one has ever been a non-human animal, just as
no one has ever been dead. The truism speaks to the unsurpassable abyss in

both cases. And yet, unlike with death, we never stop making statements such as "animals are good to think with" (Tambiah 1969). Two different kinds of difference are involved here, one abyssal, the other representational. The contrast in the intellectual career of the two kinds of animal difference cannot be more absolute: one puts a stop to thinking (or abandons it to banality), and the other seems to animate it to productivity. The suspicion is that the latter's productivity is purchased at the price of holding the banal former at bay. The ambition of this chapter is to hold both firmly in a steady focus. The aim is to make the case that the animal, precisely because it obtains a *nondescript* abyssal difference, is generally a privileged resource for *representational* thinking.

Nancy's epigraph condenses everything I want to say in this chapter. Without the benefit of the meat of this chapter, let me foreshadow the argument to come by repeating Nancy's formidable line: "Representation . . . determines itself by its own limit." It is a reminder that any representation is also a self-representation, thinking of difference also that of delineation of self-identity. Nancy is not thereby talking about Saussurian differentials—how to think what is "not me" is to oppositionally affirm what is "me." Rather, the "planetary, galactic, universal vocation" of representationalism is such that its operation is always reflexively doubled: not only does it apprehend that there is "not-me" (qua Other-authored representation) but it quickly recuperates this experience of "limit," shall we say, by (representationally) capturing this very relation from a point of exception—that is, by occupying the position that escapes both "me" and "not-me." For representation then, to think its limit is simultaneously to appropriate what Nancy calls the Outside, that is, what it, by its own definition, cannot think. The "humble" gesture of delimiting itself, it turns out, hides its universalist ambition of deeming itself an all-encompassing plenitude.

In other words, representationalism cheerfully admits to its own particularity, but it refuses to relinquish the universal applicability of this very representation (of the fact of its particularity). Representationalism may declare that everything is according to Saussurian differentials—wherein any identity is posited oppositionally, conditional to the existence of the Other—but it exempts this very declaration from the alleged "everything." Representation thus presents itself as self-motivated and self-standing. "It opens the world" but only to lead it to the "closure that it is" (Nancy 1993:1). And to that extent, to the extent that it is its vocation to contain and appropriate the

Outside, the Outside becomes representation's unspoken preoccupation and obsession. That is why it "limitlessly . . . extend[s] its own delimitation."

We might conjecture the role of animal's abyssal difference (qua Outside) for representational thinking in the same terms. Any self-assigned vocation to traverse the cross-species divide through representation—in both senses of signification and delegation (as in "speaking for")—is a double-faced gesture: it "opens" only to install a (hegemonic) "closure." In the following, I take the idea of representation in this rigorous, metaphysical sense. The aim is to realign the meaning of the political at the contestation in Hegins. For no meaningful re-imagination seems possible insofar as the doxic binarism—between the "for" and "against," between the scholarly and partisan advocacy—continues to define what is political.

Symbolism

The Labor Day Shoot had the fortune of receiving erudite scholarly attention from the esteemed American folklorist Simon J. Bronner. Titled "Contesting Tradition: The Deep Play and Protest of Pigeon Shoots" (2005), his intervention is emblematic of the symbolic/representational approach to animal issues at its best. Allow me to cite his summary statement at length:

> Compromise became impossible in controversies over pigeon shoot because the sides perceived *symbols* so differently. For protesters, the shooters *represented* predatory, phallocentric rapists who promoted violence for its own sake, whereas, for supporters, they symbolized a pioneer and biblical heritage based on human dominion over the bountiful land. For protesters, the process of the ritualized shoot perpetuated cycles of abuse and patriarchy; for supporters, it acted to regenerate the land, confirming the wholesomeness of agrarianism. The pigeons could be *symbolized* as profane, dirty pests or sacred doves of peace. The widely publicized controversy implied larger questions, and *fundamental conflicts in America*, about the role of tradition in modernity. (409, emphasis added)

A justifiable summary of Bronner's exegesis is difficult. His prose is voluminous, his facts precise and detailed, and the scope of his theoretical import prodigious. It is a must read for any scholarly attention to the controversy of the Labor Day Shoot. I only home in on the structure of his rhetorical strategy below.

Bronner's primary theoretical task is to adapt traditional anthropological theories of animal symbolism for the context of *contestation* at hand. For this, he first revises what he deems one-dimensionality (dubbed "shallow play") in Clifford Geertz's famous work (1973). He rejects the Geertzian assumption that animal-related practices such as the cockfight directly and textually reflect social structure, such as the status hierarchy. Instead, Bronner argues, we need to explain why certain animal-focused "events" are deemed reflective of human society in the first place. For him, an event becomes a focal point because of multidimensional "layering" of heterogeneous symbolisms conversant with each other across time. An event such as the Labor Day Shoot became a symbolic focal point only through and because of such "processes of contestation" and of "symbolization" in time (Bronner 2005:414)—not due to its inherent metaphorical suggestiveness of a larger social structure. Without this "frame of the contest," he argues, we cannot grasp the multiplicity of pigeon symbolism operative in the Hegins controversy (414). The Geertzian commitment to a unified "social structure" would not suffice when the issue here is precisely over a disputed meaning of the animal in concern.

Bronner's problematic is a classical one: that of introducing temporality to structure; that of allowing difference within unity. Emphasis on difference alone would not do. For it is merely a truism to state that the opposing sides in Hegins had differing histories behind them, which resulted in differing attitudes toward pigeons. Even conflicting meanings must be communicated to each other; insults need be registered by the foe. Two intersecting concepts provide the required "sameness" against which the difference in dispute becomes legible: (1) "the ancient folk root for the symbolism of the pigeon"; and (2) the "symbolism of the center." According to the ancient folk root, "killing the pigeon as one would kill a mouse or a rat offers sacred human redemption, because the bird is associated with an unclean state. Killing them ritually establishes the "symbolism of the center" by emphasizing sacrificial elimination of all that is unclean, thus offering spiritual purity" (Bronner 2005:432–33).

The reach of Bronner's "ancient folk root" evinces an impressive historical continuation, from the Bible to pioneerism: "The 'clearing' of the pigeons to the sportsmen is a metaphor for the opening of the Western frontier and the rising national optimism growing out of a pioneer heritage and violent eradication of natives" (422). "For the supporters, the shooter embodied the pioneer hunter, because pigeon shooting was considered an antiquated kind of pursuit. The shooter served to eliminate the unclean from the land and thereby consecrate it. The result is socially regenerative. . . . Supporters were not so much defending the shoot as they were their agrarian tradition revolving around the idea of dominion of humans acting as a community over animals and land" (435). This pioneer heritage took on an added meaning in the region's contemporary history: "Particularly in the historical context of the region's economic decline, the pigeon shoot annually provided a ritual reaffirmation of a regional worldview based on a pioneer hunting legacy" (429).

Only superficially is this ancient folk root relevant to supporters exclusively. Protesters, too, according to Bronner, derived their rhetorical power from what one might call the ritual value of pigeons just mentioned.

> [The] ancient folk root for the symbolism of the pigeon may seem a long way from contemporary images of the pigeon at shoots, but it is related because of the clash over conflicting modern categorizations of the bird as symbol of *both sacredness and profanity*. Indeed, the connection of the Bible as a source for opposing sides in the pigeon shoot controversy at Hegins was explicit in protestors' appeal to protect a sacred dove of peace, while supporters often cited the opening passages of Genesis dictating that humans rule, master, or have dominion . . . over the "birds of the sky, and all the living things that creep on earth." (431–32)

Bronner reports that, deriving their argument from the Bible, protesters invoked the pigeon's figuration as a "sacred dove of peace" (431) and foregrounded the "symbolic equivalence of birds and children" (434). In this light, the "shoot was a metaphor for a predatory, patriarchal society responsible for violence and social injustice" (438). The vernacular association of shooting with sexual conquest particularly invoked the image of rape victim in the birds.

Hence, the "ancient folk root" informs both parties, supporters and protesters alike. The mythical resource that inspires the contemporary passion is primally ambivalent or "contradictory" (415), libidinally rousing both supporters and protesters. It is only through the historicity of the "frame of contestation" that the current polarization can be understood: mutually reactive, protesters embraced the sacred half, and supporters the profane.

The second facilitator of "sameness" I identified was the "symbolism of the center." Citing Mircea Elieade, Bronner defines the notion this way: "the center is outlined and made sacred by establishing and ritually eliminating what is unknown or profane" (416). The notion's applicability to supporters is self-explanatory from the foregoing. Counterintuitively, Bronner deploys the same notion for protesters. Deploying the argument such as "symbolic equivalence of birds and children," he observes, protesters too, waged their battle of "symbolism of the center" (443): if the supporters' rhetoric produced "inside" families and communities versus "outside" urban centers and government policies, "the protest sought to subvert [this] 'symbolism of the center' and show[ed] it as marginal" (443). Bronner concludes: "Both arguments for centeredness laid claims to representing the heart and soul of America in Hegins" (443).

The picture Bronner paints is very complex. The intractable complexity for me lies at the heart of Bronner's aspired theoretical innovation; of thinking together symbols with the process of contestation; of collapsing the ritual consecration of the land (by cleansing the profane) with the battle for the "center" of the national ethical mainstream. These two clusters of reconciled notional opposites, which are said to crosscut both parties' ideological apparatuses, irresolvably remain in different analytical registers. One is timeless and cognitive while the other is historical and performative; one is biblical while the other is of the nation-state (that is, of the "heart and soul of America"). In the end, I fail to comprehend what Bronner means by "symbol," despite its profuse adjectival combinatorics throughout the article—"symbolic shift," "symbolic equivalence," et cetera. My impression is that as the conceptual counterpoint to history, symbol for him means something more unconscious, primal, and primordial—hence, "cognitive" (see 414). "History," in contrast, seems to designate the polemically inspired emplottable discursive positionings in time, explicitly strategized and consciously maneuvered. For the purpose of impartiality, Bronner deploys the symbol-history combination equally for the analyses of supporters and protesters alike. However, the depth of historicity allotted to each side of the polemic is very different. Supporters' history mainly reckons with the times of the biblical past and pioneerism; protesters' with the nineteenth-century animal advocacy at the earliest (with a minimalist tangential reference to the Bible).

This is hardly a shocking observation. Bronner himself explicitly describes the polemic in terms of "tradition" versus "ethical modernity." Nonetheless, it is worthwhile to question the obvious: why is it acceptable to prejudge the supporters' polemic under the auspice of "tradition"—passing, remnantal, and so reactionary—and not the other way around? And what do we make of the fact that tradition-versus-modernity is precisely the term deployed by animal rights protesters? This is an analytical and theoretical question, not a distrust of Bronner's empirical diagnosis (as to the history of deindustrialization, as to the longer legacy of the shooting tradition, and so forth). It is the question of why, in other words, the supporters' politics should be more readily available to a "symbolic" reading (rather than that of discursive positionings and strategies). I pose this question in light of the fact that I described the supporters' polemic in terms of the "excess of the present" in the previous chapter. Why must we assume supporters' unsuspecting and unaffected subscription and allegiance to the verity of the obviously fading "tradition," and view all their current projects as reactive and recuperative? Is it because of the informants' explicitly uttered statements—which anyone can sample from newspaper reportages, the NRA's leaflets, and even tabloid magazines? Is it possible to let contemporaneity abide by the supporters' politics on a par with that of protesters? Could we entertain, on the part of the supporters, something like a performative commentary on the state of change rather than denial and wished-for reversal of that change? I have argued in the previous chapter that it is historical discontinuation, rather than continuation, that legitimized the present shoot. Allow me to repeat the formula of this excess (which is at the same time lack): there was a loss of the past . . . and so pigeons must be killed. It is as though the amassment of Bronner's lucid symbolisms of weighty consequence—no less than the definition of the national ethics is at stake!—is a measured defense against such an unreason.

There is no doubt that Bronner's symbologist erudition will endure as the most authoritative account on the legacy of the pigeon shoot and its protest. Aside from the Spanglerian tropic flair (that freely traverses biblical time and even that of Greek mythology), part of the account's appeal consists in its sense of balance and impartiality afforded to this hotly contested issue. In my opinion, this sense of impartiality is purchased by the symbolic approach. A contestation here, for him, is a matter of disagreeing symbolic interpretations—as has been cited in his summary statement—and scholarly impartiality, one surmises, that of granting equal spaces to the predicative edifices of each communitarian interpretive subset in dispute. The operation is basically that of cultural relativism. There, to be ethically impartial is to entertain a meaning system "big" enough to hold and impartially assign recognizable identitarian particularities to all factions in contestation. The goal is to provide a neutral analytical language whereby all factions find their proper allotments, no matter how hotly contested a dispute is. Bronner's idea of "symbolic layering" answers to such a relativist multicultural protocol. The theoretical solution that reconciles structure and history—joined in the wording "symbolic layering"—is promised to achieve the sought after ethical impartiality too.

In the symbologist narrative, contradictions are effortlessly rendered amenable to the unity of intelligibility. Opposing forces in conflict are symmetrically balanced as though sharing a fair-game rule—as the image of "symbolisms of the center" in contest attests to. In the symbologist scenario, oppositions are eagerly made familiar in normative binarisms: insiders and outsiders, the rural and the urban, conservatives and progressives, right-wingers and left-wingers, and dare we say, Republicans and Democrats. In this symmetric relativism, no meaning is lost.[2] In this capacious binarism, historical parallelisms abound. For example, a direct historical continuation is read between the current protest and the anti-pigeon-shoot campaign of the late nineteenth-century. Bronner identifies both "culture wars" as fin-de-siècle phenomena.

Despite what the processual notion of "layering" suggests, in the final analysis, Bronner does *not* find the necessary "unity" in the historicity of the event itself—where both protesters and supporters are co-authors. Rather, the actual so-called historicity he taps into is what one might call a "larger" unity that comfortably contains both sides of the conflict as instances of timeless dyadic opposition: (Judeo-)Christianity plus "America." In other words, his rigorous pursuit of historicity stops at an allegedly more universal "social structure" that contains and neutralizes even conflictual histories. Christianity and the American culture serve as final authorities in this symbolic reading—the ultimate symbolic structure beyond which historical analysis cannot traverse. Perhaps, here, we witness symbolism's limit and inherent conservatism: a self-authorizing, self-standing unity of meaning system—such as Christianity or America—has to be axiomatically presupposed as an empirically homogeneous actuality. And no political difference or contradiction—such as between supporters and protesters—can effectively question such a unity.

How about animal difference? Is it possible to think about symbolism's conservative treatment of political difference side by side with that of animal difference? Bronner readily identifies the shoot as a case of sacrifice—that privileged practice singularly consigned to the academic question of animal difference (identification? substitution? contact?). As can be imagined easily, his analysis of sacrifice is heavily circumscribed by the wealth of data on the positivity of what had been explicitly and consciously uttered. The folklorist and the historicist in me happily embraces the veracity of this elaborate path laid out by Bronner. However, the writer in me wants to pique some more— somewhat irresponsibly. Bronner gives us an exhaustive tabulation of how the pigeon is a symbol for this and a representation for that. But I want to insist—irresponsibly—on the question of the role of animal difference, that is, the fact that they are non-humans (before they bear human meanings). I want to ask not what animals are "about" positively and legibly but what they are negatively and illegibly; not the end product of how we render them legible with human meaning but the illegible gulf or difference that facilitates such a reading in the first place. For this reason, in a stark contrast to Bronner's complexity, the formula I entertained in the previous chapter was brutally simplistic: There was a loss of the past . . . and so pigeons must be killed. My hypothesis is that something in the animal difference is allowing this jump in logic. But, first, let me situate Bronner's theoretical heritage within representationalism generally.

"The Great Cat Massacre"

The idea of the non-human as a symbol, a metaphor, a cipher, or a coded message for human relations had been much in vogue since the mid-1980s in the loose body of works coined "new historicism" (for example, Darnton 1984, Scott 1990, Stallybrass and White 1986). In pursuit of "minor histories," new historicists turned on previously neglected fields of inquiry, which often led them to matters concerning non-human animals. A parallel to the emergent hold of Michel Foucault's works on the Anglo-theoretical scene, if not directly filiating itself to him, the reigning aesthetic among the new historicists was to excavate meanings "hidden" from (human) discursivity. In so uncovering the hidden, and doing so across the species divide, the trend came to epitomize the trappings of representationalism—in both senses of signification and delegation. Hence, although dated by now, a contemplation in its representationalist bias proves instructive for appreciating the full political import of a statement such as "the Jew as vermin" (Sartre 1986[1948]). Such an interrogation is especially timely given the recent explosion of interests in the linkage between holocaustal biopolitics and the West's representational/metaphysical heritage (Agamben 1998, Lacoue-Labarthe 1989,

Norris 2005). It is nowhere more appropriate to begin with Robert Darnton's famous work *The Great Cat Massacre* . . . (1984).

Robert Darnton's case is an account of a group of mistreated apprentices at a Parisian print shop in the late 1730s who vented their anger by torturing and killing in a riotous mock execution the beloved pet cat of their mistress, along with sackfuls of alley cats whose provoking of an extermination order had provided the workers with a pretext. "Roused by the gales of laughter," the master and the mistress arrived at the scene of carnage. The mistress, suspecting that her pet cat was included among the abused, shrieked out an accusation of murder; the master instead complained of the general stoppage of work before helplessly retiring from the scene, humiliated. Darnton continues: "The laughter did not end there. [The apprentices] reenacted the entire scene in mime at least twenty times during subsequent days when the printers wanted to knock off some hilarity" (1984:77).[3]

Darnton's theoretical import—expanded and elaborated in a later article (1986)—follows an intuitive path: it centers around a symbolic *displacement* of violence from the intended human target, that is, the master and the mistress, to cats as a substitution. An exclusive attention is paid to what facilitated this displacement or substitution: the "ritual value" of cats. For this, he draws heavily from the works of Edmund Leach and Mary Douglas (although Ralph Bulmer and Stanley Tambiah also receive a "Leacheanized" representation).[4]

Darnton's synthesized rendition of the well-known arguments of Leach (1964) and Douglas (1966) goes like this: ritual values are determined in reference to "a set of categories that serve as a grid for sorting out experience" (Darnton 1986:223). Language is the most basic grid. In naming things, we slot the world into linguistic categories that help us order the world. To name, he argues, is to "fit something into a taxonomic system of classification" (223). Then there are things and creatures that straddle the boundaries prescribed in the cultural grid. Such things are powerful and dangerous, and are tabooed objects. But precisely because such hybrid categories are monstrous and dangerous they prove potent in ritual contexts. In short, the normative use of these creatures derives from the cognitive order, in the sense that they are rejected from the classificatory affirmations.

Why cats, then? Darnton states that "cats epitomized a parting of the folkways"; between the growth of an extravagant genteel culture, for example, of pet keeping among the master class, and the deteriorating condition of workers, who did not think of animals as pets. For Darnton, the incident involving pet cats dramatized the development of these "incompatible sub-cultures." Then, how is the clash of incompatible subcultures to be explained in terms of a classificatory theory à la Douglas and Leach? Here, Darnton appeals to a sort of unifying classification he calls "commonplaces of French folklore" (Darnton 1986:229), which are supposed to be shared by both the *bourgeois* culture and that of the workers—I might add, despite their "in-compatibilities." According to this "conventional notion," cats are "liminal creatures," occupying an ambiguous space between the outside world of ani-mality (of alley cats) and the intimacy of domesticity as beloved pets. The apprentices in printing shops occupied an analogously "liminal" space, be-tween childhood and adulthood, between the untamed world of the streets and the shop. In the newly emerging order of bourgeois culture, the cats usurped the apprentices' position, so the apprentices were shunted off to the kitchen, while the pet cats enjoyed free access to the dining room (233). By executing the cats, Darnton concludes, the workers reversed the situation and restored order in the liminal zone, where the danger of confusing cate-gories was greatest. The route through which the violence was displaced (not Darnton's term), and thus how the cat emerged as a substitute, hinges on a certain conceptual link between the cognitive and the ritual that Darnton inherits from Leach and Douglas. To examine the thesis of displacement, then, this link must be critically interrogated.

Leach's inaugural proposition is that "we can only arrive at semantically distinct verbal concepts if we repress the boundary percepts that lie between them" (1964:23). Taboo is to serve that purpose of "repression": it serves to "discriminate categories in men's social universe," and in so doing "reduces the ambiguities of reality to clear-cut ideal types" (Leach 1971:44). "While language gives us the names to distinguish discrete things, taboo inhibits the recognition of those parts of the continuum which separate things" (Leach 1964:35). Similarly, for Douglas, "our mind tends to impose order on the world and does not tolerate ambiguities"; we have "horror for ambi-guity as such" (1975:285). Thus, our feeling of pollution, or "matter out of place," exists as an aid to impose system, "in the face of an inherently untidy experience" (Douglas 1966:4). Bronner makes essentially an identical argu-ment when he defines the "symbolism of the center" as the clearing of the "*unknown*" qua the profane (2005:441).

So how do boundary percepts as a cognitive "ambiguity" turn into ob-jects of ritualistic manipulation? A contradiction is patent in the way I put the question. As Leach theorizes, "taboo *inhibits the recognition* of those parts of the continuum which separate things" (1964:35, emphasis added), but in his actual analyses, taboo does not concern intermediate percepts but intermediate categories of objects, *with a full conceptual status*.[5] Then, the system and the intermediate category that is rejected from it are locked in a curious circularity. Our cognitive order is said to uphold itself by suppressing interstitial categories, on the one hand, and by rendering the same categories as the focus of (ritual) activities, on the other. The interstitial category is thus simultaneously *residual* and *constitutive* of the system; it is at once rejected from the system and an instrumental guarantor of the very system. The anomalous inter-category is both an inside event and an outside remnant.[6] In other words, the system is conceptualized both as an *actuality* (in which the interstitial is residual) and a perfected *potentiality* (an outcome of ritualistic manipulation of the interstitial).

As will be elaborated, this causal or temporal indeterminacy bears witness to the constitutive requirement for human participation for any moral imperative. However, Douglas and Leach incessantly privilege the moment the system logically precedes human participation as an unambiguous, actual presence. For the primordial drive toward classification for them cannot but be a descriptive impulse toward "imposing order on the world" (Douglas 1975:285). All others, such as subjectively motivated sanctions, are secondary derivatives. Hence, for Leach, it is the law of prohibition that gives birth to the very idea of (subjectively felt) pollution, which is merely an aid to impose system. In short, a classification is self-motivated. It possesses itself, as it were, simultaneously as the classifier and the classified.

Here, we have all the ingredients for representationalism as critiqued by Nancy. As we recall, representationalism's unspoken goal is to establish itself as a self-standing, all-encompassing plenitude. For this, a representation has to include within its referential field even what it allegedly cannot think, that is, the Outside. Isn't this precisely what Leach's and Douglas's anomalous category is about? It is what escapes the descriptive capture that is, however, internally assigned a semantic place within the same descriptive order precisely *as what is outside the order*. Hence, it is both an inside event and an outside remnant.

"Incompatible Cultures"

We don't have to resort to philosophy. Even in common sense, there is an apparent implausibility in understanding a moral universe in terms of a

self-standing and self-motivated injunction qua "imposed order." The implausibility is most palpable in conflicts, such as the contention at the Labor
Day Shoot. For one, moral disputes bear upon impassioned, absolutist, and
categorical proscriptions, rather than descriptive disagreements. Proscribed
is not only the "content" of the classified, but also the classifier. To be in
conflict (with the Other's classification) is not only to disagree on how things
are descriptively predicated upon, but also to reject the predicator's horizon
itself, that is, the Other's subjective investment in that predication.[7] An impassioned reactiveness to the presence of the Other (and its perceived heretic
system of ordering) constitutionally robs any moral order in conflict of its
hoped for self-closure and autonomy.

Let us remind ourselves of representationalism's ruses. If we are to grant
a moral universe as so many representations—which is what descriptivism is
about—we must heed to Nancy's criticism: representation thinks "both itself
and its outside," thereby aspiring to establish itself as an all-encompassing
plenitude. When different representational systems are in conflict, the "planetary, galactic, universal vocation" of representation is such that the Other's
representational horizon is not simply left as its own unthinkable limit qua
Outside. Instead, to repeat my formulation above, representationalism assigns that Outside an *internal* semantic place precisely as what is outside of
its order. If I may repeat again: representationalism cheerfully admits to its
own particularity, but only to assert the universal applicability of this very
representation (of the fact of its particularity). We might call such a cheerful
admission of one's own (mere) particularity relativism. Relativism is a peculiar thing: it is consubstantial with a hysterical obsession with, and a *universalist* drive to determine, the Other and Other-authored representations side
by side with itself. Relativism thus forecloses any meaningful engagement
with the abyssal limit that divides itself and its Other. Among that Other, we
must include, foremostly, the non-relativist, including non-human animals
(see Fish 1997). Relativism cannot think such a horizonal difference.

Such a foundational "disagreement" Ernesto Laclau and Chantal Mouffe
called "antagonism": "we have a case of antagonism when the presence of
the Other prevents me from being totally myself" (1985:125). We might call
relativism a symptom of this failure at self-possession for it is a hysterical
attempt to render thematic both what it is and what it is not simultaneously.
The notion of antagonism was offered to amend the Saussurian idea of differential oppositions, whereby identities/oppositions are determined on account of their relative location in a shared system and along the shared plane

of comparability (see Song 2006). For Laclau and Mouffe, what antagonizing parties in conflict lack is precisely the presupposed shared system of comparability, each importing its own version of "universality" qua the horizon of meaningfulness. The notion reminds us of the fact that not all differences can be assigned places within, to paraphrase Bronner's term, a "more layered" system of descriptive order—similar to Darnton's "incompatible cultures" within "common places of French folklore." Rather, if I may repeat, radical, antagonistic differences differ precisely in the definition of what consists of such a "universal"—qua (not the "content" but) the very condition of possibility for difference. All "antagonizers" aspire to define their own particularity—that is, why they differ with the Other—in universalizing, all-encompassing terms. They thus inscribe themselves doubly, both inside and outside, as the subject and object, of their own version of "more universal" descriptive order—in other words, both as the universal, horizonal frame of differences and as one particular "moment" in that frame.

Leach's and Douglas's idea of moral universe as a *self-motivated* actuality merely reproduces such a hoped for hegemony of an antagonizer and fails to analyze it. A hegemonic classification supposedly classifies itself, and so presents itself as self-standing. There, the classifier and the classified, the subject and the object of classification, coincide. The notion of antagonism, in contrast, problematizes that coincidence: insofar as there is the Other (classification)—which is always the case—such an operation can only be hoped for. Insofar as there is the Other, the classifier cannot firmly situate itself within its own classification. For there intervenes a structural disjointedness between "what I am for myself" and "what I am for the Other"—that is, between the subject and the object of classification. Hegemony, according to Laclau and Mouffe, is an attempt to obfuscate this inherent fracture.

The Politics of "Displacement"

Bronner and Darnton ensure that no "incompatibility" enjoys antagonistic absolutism. Antagonizing parties remain fundamentally legible to each other, made to cohere within the cultural-relativist multicultural plenitude. Subtracted from the dimension of subjective investment, the specificity of a culture's descriptive classification becomes liable for "arbitrariness." Discredited thus is any claim to necessity beholden to the dimension we called "existence" in the previous chapter. Such a relativism is not only analytically defunct but always already partial. In Hegins, the same language is spoken by animal rights activists. The truth of its partial politics may be shown in bolder relief via animal rights discourse. According to Heidi Prescott, the national director of the Fund for Animals, "This [that is, southwest Schuylkill County] is an economically stressed area. But people still live with the dream of a glorious past [of the mining boom]. They think people in the city and the government are responsible. And so they vent their anger at pigeons [which are city birds]" (interview, 1996). Studied, dispassionate, and even potentially empathetic, this line was delivered with an impeccable tone of relativist impartiality. Theoretically, it states that the shoot's supporters regard the pigeon as a metaphor, a symbol, a coded message, or a disfigured representation of social antagonisms they are unable to grasp. Prescott tacitly declares the shoot's supporters' "real" political consciousness thus *displaced*.

A scholarly affirmation of such a reading is readily available in the new historicist literature. Peter Stallybrass and Allon White's notion of "displaced abjection" is such a case (1986). It is "the process whereby 'low' social groups turn their figurative and actual power, not against those in authority, but against those who are even 'lower' (women, Jews, animals, particularly cats and pigs)" (Stallybrass and White 1986:53). Difference from Darnton, Leach, and Douglas is minor: "displacement" here follows two routes, "higher" to "lower" and from humans to non-humans. For example, "Like the pigs in the Venice carnival, which were chased across Piazza San Marco and stoned, in Rome Jews were forced into a race at carnival time and stoned by the onlookers. This similarity between the fate of Jews in Rome and the fate of pigs in Venice during carnival time points up a frequent association whereby the pig became a focus of what we call displaced abjection" (53).

The category of the "lower" here contains both humans and non-humans—that is, "women, Jews, animals, particularly cats and pigs." How exactly the two routes of displacement, higher to lower and human to non-human, relate to each other is unclear. For at least Leach himself, the routes of displacement are straightforward: there is a structural "homology" between the categorization of humans, of animals, and of living space (1964). With their vague Marxist gesture toward the "lower," Stallybrass and White are reluctant to wholeheartedly endorse Leach's structuralist solution. However, although they indirectly criticize Leach's exacting homological pairing—specifically, the Leachean model's agricultural-milieu-centered bias, which they propose to augment with the multiplicity of cultural "grids" in different sites—the "value" of the pig retains ambivalence across different sites throughout their work, as if the pig retains its originary memory as an interstitial creature in the agricultural milieu (1986:45–47). In effect, Leach's homology is fully operational in them. Displacement and homology prove to be inalienable concepts. Each supposes the persistency of the other.

The Hegemony of Representationalism

The notion of homology holds the truth about the politics of the idea of displacement. If homology by definition requires both difference and sameness, then the somewhat ironic conclusion we can draw from Stallybrass and White is this: even as the notion enables prodigal human/non-human comparisons, the comparability is purchased precisely at the expense of presupposing the givenness of the human/non-human divide. Otherwise, "displacement" remains illegible. The rigor of homological representation relies on this kind of silently and categorically posited apriorism.

Let me contextualize such an apriorism within new historicism's liberal imperative. For the new historicists, descriptivism's appeal lies in its seeming anti-humanism or anti-human-centeredness: it captures, in one and the same empirical representation, humans and non-humans alike—printing shop apprentices along with cats, pets with mistresses, Jews with pigs, and so on. The new historicists' enthusiasm for anthropology's descriptivism partially consisted in irreverently unleashing such an anti-humanist, trans-species theory—sampled from the non-West—on the humanistic canonical historiography of the West. Its species relativism, so to speak, is motivated by cultural relativism. Relativism's ambition is to humbly capture the Self side by side with the Other, be it of other species or other culture, along one and the same representational field. As in Nancy's representationalism, it represents "for itself, both itself and its outside, the outside of its limit" (1993:2). However, to repeat the above point of irony, the more it captures itself as merely one of the "classifieds," as it were, the more obscure its status qua the "classifier" becomes. The more it presses upon trans-species universalism, the more axiomatically presupposed and homogeneously self-standing "humanity" becomes. Thus, antagonism is (hegemonically) elided.

A similar observation can be made of the trans-species universalism of the animal rights movement. It is a well-known fact that a homology of sorts inspired the rise of this movement. Ceaselessly commented upon by both its devotees and its historians alike is the movement's conscientious filiation to the women's and civil rights movements (for example, Singer 1990[1975]). The explicitly drawn parallel is the one between animal victims and victims of sexism and racism (see Chapter 2). Stallybrass and White's trans-species category, "women, Jews . . . cats and pigs," may as well have been uttered by Prescott.

However, to state the obvious, the animal rights polemic does not promote relativism but institutes moral proximity between humans and non-humans, as is encapsulated in the following well-known catchphrase: "A rat is a pig is a dog is a boy" (Ingrid Newkirk cited in Bronner 2005:432). That hardly any animal rights devotee would adhere to such a motto to the letter, in reality, is beside the point. Its rhetorical effectiveness consists precisely in its "virtual," axiomatic status: it is against the background of such an a priori "literalism" that all *other* animal-related practices become legible as symbols, metaphors, or displacements. Even meat eating, for example, is deemed a *metaphorical* expression of the violent patriarchal society (Adams 2000[1990]). Or, "the domination of nature, rooted in postmedieval, Western, male psychology, is the *underlying cause* of the mistreatment of animals as well as of the exploitation of women and the environment" (Josephine Donovan cited in Bronner 2005:424). Animal rights activism's own place abides, as an epiphenomenon of sorts, in a relativist kind of representational rigor and prolificalness. All other animal-related practices fall under the unity of the protocols of such a rigorous representation as so many regimes of (folk) classifications (articulable by homology). And just as in academic relativism, representational productivity of animal rights philosophy is purchased by absenting itself from the "commonplace" classifications thus enumerated—in other words, by obscuring its own status qua (merely) another "classifier." Once again, antagonism is hegemonically elided.

When animal rights discourse explicitly assigns itself a historical place next to other human-animal relationships, it is in terms of evolutionary progress; how trans-species ethics is, as it were, the final stage of what we might call the *modernity* of humanity (Nash 1989). As many have critiqued, the "planetary, galactic, universal vocation" of the idea of modernity is such that it marks historical multiplicity under the seal of its always seamlessly uniform and always most up-to-date homogeneity. As Nancy aptly writes, "It opens the world to the closure that it is" (1993:1). Evolution is a signature modernist rhetorical device to demarcate oneself as a frontier, as though on the edge of time itself. Thereby, once again, animal rights discourse installs itself in an axiomatically presupposed "virtual" place, outside and beyond empirically representable historical multiplicity (in which other folk classificatory practices presumably belong). Allow me to repeat: as a case of "antagonizer," the animal rights discourse defines its own apparent particularity in *universal* terms.

So far, I have engaged with the idea of displacement by focusing on its rhetoric of inter-species analogy. Its political import is sought by examining its telling resemblance to animal rights advocacy, a discourse that explicitly politicizes trans-species universalism. The resemblance lies in the seemingly self-critical, anti-humanist gesture toward descriptively arresting itself side by side with its radical (non-human) Other. However, I have argued that this "relativist" gesture of condescension is ensconced in an unspoken fantasy of affirming itself as an unbroken, self-standing, axiomatically presupposed homogeneity. Descriptivism cum representationalism in the last analysis has to logically beg such a presupposed global category, which normalizes and accommodates antagonisms—at both levels of inter- and intra-species, of both species and cultural differences.[8] For Bronner, the axiomatically presupposed apparatuses are Christianity and the American culture. What we might call the folkways of Christian-American culture provide a shelter of meaning in which all conflicting parties find their proper places in a symmetrical opposition dubbed "culture clash" (Bronner 2005:414).

Beyond Representationalism

Descriptivism equates our moral universe with how we organize the order of things. It is somewhat comical as a theory of ethics because it does not explain why humans endure the futility of perpetuating fears of pollution and restricting taboos. If a classification's self-contained motivation is perceptual and logical rigor, then there is no reason for it to allow anomaly in the first place; a "description" more faithful to the reality, and hence free of threatening anomalous categories, can be always modified (Valeri 2000:44–45). Descriptivism's glaring omission is the dimension of subjective investment in any ethical enterprise.

Valerio Valeri's correction of this omission is instructive for my purpose of rendering the dimension of antagonism operative. First of all, he corrects Leach's usage of the term "repression," from the sense of unilateral suppression—as when Leach says: "repressing the boundary percepts"—to its original, Freudian sense. Valeri argues that repression as such can be talked about only when prohibition runs into conflict with desire, that is, precisely when prohibition's self-generating and self-standing unilaterality is constitutionally undermined by the subject's desiring of the prohibited object: "It makes no sense to apply the term 'taboo' to a situation where there is no *conflict*, or at least potential conflict, between spontaneous attitude to an object—attraction or simple lack of fear or aversion—and the attitude that is prescribed or recommended by a rule" (2000:27, emphasis added). Even more, Valeri continues: "The prohibition *must* encourage a sense that its object is desirable, otherwise obeying it could not have the religious significance it has (i.e., *renouncing* the satisfaction of one's desire in order to fulfill God's will)" (27, latter emphasis added).

For him, the law of prohibition does not logically or ontologically precede but is rather dependent on what it "represses," that is, the possibility of transgression. Just as in Kantian ethics, which is elaborated below, Valeri defines the ethical dimension of prohibition as the subject's capacity for a negative self-relating—the capacity to "conflictually" relate to one's self-interest (or attraction). Hence, Valeri's celebration of renunciation—which he calls "negative morality"—as the core of religious significance. For Kant, the moral value of an action performed for the sake of duty is increased in proportion to a decrease in inclination to perform the action. Similarly, Valeri has it that what is prohibited is necessarily desired by the subject. In this sense, one can risk calling Valeri's notion of taboo a sort of Kantian "categorical imperative" with its necessary presupposition of a discord between the moral law and the subject.

I suggest this comparison with the Kantian notion of "categorical" in order to highlight Valeri's awareness that ethical injunctions are in the end axiomatically presupposed "virtual" things, not self-motivated actualities. The lesson here, however, does not stop at how ethical injunctions are actually "man-made." The lesson rather touches on how such a man-made thing necessarily assumes purity and homogeneity. It is because ethical injunctions are posited *on account of the subject's constitutional displacement* from intuiting it. It is this Kantian twist to the common-sense constructivism, which I develop more methodically below, that is missing from descriptivism. Hence its mystification and perpetuation of such silently presupposed axiomatic categories—for example, "the French" for Darnton and "America" for Bronner.

What is relevant for us is not Valeri's psychology.[9] Rather, what is of pivotal importance is how he renders "ambivalence" as something other than what can be an empirically or descriptively locatable phenomenon:[10] "Ambivalence attributed to the object of the prohibition is in reality an ambivalence of the subject. One is afraid of violating the prohibition and yet one desires to violate it. But this ambivalence remains unconscious and is only apparent in a reified form—as a combination of attractiveness and loathsomeness in the object" (Valeri 2000:22).

Descriptivism, then, which derives ambivalence from empirically identifiable "interstitial"-phenomenal categories, confuses a "reified" *result* for the proper ethical dimension. The properly ethical dimension is neither in the subjective nor in the objective alone. It is certainly not in the descriptive and empirical world of objects that prohibition manifestly deals with. Rather, for Valeri, if I may so paraphrase, there is ethics because the subject, on account of its "desire," is constitutionally *displaced* from the world of objects that the law prohibits. This means that the subject's status as an object, locatable and describable in relation to other objects, itself is problematized. I am here repeating the point about the necessary gap between "what I am for myself" (that is, the subject) and "what I am for the Other" (that is, an object)— between the moment of the categorizer and that of the categorized. In other words, antagonism. The law as an axiomatically presupposed category comes into existence because—to repeat Laclau and Mouffe's definition—"the presence of the Other prevents me from being totally myself" (1985:125).

The Transcendental

This point is unreservedly Kantian—although Kantian reference is nowhere to be found in Valeri's work. Kant's foundational proposition—for both *Critiques* of "pure reason" and "practical reason"—is that we humans lack an intuition into our objective status as to "who we are" in the order of things. The Kantian moral subject is thus one who is in permanent discord with its status as an object, being unable to "sublate" or mediate it, and experiences its objective state only residually. It is through the capacity for a negative self-relating to the substantial and objective support of one's being—which he called "pathological particularities"—that the Kantian moral subject purchases a moral standing (Zupančič 2000: chap. 1). Hence, for Kant, moral knowledge is something a priori, antecedent to consideration of human nature and its empirical conditions. The goal of his *Critique of Practical Reason*, which he called the *metaphysics* of morals, is to find "the ultimate source of the principle of the moral law in reason considered in itself, without reference to specifically human conditions" (Copleston 2006[1952]:4). Hence the enigmatic formula, if I may repeat: the moral value of an action performed for the sake of duty is increased in proportion to a decrease in inclination to perform the action, that is, to the extent that it is performed against "patho-logical particularities."

Two propositions can be drawn from Kant's articulation of moral law. First, the Kantian moral subject has no way of subjecting itself to the "knowledge of objects"—morality simply belongs in a different realm for Kant. Thus, the moral subjects are bound to experience their substantial contents (or their status as objects in the phenomenal world) as contingent and arbitrary; the knowledge as to why they are phenomenally this way, rather than the other way, is constitutionally excluded from them. Second, due to this incomprehension of self-as-object (for example, Descartes's *res cogitans*), the inner voice of the moral law, which calls for the renunciation of these very objective particularities of the subject, is felt as a senseless and irrational injunction. The outcome is the groundless, incomprehensible, and aimless sense of guilt in the subject (burdened with an incomprehensible object despite him- or herself), which is the force on the side of the subject that binds him or her to the irrational command of the moral law. Paradoxi-cally, Kant saw the triumph of the autonomous moral being precisely in this blind compliance by the subject branded by an irrational sense of guilt—as in duty for the sake of duty—in total disregard of, and in an active censure of, one's particular "contents."

This seeming detour through Kant's moral philosophy is intended to comment upon the nature of social or historical unity that representational-ism, from Bronner to Darnton, comes to presuppose. Its implications are pivotal in the Hegins context; from how we understand the space-time of an event to the definition of history/tradition. Kant's lesson so far has been on how human beings come to posit axiomatically presupposed categories. Un-like representationalism, he does not deem these categories "constructed"—hence, conventional, contingent, and even "arbitrary." On the contrary, these categories are in the realms of the ideal, the pure/homogeneous, and the absolute. Yes, they are constructed, but constructed precisely and "categori-cally" to belong to a different register than the world of their "constructors." Yes, moral laws are constructed by humans but only insofar as the construc-tors constitutionally exile themselves from intelligible access to what they have "made."[11]

In this sense, the target of Kant's critique is entirely different from that of representationalism. His critique is not on the errancy of a constructed category's false hypostatized predicative edifice—how it is "really" not there as an actual, objective presence. (Such a target is that of historicism, whose exclusive job is to demonstrate the becoming-real of an event, of a tradition, in time through the microphysics of power relations—to put it in a Foucauldian fashion.) His critique, is rather on the *necessary purity and self-sameness of a category presupposed by axiom in advance as a non-place.* The critique is not on its phenomenality, but its epiphenomenality and apriorism—dubbed the transcendental.

But a representationalist might protest: is Kant's project not complicit with the ideological effects of these constructed categories by affirming them as ideal, pure, and absolute? Is his moral philosophy not another reactionary conservative ruse to maintain moral imperatives in the domain of the unassailable (in the face of its crisis that modernity has brought)? Certainly, there is no paucity of these complaints against German Idealism in contemporary social science particularly as it is touched by the postmodernist sensibility either directly or indirectly. The Kantian superlatives—the absolute, et cetera—are intended to awaken us to the power and persistent weight of these transcendental categories, whose persuasion subsists precisely on their "unreality." His critics often regress Kant's distinction of the phenomenon/transcendental to the conventional duality of phenomenon/essence or surface/depth.[12] Kant cannot possibly be accused of presupposing such a duality because his "critiques" are none other than attempts to explain how humans come to presuppose such a duality. His question can be stated as follows: how in the world do humans, finite beings caught in the contingent phenomenal world, come to posit categories that are never to be encountered in the experience of the phenomenal world—that is, necessary, absolute, pure, homogeneous, and so forth? To put it more paradoxically: how in the world do phenomenal beings volunteer to posit categories from which they themselves feel constitutionally alienated and barred?

Kant's greatest innovation is said to consist in his refusal to assume a "neutral" vantage point from which the difference between the phenomenal and the transcendental could be determined. Instead of so starting with a duality, he assumes that there is nothing but the finite, phenomenal world. From that, he shows how the transcendental rises out of the phenomenal. The transcendental, in this sense, is nothing but an illusion of a finite being, but an illusion whose effect is brutally real—as can be testified from our example of the nation-state.

More specifically, the transcendental dimension opens up on account of the fact that there are other consciousnesses or perspectives besides my own. Kojin Karatani attributes the root of Kant's "transcendental turn" to

his emergent concern with the effect of the "otherness" on the consciousness of the ego. Kant wrote: "Formerly, I viewed human common sense only
from the standpoint of my own; now I put myself into the position of an
other's reason outside of myself, and observe my judgments, together with
their most secret causes, from the point of view of others. It is true that the
comparison of both observations results in pronounced parallax, but it is
the only means of preventing the optical delusion, and putting the concept
of the power of knowledge in human nature into its true place" (Kant cited
in Karatani 2003:47). Karatani immediately cautions: "Here Kant is not expressing the commonplace, that not only must one see things from one's
own point of view, but also, simultaneously, from the point of view of others"
(47). In other words, the key is not some kind of synthesis between incompatible vantage points. Rather the key is "pronounced parallax," the notion
that lends a positive conceptual import to the state of being suspended in
between incompatible vantage points. The example of the parallax, Karatani
entertains, is the uncanny experience of seeing oneself in a photograph or
hearing one's own recorded voice for the first time. Both technologies purchase a severe rhetoric of "objectivity" qua seeing (hearing) as others might
see (hear), that is, what I am for the other. No mediation or identification
is possible with such an indefinite and infinite suggestion of heterogeneity.
"The hideousness or uncanniness one experiences is due to the *viewpoint of
others that intervenes* therein" (48; emphasis added). "To be objective," for
Kant, is to experience such a "displacement or derangement" on account
of the existence of the Other (48). The objective of his transcendental philosophy is not simply to speculate on a transcendental entity beyond our
grasp, but on something that is discernible only via the irreducible difference among positively identifiable "points of view."

For Kant then, to be in society is to be "displaced" from oneself qua positive positionality. Slavoj Žižek equates this notion to Laclau and Mouffe's
"antagonism" (Laclau and Mouffe 2006:20). Recall Laclau and Mouffe's
definition: "We have a case of antagonism when the presence of the Other
prevents me from being totally myself" (1985:125). We have introduced the
notion in order to entertain the idea that irreducible differences—this "in
between"—itself is the society as such. We contrasted this notion to Bronner's and Darnton's idea of society as a "more layered" meaning system, in
which all differences can be assigned reconcilable places within—each "culture" being a particular subset within a global edifice called "American" or
"French." The latter are emblematic of *defenses* against the transcendental

nature of sociality, its constitutive displacement proper to being-in-society. Just like the relativism I criticized above, these are symptoms of antagonistic failure at self-possession here dubbed displacement.[13]

Beyond the "Order of Things"

We are now ready to critique representationalism's use of animal difference in earnest. In *The Order of Things: An Archaeology of Human Sciences* (1970), Michel Foucault speaks of a certain "doublet" that hounded human science's descriptive project: "man appears in his ambiguous position as an object of knowledge and as a subject that knows: enslaved sovereign, observed spectator" (312). I might add: the categorizer who categorizes himself. "Man," shall we say, is a paradoxical creature that from the vantage point of absolute privilege and exception "sovereignly" declares that it is only a humble part of nature.

Two different levels of difference are simultaneously deployed here: (1) the descriptive "content" of the representation of nature; and (2) the difference between what performs this very representation (that is, humans) and what does not. For Foucault, human sciences' representational way of thinking is unable to think the relation between these two "levels" of difference. This gap that remains unthought in human sciences Foucault calls "dispersion." We may call the gap antagonism—for antagonism pertains to the parallax displacement of one's representational "categories" on account of the existence of the Other "categorizers."

Difference at the second level, for Foucault, is not a phenomenally describable difference but a transcendentally presupposed position of "identity" necessary for human sciences' difference at the first level to be possible. In other words, "man" has to be presupposed silently for the rigor of empirical "descriptivism" possible for human sciences. The folly of descriptivism is its ceaseless effort to locate the second level, that is, the very condition of possibility for representational difference, within the first level, that is, what appears among those representations. In other words, it cannot think the point of exception from which it speaks. And for that reason, it is unaware of the fact that the so-called outside it represents is already captured within its referentiality—as part of the "inside" (see my discussion of Bhabha in Chapter 2). We have seen this operation in Leach's and Douglas's notion of anomaly.

Jean-Luc Nancy puts it succinctly: "Man attains what the animals do not only because identity, in him, has preceded and established humanity in its very difference" (1993:10). In other words, the animal difference is always already captured "inside" the homogeneous identity of the human as precisely what it is not. The key here, once again, is that "man" is an *axiomatically* presupposed category. What Foucault calls human sciences names the epoch consumed with the absurd task of *empirically* locating what had been axiomatically presupposed always already.

Its excellent example we find in the pursuit of the *animal* origin of humanity. At the dividing line was the problematic of language. Dividing the linguistic from the pre-linguistic came to coincide with dividing human and non-human. On that futile task (of trying to empirically discover what had been presupposed already) the linguist Heymann Steinthal left the most memorable reflection: "Without realizing, I presupposed this origin: in reality, man with his human characteristics was given to me through creation, and then I sought to discover the origin of language in man. But in this way, I contradicted my presupposition: that is, that the origin of language and the origin of man were one and the same; I set man up first and then had him produce language" (cited in Agamben 2004:36–37). To paraphrase, the linguistic cannot be deduced from the pre-linguistic, for the definition of the pre-linguistic already contains that of the linguistic.

The Violence of Representationalism

For Giorgio Agamben, this way of relating to the non-human animal has inaugurated a new epoch of violence in modernity. Agamben's controversial provocation in the Anglo theoretical scene first came with the thesis that the violence of a holocaustal proportion became imaginable for the first time by the metaphysico-representational complex of the West (1998). Then, as its sequel, Agamben wrote *The Open: Man and Animal* (2004). In it, he details human science's ambition to descriptively settle the age-old question of the definition of humanity with the newfound natural scientific rigor, that is, vis-à-vis non-human animals. The irresolvable problem was localizing, along one and the same unified analytical horizon (that is, the natural order), the human intellect—that is, the fact that it is the human that is the sole author of this very analytical horizon; in other words, Foucault's second level of difference along his first level of difference. Due to the irreducible situation of what we have referred to as Foucault's doublet, Agamben observes (though his own reference is not Foucault) that a unified vision remained elusive. What they got every time was either "animalization of man" or "humanization of the animal": "The animal-man and the man-animal are the two sides of a single fracture, which cannot be mended from either side" (Agamben 2004:36). This fracture is none other than that of antagonism.

Agamben's innovative point is that this fracture was not just a scientific and epistemological failure (concerning inconsequential non-human animals) but one with political consequences of catastrophic proportions (for humans also). He calls the resulting epistemologico-political complex an "anthropological machine." It was an ideological apparatus that instituted what one might call a conceptual cleansing, which was necessary for the advent of modern societal unities, such as man or nation, endowed with Kantian purity and absolutism. The machine has inaugurated an unprecedented way to imagine territorialization, both spatial and conceptual.

> Insofar as the production of man through the opposition man/ animal, human/inhuman, is at stake here, the machine necessarily functions by means of an exclusion (which is also always already an inclusion) and an inclusion (which is also always already an exclusion). Indeed, precisely *because the human is already presupposed every time*, the machine actually produced a kind of state of exception, a zone of indeterminacy in which the outside is nothing but the exclusion of an inside and the inside is in turn only the inclusion of an outside. (37, emphasis added)

Rehearsed here is this chapter's recurrent point of how the "outside" is appropriated only in the form of that which is already included as part of the "inside"; how (animal) difference is inscribed only as that which is already captured within (humanity's self-) identity. But the curious feature in this statement is the sense of unmediated, direct, automatic causation: ". . . because the human is already presupposed every time, the machine actually produced a kind of state of exception," Agamben writes (2004:37). Let me put the same this way: when a "territory" such as the human is axiomatically presupposed (absolutely, transcendentally, and categorically), there (automatically) abides a "state of exception," which, for him, is an extralegal space that supports the holocaustal potential that he calls "biopolitics," after Foucault. Why this automatic equation? What exactly is the state of exception? A bit of unpacking through his earlier works is necessary for these formidable suggestions.

The state of exception is the name Agamben gives to the intellectual-institutional apparatus, centrally responsible for the operation of the modern metaphysico-representationalist regime and its holocaustal potential (1998). It is a sort of stopgap for representationalism's aforementioned constitutional "fracture." The elision of the fracture enables representationalism's phantasm (of installing itself as a self-standing, self-motivated, and all-encompassing plenitude). For, to state the obvious, representationalism's ambition is to articulate self-evident referential differentiations (between, say, inside and outside, legal and illegal, cause and effect, et cetera) and maintain the purity of boundaries. The "state of exception" or the "zone of indeterminacy" is a designated conceptual-institutional space of incoherence, which renders this otherwise impossible operation of coherence possible. It is a circumscribed zone of irrationality, which founds rationality, an *exception* to the law that founds legality itself. It is, in still other words, an unlawfulness in the middle of the law, an outlaw dimension internal to the law.

Agamben relates its origin to the figure of the sovereign in antiquity. For the sovereign is the one who pronounces: "I, the sovereign, who is outside the law, declare that there is nothing outside the law" (Agamben 1998:15). The sovereign is a figure of extra-legality who, from outside the law, so to speak, enables the distinction between the lawful and the unlawful, or the inside of the law from its outside.[14] The sovereign, we might say, is a "stop-gap" who screens (from view) law's constitutive fracture, its inherent impossibility. By so controversially reviving the logic of sovereignty in theorizing modern biopolitics, Agamben tried to show the unlawfulness residing in the middle of modern law. And to that extent, to the extent that the law is already outside itself, he further showed, politics came to unmediatedly, directly, and automatically reference biological life itself. A similar dynamic I described in the Introduction this way: there, I talked about how an injunctional impossibility directly acquired the opacity of the body in me. But how exactly does this "automatism" work? How does the law/injunction directly concern the body? This is a crucial question not just to better understand Agamben's work but also to shed light on why I embarked on this book with my own bird phobia.

Agamben's unspoken indebtedness here—the indebtedness made explicit by Eric Santner (2006)—is to Sigmund Freud's *Totem and Taboo* (2000). Arguably, the central problem in the latter is also the paradox of the law: how is it that taboo (qua the law of prohibition) maintains its legitimacy despite the fact that its constitutional origin is invariably unknown? Put simply, how does such a law apply to "new" cases—without the clearly stated "rational" injunction of what is lawful and what is not? Freud's answer is this: "anyone who has violated a taboo by touching something which is taboo becomes taboo himself" (2000:48). The law of prohibition is so maintained by such a mechanism of "example" (57). At work here is the logic that precisely captures the law's (sovereign) paradox that concerns Agamben: the one who violates the law becomes—by "example"—the enforcer, as it were, of the same law. The point is that this Freudian law of prohibition does not enforce itself by constituting (at the origin) what is lawful and what is unlawful, what is inside and what is outside. Rather, it enforces by (directly and automatically) constituting in the embodied example of the violator a category—a sovereign category, shall we say—that disrupts the distinction between lawful and unlawful.

It was this kind of experience of exposure to the law that I tried to capture when I wrote in the Introduction: "I became my own ridiculous material embodiment of the failure of assimilation." It was this way that "the injunctional impossibility directly acquired the opacity of the body." The "body" that subsists in such an exposure to the strange ontological status of the law/injunction I called "creaturely life," after Santner. Agamben's name for the same is "bare life." The difference from totemic law (which is the concern in *Totem and Taboo*) is that modern law hides such an "irrational" aspect inherent to law from our view at all costs—so that the law maintains its rational guise and its "eternal validity" (Santner 2006:21). The modern law achieves this, so Agamben tells us (following Foucault), precisely by rendering the (irrational) biological life its exclusive concern.

What is policed thus, in modern biopolitics, for Agamben, is not the material body or the empirical animal as we know them. Neither is the policed "man-animal" nor "animal-man." Rather, what is policed is creaturely life or bare life in its precise senses that are conceivable only in relation to the function of the law. "On the one hand, we have the anthropological machine of the moderns. As we have seen, it functions by excluding as not (yet) human an already human being from itself, that is, by animalizing the human, by isolating the nonhuman within the human. . . . And it is enough to move our field of research ahead a few decades . . . and we will have the Jew, that is, the non-man produced within the man, or the *néomort* and the overcomatose person, that is, the animal separated within the human body itself" (Agamben 2004:37).[15] It is to bring out this "animal" that divides from ourselves—the "animal" that is ex-cited under the "third gaze" of "imagined communities"—that I made a detour through my own bird phobia.

Multiple Humanities

At least, we should be confident to state now that how we conceptualize non-human animals is a political matter through and through. In fact, I have argued at the outset that the animal is a privileged resource for representational thinking. Agamben confirms this insight in the most damaging criticism possible. He is not thereby arguing that animals are metaphorical human beings—for example, comparing how animals were imagined by the nineteenth-century human sciences *homologously* to the treatment of the Jew in the twentieth century. Rather, the animal in Agamben's exegesis emerges as a paradigmatic "outside" in precisely Kant's and Nancy's senses. In other words, we are talking about the privileged Outside that is enlisted in the service of representing the homogeneous non-place of the inside. It keeps the axiom of the homogeneous inside from "antagonistically" fracturing from itself. To that extent, I wrote at the outset, the Outside is representationalism's unspoken preoccupation and obsession. Also, to that extent, representationalism cannot think animal's illegible abyssal difference, which facilitates a representational reading in the first place. But how can we think such an abyssal difference if not symbolically and representationally? Am I not presupposing the horizonal boundary between human and animal yet again by deeming the animal abyss a self-apparent given?

In order to avoid this trap, thinking animal difference seriously must accompany a willingness to jeopardize the givenness of humanity's presupposed homogeneity. This is the conclusion Nancy draws by strictly following the logic of the paradigmatic humanism. For example, Hegel wrote that "identity, as self-consciousness, is what distinguishes man from nature, particularly from the brutes, which never reach the point of comprehending themselves as 'I'" (cited in Nancy 1993:9). Self-consciousness is here defined as without content. Lacking content, it is by axiom without division in extension. It is merely an empty awareness of its indivisible self-sameness. It is nothing else whatsoever. It is merely an awareness of the fact that it does not differ from itself. Hence, by definition, it is indivisible—*in-dividual*. Defined as self-sameness itself, "man" qua humanity cannot but be equated with Hegel's "I." Individualism is irreducible. Then, Nancy asks humorously, "Why is there more than one individual?" (1993:10). Logically speaking, there cannot be more than one self-same exception that is without content, without extension, and in that way, and only in that way, different from all the others. Such a category cannot assign difference at all. In fact, "if the subject did not differ from itself, it would not be what it is: a subject relating itself to itself" (11). In conclusion, the definition of humanity in terms of (Hegel's) self-consciousness is thoroughly antithetical to the *fact* of our multiplicity. If we follow Hegel here, Nancy continues, nothing prevents us from defining humanity in terms of one individual person, with whose contrast we define nature and animal in toto.

In the following chapter, I want to introduce an individual who may as well ask, "Why can't there be more than one humanity?" Parroting his "irresponsibility" I might also be moved to ask: Why is humanity always conceived in terms of homogeneous Oneness? If presuming that there is only one individual is preposterous, then so is the presumption that there is only one humanity. Our willingness to accede to the fact of multiplicity in humanity must also destabilize the boundary between humans and animals.

CHAPTER SEVEN

The Line of Flight, Out of Bird Phobia

Too often . . . we imagine that the relations of a certain animal subject
as to the things in its environment take place in the same space and
in the same time as those which bind us to the objects in our human
world. The illusion rests on the belief in a single world in which all
living beings are situated. . . . Such a unitary world does not exist, just
as a space and a time that are equal for all living things do not exist.
—Giorgio Agamben, *The Open*

After the Event

Sitting on a swing on the western end of the park, I watched ripples made on
a puddle by my cigarette butt. Dense fog and drizzle seemed to muffle what
little sound there was in the first place. It was eleven-and-a-half months
till the next Labor Day Shoot. For me, the post–Labor Day depression was
almost unbearable. I suspect that the mood was common throughout the
Hegins community. But the official rhetoric of the shoot having been about
an "outsider intrusion" prevented anyone from complaining about the anti-
climax. There were obvious absences that could have caused the depression:
the crowd had dispersed, the media buses had left, the state troopers had di-
verted their attention elsewhere, the protesters had moved on to more enterprising issues, et cetera. But it was not just that. There was something special
about the excitement of the Labor Day Shoot. The world "made sense" then,
even when one did not subscribe to all the conspiracy theories that happily
carried the day.

Of course, it was this quiet around Hegins most of the year. But the time leading up to Labor Day was different. Anticipation magically imbued the everyday leaden boredom with a quality of duplicity. It was as if the quietude could not be trusted already. One almost felt like imagining a sinister agent behind it—behind the reason why nothing was happening yet. The mundane quietude of the park, especially, had that quality of artificiality, as if something was being willfully withheld. It was a strangely animated kind of absence. But now, the deadness was almost godless. It was as if the "gap" had closed and the here-and-now contingency was nothing but that—a contingency, powerless and mundane.

Now, feeling abandoned after the event, I felt as though I had fallen into a different space-time altogether. Especially different was Hegins Community Park. The park, the center of it all on Labor Day, bore the eerie abandonment like an injury. I hovered about the empty park day after day like an afterthought. I, the only outsider left behind, as it were, was like a silly partygoer whose wished-for merriment is ill-timed. I spent countless hours pacing up and down the park's grounds, panicking somewhat from all this sudden mundane meaninglessness. Space-time itself became an enigma. Now, boredom became desperate.

Along Came Monk

Breaking this boredom came Monk. Monk was already in his early eighties when I first met him. A frail man with black lung, he was also called "Pop" by everyone; he was everyone's grandfather—to be distinguished from Shally's father, who was introduced in Chapter 4. Nothing about him particularly stood out except for the shrillness of his voice and an unusually grave reticence. But after close inspection, I realized that both traits made him quite unusual indeed; he was everyone's grandfather only in looks. His voice had a high-pitched, metal-grinding kind of tone that made him sound cranky all the time. But he did not merely sound cranky; the man carried an aura of disappointment all around him. His defiant reticence, though, hinted at a friendly side of him, as if he did not want to burden others with his profound aura of disappointment. But his unusually determined reticence generally made others nervous—I mean, among those who bothered to talk to him, which were few. I, in contrast, liked talking to him very much because unlike the others he did not ask a single question about me. Not one question. He sort of acknowledged my presence as a non-human creature would.

One day, he looked me up and left his phone number at the front desk of the motel I was living in. The year was 1996. We met at a diner in Pottsville the next morning. I didn't know whom to expect, but I recognized him as he entered. He was one of the row of elderly men who were perched year after year on Labor Day on the same bench near the entrance of the park. That bench, in turn, was adjacent to the book-signing and selling table, annually set up by Patrick Canfield (1993), the author of the only existing book dedicated to the county's practice of pigeon shooting. Over the years, the bench had become a magnet for the pigeon "gangs" of the bygone era to enjoy a reunion of sorts every Labor Day. For the author Patrick Canfield—who was younger than most of the relevant generation treated in the book—having the entourage of "real" protagonists was not only a selling point but a deep honor. But no one paid attention. The book sold only to a handful of visiting (and thus "outsider") gun enthusiasts or militant supporters of the NRA. But Patrick tirelessly pressed on with his ballyhooing of the elderly men: "These chaps you see here are the real legendary hell-raisers you read [about] in the book!" This somehow made them look older and shabbier. I first hung around the bench just to have a place to hang around. The bench offered me just about the only place in the whole eighty-acre-wide park where I could lay down the burden of my conspicuous presence.

Monk did not waste any time getting down to the business of his visit. Abruptly, he produced a strange-looking object from his pocket. It was a little bell—the kind lined up in jingling instruments—attached at the end of a three-inch-long metal stick as thin as wire, surrounded by a bush of red crepe paper strips. It looked like a bell Korean shamans might use, only smaller. The red crepe paper gave it the air of a Buddhist aesthetic. The strangeness was uncomfortable. I didn't feel like touching it. I drew in my hands from the table and asked suspiciously what it was. He said he used it to train pigeons. I had not become acquainted with this kind of training tool from Shally.

"What do you train pigeons for," I asked dismissively, feigning ignorance.

So that "they get to know the land," he replied in these exact words.

He preempted my predictable, ill-informed barrage of queries with his own question: "Can you get this kind of bell from your country?"

"Where did you get those?" I asked.

"From Taiwan," he said.

"I am not from Taiwan; I am from Korea," I said, irritated.

Amazingly, he repeated his question as if he didn't hear me, "Can you get it for me?"

In disbelief, I carefully studied this man, this grown-up man who was holding the silly toy of a bell in front of him with great care and talking about his need for more of them almost in desperation. His seriousness was comical. I wondered if he was senile and told him that I would try to find one. I could see that he did not believe me. I did not believe myself. His request exited my mind with the closing of the diner's door behind me. But the counterintuitive turn of conversation and that odd bell stayed with me like an episode of indigestion.

My mind kept returning to the rabid bushiness of the dull-red crepe paper—like the hair of a mad woman, as Koreans are wont to say—the wire-thin metal stick that could poke, and the unquietable jingle of the lone bell. Having been raised in a Presbyterian family, I was brainwashed to fear religious icons. With Buddhist ones especially, which are interchangeable with those of shamans in the Korean context, I didn't need any more encouragement. I could hardly believe that someone had the audacity to suggest that this matter could be even further aggravated by adding matters of pigeon to the mixture. My mind swam uncontrollably in images of pigeons poked at with that thing. I pictured that three-inch thing on the back of a pigeon's neck, like a machinic growth in all its inanimacy, immobile even as the bird kept on with its hideous bobbing. I thought of the sound of the bell accompanying the extant mechanical jingle of the pigeon's wing flapping. And "getting to know the land," for Christ's sake? I thought of the bleeding pigeon wildly flying around, defiling everything. Shally's demonstration did not touch me like this. But something about Monk's pious dedication deeply bothered me. And so, by and by, a new "landscape," shall we say, a new time-space of phantasm opened up in my mind, the landscape of a mineral inanimacy that is befouled—literally—and made organically alive in all its monstrosity, just like that hideous combination of flinty beak and warm body. . . . Intellectually, I was intrigued. I was intrigued by the ease with which this brief encounter with Monk dislodged the leaden mundaneness of the landscape around me from itself both spatially and temporally: now, the killing and the excitement were confined neither to the park nor to Labor Day. Somewhere, pigeons were flying with that hideous thing stuck to their bodies. Somewhere they were defiling the land as we spoke. Intellectually, yes. Viscerally, though, I felt I was already too close to pigeons. I dropped the subject from my mind till the next Labor Day.

Reed

On Labor Day, Monk sat himself in his usual position, on that bench of elderly men. We acknowledged each other and didn't say anything. I was made uncomfortable by neglecting his request, and he seemed to have no interest in pressing the subject further. My attention was quickly attracted by a new man by the name of Reed. Reed was a quick-talking elderly man who wore his age with resentment as if it should belong to someone else. The man was filled with a repertoire of carefully mastered magic tricks and jokes to prove his continuing relevance. He filled hours of my audio-recorder with useless jokes, which were always followed by promises to get to the information of real substance. He was good enough to trick me time and again.

In the afternoon, a cart filled with crates of pigeons towed by an ATV was passing by us. A pigeon poked its head out slightly—perhaps seeking relief from the deadly heat. And the man who was tending the transport viciously kicked the side of the crate to scare the bird. Suddenly, Reed, the avid talker, stopped talking. In a resigned murmur he talked to himself: "These people don't know a thing about pigeons." Monk, sitting next to Reed, quietly nodded. This interested me. For the first time, I saw a real division among the supposed supporters of the shoot. "What's wrong with these people?" I asked as an encouragement. Reed stopped his jokes and largely repeated what I already knew.

There are largely two kinds of pigeon shooting practiced in Schuylkill County. "Straight shooting" is a relatively recent invention employed at the Labor Day Shoot. For Reed and Monk, this style belonged to "doctors and lawyers who shot hundreds just because they can afford them." These were the exact words repeated on later occasions. The traditional miner's style is called "trap-and-handle," or, simply, "trapping." Reed assured me that this type of shooting was the only "real one."

This discriminative evaluation, back then, was news to me. Patrick Canfield's book also mentions both styles, but not in these terms. Not at all. And neither did Shally or his father. Having written the book as a response to the animal rights protest, Patrick was much more interested in seeing one unified tradition that could clearly demarcate insiders from outsiders. His book ends with "To Animal Rights Protesters—let the pigeons fly." Feigning ignorance, I immediately asked Reed, again, to show me how trapping was done. This was a sociological interest; I had no intention of getting to know more about the business of pigeons per se. Surprisingly, for a man who was desperate to sustain my attention a minute ago, he looked reluctant, almost dismissive. He waved his hands in the air and dropped the subject. Toward the end of the shoot, after Reed was gone, Monk suddenly picked up the issue in a feeble voice. Unannounced, he abruptly turned to me as if he had been thinking about it all along and said: "Reed don't know trapping too good; he is a shooter, you see." At first, I did not know what to make of this series of discreditings—first, straight shooting, and now, Reed the shooter. I had to find out. I coaxed Monk to take me to Reed's place several days later. The visit confirmed that Monk was right: Reed was much more interested in talking about guns and shooting. I asked how the trapping was done, and he kept bringing out an arsenal of guns from his collection, along with piles of yellowed newspaper articles that bore testimony to his once legendary marksmanship. All the while, Monk kept quiet as if bemused by Reed's buffoonery at my naïveté's expense.

Reed's place was hard to find, hidden deep in the woods past a labyrinthine web of dirt roads. I could never have found my way back to it. Monk's place, in contrast, was right by a major road. For this reason, I had to rely on Monk for rides numerous times. A ride in his truck was an awkward affair, Monk being a tortuously silent man. But in time, I got to know him a little. I got to know, for example, that Monk's truck—which was taking me to and from Reed's useless sessions—turned out to be, practically speaking, a classroom in trapping. In the capped flat bed, he had all kinds of equipment related to trapping, except the birds themselves. I got irritated by this deception and protested it. He said that there was no point in learning such a "useless skill." "People will think you are a troublemaker," he said in these exact words.[1]

Besides, he added: "You ain't no miner."

"What does mining have to do with pigeons?" I asked. After some ramblings, out of Monk's mouth came the syllogism that was to become his mantra: "To know pigeon, you have to know the land, and to know the land, you have to know coal."

I was taken aback by the possible accuracy of my fancies. I shuddered at the returning thoughts on the shamanistic, blood-letting orgies that I came to attach to the phrase "getting to know the land." So it is true, I thought, that these guys do indeed promiscuously confuse flesh-and-blood substance with mineral matters, organic life with the inanimacy of landscape. The way Shally fed charcoal to his birds suddenly came back in a new light. And how appropriate that the culprit was—yet again—birds! The poetic justice of it all at the expense of my nerves was too complete to pass up. Before I knew it, this association, this new "landscape" opened up in my phobic imagination, became my nervous intellectual obsession. After about a month, I surrendered myself to Monk and asked to be taken in as an apprentice of sorts.

The Apprentice

Monk did not take me seriously at first. But after much coaxing, he agreed to one demonstration of brushing, which was generous given its practical illegality (see the Introduction). We went to his pigeon pen. Monk caught eight birds for demonstration. With the birds in a portable cage, a trap, and training instruments in a box, we drove a short distance to the center of a shabby private gun club where he was a leading member. He put down a trap with its top open, grabbed a bird and held it snuggly against his abdomen with one hand, and tied thread-like instruments on the bird's body after moistening them with his saliva. The rest was not much different from Shally's demonstration. But this time, I thought I had to learn to do it myself.

Emboldened, partly for having a mere eight birds in the expanse of nature, I volunteered to try my own hand. My hands were icy and stiff, and they felt far too small to wrap around the wings, which is necessary to comfort the bird. Using both hands, I held it gently and tugged its head against the folds of my vest. Since my whole body felt completely drained of blood by that time, the bird felt incredibly warm. That was a revelation: I had only thought of them in terms of flinty beaks and sinewy forks of legs. For a brief instant, I caught myself finding solace in that warmth.

But then Monk called me back to my senses, that is, back to panic: "What are you doing? Now, tie the cap [that is, the thread-like thing]." As I tried to free one hand, abandoning two-handed security to a precarious one-handed grab, and reached for the cap inside my pocket, one wing got loose. It didn't flutter immediately. Instead, the bird spread its loosened wing slowly, ever so slowly, to its full expanse, right in front of my nose. It was huge, and its plumage had a cobweb of delicate patterns similar to those I once saw magnified from an insect wing. Almost at once I noticed the wriggling sinewy claws and a smudge of droppings on my belt. Before I knew it, the pigeon had darted out.

Monk was puzzled and asked if my hand was *kaput*—broken. Apparently, my clumsiness persuaded him that I had a disability. I was comforted by the warmth in his voice. And so I confessed my fear of birds. He looked surprised, grinned significantly, and said: "I can fix that." And so my apprenticeship began.

The daily training of pigeons is also called brushing. Monk diligently applied himself to the task at least five days a week. With the chores involved in tending his pen and all, Monk, like Shally, devoted roughly four hours daily to matters of his birds. This was a little extreme compared to other trappers who were members of the same private gun club. The club facility was a modest affair, collectively owned and maintained by a few dozen local working-class men. Since the club's main activity was shooting live pigeons, its entrance was well hidden from the road. A stranger venturing into it required not a little courage. The shooting range itself, an expanse of about twenty acres, was surrounded by woods, and in the middle of the club land was the clubhouse, which housed a bar where club members hung out.

I always found that clubhouse interesting. It bore the grandeur of a bygone era when mining was still thriving. First started by mine engineers, the house was built with fine materials and an ambitious aesthetic goal. It was an octagon, with huge windows on all sides. And the bar itself was padded fat with a generous amount of cushioning and bright red leather. But because of its inaugural ambition and wealth, the house suffered badly the change in the class status of its ownership: signs of failure in upkeep were all around. The engineers were long gone—for at least forty years. But the spirit of proprietorship was still not completely transferred, as if the current owners were squatters on an abandoned property. This was evident in the way the men leaned heavily against the bar as if taunting with their unwillingness to move—yes, squatting. It was evident in their endless talk about how mine engineers "didn't know a thing about coal." One got the impression from those talks that the engineers were somehow chased away by the force of nature itself—due to their ignorance regarding the business of coal. This made the transition to the current owners a kind of natural phenomenon, and the men now lazily leaning against the bar a natural growth as inevitable as weeds—a natural ally of coal.

And precisely for this reason, precisely because the place embodied the sense of entitlement to not only the gun club itself but the entire territoriality of the region, the place was more strictly off-limits to me than any other place. The first time I ventured inside, a man named Keefer—Monk's close friend who was second in rank (after Monk) at the club in terms of seniority—confronted me. Just as might happen in the movies, he told me flat-out that "they" didn't want me to "snoop around" the club. There were a lot of men who witnessed the scene, and so Keefer's words became my official verdict: I became someone everyone felt free to tell to "go away"—even children. Children, as everywhere else, I suppose, carried out this verdict with a particularly devastating sting.

Strangely, Monk did not utter a word about the social impasse I was in. Instead, he let me tag along wherever he went or whatever he did within the club. As long as I was with him, no dramatic scene was repeated. Monk's silent protection was augmented by his grandson, Tom (not Tom Klinger), who maintained a conspicuous presence around the club and much beyond, thanks to his thugishness. Tom was one of the rowdiest hooligans at the Hegins shoot. Hence, my acquaintance with him dates back to the very first Hegins shoot I attended. Not surprisingly, our acquaintance began on a rough footing. He was one of many who habitually hurled death threats at me—some by allusion and some explicitly—whenever they saw me at the Hegins shoot. But with my repeated showing up, year after year, the threats lost steam. The threats almost became embarrassing, like a repeated joke. Strangely, I shared that embarrassment and wished that they would stop for all our sakes. By and by, I became a familiar, or an accomplice to the required task of at least toning down, if not eliminating, the mutually embarrassing scene. In any case, Tom had a bigger problem on his hands now: his finding me daily alongside his own granddad, I suppose, was a source of major embarrassment. In front of other club members, he desperately tried to dismiss my presence. He seemed to be actively, if subtly, inviting others to do the same for his sake. This had a positive effect on my well-being. Besides, my being his social liability gave me some power over him: I sadistically enjoyed seeing him cringe whenever I addressed him in a friendly way before other club members. With Tom's being the aggressive thug that he was, the fact that he tolerated my presence around the club allowed me the benefit of the doubt and gave me a modicum of license to be there.

Besides, being Monk's apprentice/help made me more knowledgeable of the nitty-gritty details of the facility than an average club member. In time, I came to be viewed as a useful—if not indispensable—hand to have around.

The fact that I became so physically familiar with the club had much to do with the location of Monk's house. His house was right behind the club, and his pigeon pen on the edge of the shooting range. He literally spent his entire life there after retirement.

His day began in the late morning with the cleaning of the pen. This was done relatively quickly. Then he worked on preparing feeds. This took a great deal of time, and in this Monk was as obliviously absorbed as he was meticulous in measurements. His feeds consisted of maize, anise oil, and charcoal—yes, charcoal again. Maize is the mainstay in terms of quantity, but the charcoal is his secret ingredient. I kept quiet about Shally's recipe. "It helps digestion in the crops," Monk said at my inquiry. For him, crops, that hideous zone of ambiguity between organicity and inanimacy, held the key to the bird's life force. That was the first thing he checked after the mysterious death of a bird. He would cut the bird open with a razor, take out the crop, put it on a piece flat wood, and squash it under his boot. This would make the sound of an organic sac bursting at first, followed by the muffled sound of sand ground against a hard surface. The characteristics of that sound would yield clues about the bird's death.

Brushing

There are no set numbers or kinds of apparatuses employed in brushing. Monk employed a variation of four kinds: whistling, bottle caps, the rig, and, the perennial etymological mystery, boogla-woogla. I have even heard that some people employ dogs. The rig is the bell I have described already. Close to what I had imagined, the wire part can be secured to the dense feathers on the back of the bird's neck. Bottle caps, as I described in Chapter 3, are punctured bottle caps with a cotton thread strung through them. They can be tied wherever a training session demands. Their hang time on the body of the pigeon can be manipulated by the amount of saliva applied when tying them to the feathers. Boogla-woogla, once again, is a bundle of strips of bright-colored sponges tied at the end of a wooden stick about a foot long. Around the bundle is a ring of bells (about six), bigger than the bells on the rig. One shakes the thing above the trap before it opens.

Brushing is exciting to watch, but its exact purpose always escaped me. I kept the burning questions to myself through the first couple of sessions. But when it became obvious that the following sessions were to proceed exactly as the previous ones, I became impatient. I began asking. But as I quickly realized, Monk was no conversational pedagogue. It was next to impossible to draw him out of his leaden silence for any stretch of time. Days and sometimes even weeks would go by before Monk abruptly returned to my question with an answer. Obviously, his memory was extraordinary, but his sense of time or of attention span was not of our species. It took enormous concentration on my part to comprehend an abruptly returned question in its proper context. Although I began anticipating his preferred intervals over time, reconstructing a semblance of dialogue retrospectively from my voluminous labyrinth of notes and my questionable range of memory required a good deal of interpretation and editing—yes, an editing out of days of irrelevant contexts. I tried to indicate a passage of time whenever I could without disrupting the conversational "rhythm."

In any case, unsteadily my questions issued forth. First, I asked what each brushing apparatus "stood for." Downcast as if ignoring me, but with a surprising patience, Monk answered them all: he repeated "the hawk" four times at hopelessly long intervals, as if struggling to recover each time.

"So, everything stands for the hawk?" I said, politely scandalized—but more disappointed.

"Them birds have to know that hawks come in all kinds of shapes and sounds," said Monk.

"But, Kenny told me that there are only two kinds of hawks in this area."

"Kenny doesn't know a thing," Monk dismissed.

I knew that "scientifically" speaking, Kenny was right. And I knew that there was no way that Monk would not know that either. I knew he knew it, but I didn't pursue it further.

The Hawk Is at Once One and Multiple

The question resolved itself as I began to try my own hand at brushing. Monk was generally very relaxed and tolerant of my ignorance and awkwardness around pigeons. But there was one rule that he was absolutely adamant about from the beginning: under no circumstances should birds *see* the brushing apparatuses. I was a little alarmed by Monk's rare mood of animation verging on agitation whenever he broached this subject. I surmised from his gravity that one visual exposure is bad enough to ruin a bird forever, or something like that.

And this golden rule was a demand of high order when it came to practice: after all, you have to put these apparatuses on the birds' bodies. Monk

demonstrated the procedure: you hide the apparatus (in your pocket when
it is as small as the bottle cap), take the pigeon out from the transporting
cage, hide the bird's head in the darkness of the fold of your shirt (by bend-
ing your torso forward a bit), hold the apparatus with your lips or teeth,
moisten the thread the desired amount, gently tie it to the desired part of
the feathers, and put the bird in the darkness of the trap. When you tie it to
the feathers, Monk warned, the bird should not "feel" where you are putting
it. Specifically, you should be careful not to pull at the feather. Also, when
you are applying the rig, you should secure the rig far enough back that the
fluttering red crepe paper shreds do not come into full view of the bird's
eyes; the bird should be able to see the rig only ever so slightly in its extreme
peripheral vision.

So, I concluded that the simulated "hawk," whatever the apparatus,
should not be *localized* by the bird either by vision or by "feel." I tested my
hypothesis: "Is the whole thing because pigeons might figure out that the
hawk, which is supposed to be stalking them, is actually a fake device?"

Monk grinned as if to ridicule and said, "Birds ain't that smart."

That was the end of the conversation that day. But several days later,
Monk abruptly picked it up again: "The birds have sharp eyes. When they
see, they think too much. They try to count."

These were his exact words. They were inscribed in my memory because
of the unusual metaphors: they "think" and "count." Regardless of whether
pigeons can really count in the proper sense, "counting" means distinction.
So, obviously, by depriving the birds of vision, Monk does not want the birds
to be able to distinguish one simulation of a hawk from another; by depriving them of bodily "feel," he does not want them to be able to *localize* a
simulation. In short, "the hawk"—which is thus made neither just singular
nor just generic—must be uncountable and, which is the same thing, *unlocatable*.

To make the origin of simulation unlocatable, sound is privileged over
sight. In the cases of the bottle cap and the rig, the pigeon in flight will experience these apparatuses as sounds of threats that are as persistent as its
own shadow—or, even as ubiquitous (if temporarily, as long as an apparatus hangs). In any case, as an amorphous stalker—at times barely accessible
in the periphery of vision—"the hawk" for the birds would be experienced
as a presence that is unlike anything they have experienced: at once object
specific and immaterial. It was no wonder, I realized, that Monk thought
my question of what each apparatus "stood for" absurd. The whole purpose

of employing a variety was precisely to make the birds "lose count," as it were, and so unable them to distinguish one source of sonorous danger from another.

How about the boogla-woogla? That bulky thing doesn't stalk like the bottle cap or the rig. That's why, Monk said, you have to be more careful with it and hide it as soon as the trap opens and the bird takes flight. The reason, he added, was because pigeons are "curious animals," and that they always want to "check out" the source of danger once they feel securely away from it. For the same reason, it was said, the place of the trap should not be visible from the pigeon pen—because after their release, the birds predictably fly back to the pen and perch on its roof.[2]

If training is done well, then, the birds are exposed daily to the same sounds of danger, whose origin they cannot visually verify, all their lives. To that extent, as Monk was wont to say, "Every time the trap opens, he is looking for them. He wakes up in the morning, and he is looking for them. He has to have this hunger. He has to search."

Then, what the birds will always be looking for in the world is, more precisely, the visual sources of three different sounds of "the hawk." For pigeons, "the hawks" will be like an invisible cabal of omniscient stalkers, a secret society made up, if counted, of three (or three kinds of) members that know the pigeons' every move, appearing and disappearing at will. They are multiple but they may as well be one.

The training seems to be designed to exploit one of the strengths that pigeons are known for, that is, vision, but only to frustrate it. Imagine the sad existence of such a creature: he will always experience the visual world as though something very important is missing from it, to say the least. One day I felt a little cynical about all of Monk's fussiness about the bird's vision and teased that a blind one would suit him best. He immediately jumped on this remark: "No, the bird has to *see* that the hawk is behind him!"

Then, what is the practical outcome? How do trained birds actually turn out different in a shoot match?

"Think about it: bird hears all this in darkness . . . alone. He don't know what's goin' on out there. And the next thing you know, the trap collapses and you are thrown into that noise. Just like that. Now, you are on your own. What do you do? Barn birds react to every disturbance. They try to see too much. Good brushed ones ain't."

"What? Why? How?"

"Brushed one thinks that it's always the same damn hawk after him."

After a long pause, I thought, this sort of makes sense. Barn birds' reaction to every disturbance will make their flight more predictable, if not monotonous. And brushed birds are trained to perceive a threat as necessarily amorphous, not specific to objects they see. If they think it is always the same hawk, as Monk says they do, they are trained to confuse an individual hawk and the collective hawk, an individually embodied source of threat and an omnipresent one. In an ideal situation, hypothetically speaking, they would not even trust a source of threat that is visually locatable in an object—which clearly will be the case at a match. They may suspect that "there has to be more" than meets the eye, as it were. So, it makes logical sense that a perfectly trained bird will not impetuously jump at every stimulus and will instead stoically ignore "obvious" ones. But, still, even if that happens—which is quite a stretch—what exactly is the brushed birds' advantage? How does such a "wisdom" translate into the way they move? After all, they are nothing but object-targets whose wisdom the shooter does not care about.

Is there really a difference in the way the brushed birds actually fly? Are they not just as much reacting to every disturbance during the training?

Monk replied: "He can see a flight line that no one else can see."

"How?"

"Because he thinks the whole world is his."

What? In the first place, how does a bird that thinks that it is stalked all the time build such a confidence—presuming that Monk means some sort of confidence? And what does confidence have to do with what "flight line" he sees? That is, how does confidence translate into an alternative time-space, if we can call it that?

Thrownness

From Monk's remarks, three "sites" of images gripped me. First, for the bird, the catastrophically shocking and exigent moment of the scene when the trap collapses. Second, in that scene, brushed birds react differently to object-stimuli (compared to barn birds). Third, such a different relation to the object-world results in the feat of "flight line."[3]

The third one is the most controversial. Monk may as well be saying that a brushed pigeon could make itself disappear, in the fashion of entering another space-time. Regardless of whether such a feat is possible, I take his belief at its face value. I am not an ornithologist but an ethnographer of human beliefs. And Monk firmly stood by that utterance at a later time. To

my disappointment, others at the gun club did not think this claim outlandish. But they could not illuminate me further either. Not that they really
tried; Monk, in their minds, was firmly in a different league of genius when
it came to matters of pigeons. After all is said and done, the truth is that
Monk's pigeons were rarely shot down.

But let me take up these three "sites" in order. First, the scene. In Monk's
subsequent portrayal of the scene—which seemed to be a very crucial part
of my training—words generally varied. But the word "thrown" was almost
always there. A touch of disgust was carried by that word whenever he repeated it. The act of throwing, for Monk, pretty much summed up humanity's misunderstanding of the creature. "You are not throwing the bird!" he
lamented often when seeing or hearing about poor techniques of trapping.
The folly of throwing, for him, reached its unsurpassable height particularly
concerning two devices. I would not be at all surprised if the privileged place
the act of throwing earned in Monk's moral vocabulary originated from
his contempt toward these devices. They were specially made traps invented
during the 1970s by two electrical engineers who were affiliated with the gun
club only for a short while. One had a spring-board mechanism and violently catapulted the bird into the air as the trap opened. The other one had
an electric shock mechanism in its stead for the same purpose. They were
mean-looking things too, made of shiny steel and as heavy as a bear trap.
The inventors must have sought consistency as much as the speed at which
the birds left the trap, much in the fashion of the clay pigeon "thrower." For,
at times, dazed birds emerging from the trap fail to take flight. Confusion
with clay pigeons, for Monk, was nothing less than a moral failing.

But in my training, Monk's usage of the word was generally in the passive voice: thrown. He was speaking from the bird's point of view, as it were,
as if exploring the other (victim's) side of the disgusting act of throwing.
Might this mean sympathy? I could not tell. In any case, Monk talked about
trappings from the point of view of birds much more than anyone else I
knew. Curiously, he used the same word—that descriptor for such a despi-
cable act as "throwing"—to describe the imagined state of the bird he himself trapped. But it was much, much more than sympathy as we know it.
Pity was definitely not it. It was more like pathos for a helpless, lone creature
that finds itself in a catastrophic situation but that, at the same time, teems
with pride and celebration precisely for that reason—as one would admire
someone else's gallant suffering in an encounter with an insurmountable
adversity.

Invariably, his figurative language for the state of thrownness was rich, eloquent, and even moving. It was clear that much was at stake in an apprentice's understanding of the richness of this "scene." I thought this surely must be very important in unpacking the ultimate syllogism, "to know pigeon, you have to know the land, and to know the land, you have to know coal." In any case, very much emphasized in describing this "landscape" were the states of exigency, the shock, the catastrophe, the brink, the verge, and the confusion of a creature willy-nilly finding itself in it. His figurative language drove again and again at a scandalous numerical imbalance between the stark singularity of the lone creature and the shocking multitude of adversities that seemingly conspire against the creature. What Monk invited me to imagine thus, I thought, was the bird's sense of incomprehension: Why am I here and who are all these people and things addressing me?—the shooter, the crowd, the referee, the alien environment, the smell, et cetera. Again, I am not interested in whether pigeons are indeed able to "think" this way. But for humans, we have a name for this kind of thinking: existentialism.

Avian Existentialism

I think that existentialism can help us link the three "sites" that compose this "landscape." The reasons are as follows. Existentialism as a literary and philosophical endeavor tries to grapple with the question of—needless to say—existence. The question of existence brings into view the "level" of human experience that is presupposed but not thematized in our usual queries on the meaningfulness of things: Why are we here in the first place—why do we exist? Such a question tries to problematize the facet of our being that we have no choice but to presume to go on even as we cannot help but question it. As long as the question continues, so the thesis goes, we are bound to experience the world as though we have arrived at it too late, or as if we have missed some very important inaugural moments. If the pursuit of "meaning" is reflective, the question of existence evokes the emotive register of immediacy, urgency, desperation, even panic. For the question aims to confound the very reasons for our being by opening up the wound of the foundational groundlessness of our existence (Kaufmann 1968:12). In thus upstaging states of crisis, an existentialist exercise frequents the situations of emergency, of the brink, and of the verge. But, more importantly, such a traumatic temporal dimension of crisis is inseparably intertwined with what I just called a certain "numerical imbalance": the lone hero versus an overwhelming heterogeneity of adversities—for example, people as well as things plus time itself—that are magically united against the hero. Hence the sense of urgency invoked is total—almost physical. I do not want to lose this sense of urgency in an almost physical/spatiotemporal sense—in distinction from the impression of cognitive meditation that existentialism is often made out to be in academic treatments—for the sake of sustaining the problematic of the "landscape." In any case, the existentialist emergency cum wisdom sounds just like the kind of question Monk's philosophically bent pigeons might ask at the scene of a match.

Precisely what vocabulary of physicality/spatiotemporality might the existentialist affect of urgency bring to bear on our understanding of the "scene" and the pigeons' experience of objects in it? Imagine once again what that scene consists of. There is the cacophony of noises, the erupting theater of a frenzied crowd, the "hawk" (as far as the birds can tell) in pursuit, the likely deluge of alien smells, et cetera. Plus, as the darkness inside the trap is abruptly no more, there is the sudden appearance of an expanse of space and the crunch of time that urge and await the bird's "decision" for a possible route of escape, and so on. Of these, we can generalize this much: the set-up of the scene renders the pigeon (subject) passive. The bird's "agency" is surpassed by the otherness of the crowd, the otherness of the hawk, and the otherness of space-time that precipitates itself into existence unannounced, as it were, without reckoning, and without due. This is for the obvious reason that none of these "others" presents itself before the pigeon subject in the present tense for the pigeon to "actively" appropriate, arrogate, exploit, regulate, or choose from.

Then, what are these "others?" They are clearly not ordinary objects—inactive, inert, dormant, lifeless, et cetera; among them are also included opposing volitions of people and the "hawk" to be negotiated with. Nor are they ordinary subjects—autonomous, self-willing, and nontransparent; for there is also the disorienting space-space itself that must be contended (if not negotiated) with. The others seem to be at once both and neither of the two completely.

Let us examine a little more closely these "others" that disquiet and afflict our existentialist hero. Existentialism often speaks of the multitude of such besieging forces in the singular: the Other. This inflectional reckoning is a correlative to existentialism's focalizing of the "ownmost" experience of the authentic and sovereign—if not atomic—self; the Other in the singular is an all-inclusive notion that encompasses everything that extrinsically stands opposed to that embittered "sovereign" subject. Hence, the Other is not an empirical individual or individuals within dyadic intersubjective relations. It could be the time itself that is and has been prior to the commencement of the subject's consciousness—that is, the time that affects the trauma of "always already." It could be another subject or a collection of subjects to whose "priority" we submit ourselves—that is, culture, society, tradition, and so forth. Especially, the latter—what one might call the social dimension of thrownness—is often articulated in terms of the enigma of the Other's *address*: I do not fully recognize myself in the role and identity that the culture/society/tradition qua Other imposes upon me. Because we are embodied beings, this lack of recognition has a "physical" implication: if I do not find myself in the entity that is addressed or accounted for by the Other; what or who is this thing that the Other recognizes and addresses as "me"? The strength of the existentialist analytics for our present purpose is its versatile interpretation of the idea of thrownness in all its heterogeneous dimensions: spatiotemporal, societal, and objectal. And this versatility directly owes itself to a peculiar logic the notion of the Other follows. For a more explicit exploration of that logic, I turn to one of existentialism's founding thinkers, Jean-Paul Sartre.

Being mindful of the centrality of the sense of vision for Monk's birds, let me turn to Sartre's section titled "The Look" in his *Being and Nothingness: An Essay on Phenomenological Ontology* (2001[1956]). Attributing a fancy philosophical move to Monk is not my intention here. I am turning to philosophy to manufacture a prosthetic aid of language, to make sense of what seasoned pigeon handlers intuitively assume due to the depth of occupational history from which the sport arose: bootleg mining. Specifically, the kind of assumption that needs to be unpacked here through existentialist language is the handlers' ready linking of the realm of what I called above the (human) address/surveillance and that of the world of objects qua time-space.

The Look

Allow me to remind you of how pigeons as prey are taught to perennially look for their visually elusive predator—all their lives. The predator is necessarily also looking, or so pigeons would presume. So, strictly speaking, the pigeon is looking at/for what is also looking at/for him—"always." In fact, in the artificially made-up world of Monk's pigeons, one cannot think of pigeons' own looks independently of those of the hawk; the hawk's look is always "on," so to speak. We may even say that among Monk's ideal pigeons— which are "always searching"—the look of the hawk should be a kind of condition of possibility for the pigeons' looks. And yet it is not a "positive" condition of possibility akin to "worldview" (whose "lens" is posited as collectively shareable). It is rather a "negative" one in that it works as a condition of possibility only to the extent that the embodied source of the hawk's look remains forever elusive and unlocatable. It is like Jacques Lacan's idea of the gaze we saw in the Introduction. The two "looks" cannot "meet" both as positive entities. The pigeon's look can consummate only in so far as it cannot look at the hawk's look; or, which is the same, the hawk's look can function as a condition of possibility for the pigeon's look only insofar as the former does not appear in the latter's purview as another look but only as something whose presence is suspected, always and everywhere. Here, Monk has constructed a peculiar chiasmic relationship between pigeons and the hawk: when the pigeon is a subject of looking, the hawk is nowhere to be found; when the pigeon is an object being looked at, the hawk's presence is ubiquitously sensed. In the pigeon world created by Monk, the two looks are locked together as if they are always on two different sides of a Möbius strip.[4] We might consider the following as Sartre's version of the "scene," in which the self and the Other find each other within the strange logic of the same kind of chiasmic "locking":

> I am in a public park. Not far away there is a lawn and along the edge of that lawn there are benches. A man passes by those benches. . . . I apprehend him as an object and at the same time as a man. What does this signify?...If I were to think of him as being only a puppet, I should apply to him the categories which I ordinarily use to group temporal-spatial "things." That is, I should apprehend him as being "beside" the benches, two yards and twenty inches from the lawn. . . . His relation with other objects would be of the purely additive type. . . . In short, no new relation would appear *through him* between those things in my universe. . . . Perceiving him *as a man*, on the other hand . . . is to register an organization *without distance* [that is, not of space-time] of the things in my universe around that privileged object [that is, the man]. To be sure, the lawn remains two yards and twenty inches away from him, but it is also as a lawn bound to him in a relation which at once both transcends distance and

contains it. The distance is unfolded starting from the man whom I see and *extending up* to the lawn. . . . We are dealing with a relation which is without *parts*, given at one stroke, inside of which there unfolds a spatiality which is not *my* spatiality; for instead of a grouping toward me of the objects, there is now an orientation *which flees* from me. (2001[1956]:230; emphases in the original)

The emotional tone with which Sartre opens his discussion is one of panic and exigency, not that of calm reflection. What causes this panic is one's becoming aware of the existence of another consciousness, another subject. An alien "orientation" is thus introduced. But it is also an introduction of an alien object, because the look of the Other as an embodied "thing" disrupts the entirety of the object-world; the result is a world "without distance" and "without parts," Sartre writes. If the Other's consciousness were an ordinary "orientation," a coincidence with its "viewpoint" should be potentially available to other subjects, as in sharing a pair of binoculars. We know this is impossible. If the Other's consciousness were an ordinary object, we would not bother with thoughts on the possibility of "coinciding" with it. This is also not true. It is neither a pure orientation nor a pure object—akin to "glassy eyes" and injunctional impossibility that simultaneously invites identification and rejects it. The Other's consciousness introduces into the world an orientation that is other than mine, but it is an orientation only insofar as access to it is necessarily barred to me, hence opaque to me like an object. À la the hawk, we may call the Other's consciousness a negative condition of possibility or horizon, whose presence the subject must acknowledge but whose "content" remains inaccessible to the latter. That horizon exerts its influence on us by announcing its existence without lending its content (as in worldview) to us.

It turns out that the Other's look as an orientation and look as an object are structurally exclusive of each other. As Sartre puts it, "if I apprehend the look, I cease to perceive the eyes" (2001[1956]:234). Vice versa, when the look is located, it stops being all-pervasive. That is why Sartre describes the look as a "drainage hole" in one's universe; the Other's look, *while being in the object-world* (more precisely, whose presence is suspected to be part of the object-world), drills a gaping hole in one's universe, as it were. The important point here is this: the Other's look qua object is not an "otherworldly" object somewhere outside the purview of my world; rather it is an object that persists as part of my object-world, but only to announce that what I see *might not be* all there is to see—that it might be incomplete. For the object aquires a "face" turned away from me—on account of its "facing" the Other's orientation. As will be elaborated below, Sartre introduces the notion of "probability" to describe this experience of uncertainty or incompleteness. This is not a skeptic's point of how our world "may not exist."[5] Rather, "probability" is an effect caused in the entire object-world due to the introduction of a strange object that is Sartre's Other. The former is thereby disjointed from a unified spatiotemporality.

Isn't this object exactly like Monk's hawk? Recall Monk's rejection of the idea of a blind pigeon in his squad: the pigeon has to "*see* that the hawk is behind him." The hawk from the pigeon's point of view is not an otherworldly object but an object that is, just like Sartre's look of the Other, "there" and "not there" at the same time, thereby rendering the pigeon's entire object-world always somehow incomplete. That is why Monk's pigeon is perennially "searching": "every time the trap opens, he is looking for them [the hawks]. He wakes up in the morning, and he is looking for them." In other words, the hawk dislocates the pigeon's objective world from itself while appearing as a part of the same object-world. It is "the appearance among the objects of my universe of an element of disintegration in that universe" (Sartre 2001[1956]: 231).

We might try a positive description of the hawk as an object. It is simultaneously a specific object and a ghostly omnipresence; a specific object with a locatable sound (before the trap opens) but an object that is magically "everywhere" wherever the bird goes, like a shadow, however erratically he tries to fly to lose it. And, moreover, the "same" hawk never fails to show up every day. To bring back the existentialist language, such is simultaneously experienced as a generalized "address" to whose exposure our very existence is foundationally given *and* as a singular object potentially locatable. If the hawk could talk, it would whisper into pigeons' ears: "I am there and not there at the same time"; "I could be a locatable, singular individual object and multiple all at once"; "I am everywhere but always there for you particularly, too." Sartre gave the name "nomadic gaze" to such an "object." It defies not only our sense of spatiotemporal coordinates but of number, for it is singular and multiple at once. On the latter's account, Sartre calls it "prenumerical."

Let us pause here and take stock of what existentialism has afforded us about the scene so far. We began with the image of a traumatic exigency at the moment of the trap's collapse. Existentialism articulated the "trauma" in terms of the enigma of the address of the Other. And the Other, just like the hawk, affects our pigeon's relation to the object-world itself. Then we might say, along with existentialism, that Monk's goal of introducing the hawk into his pigeon's world in a particularly designed fashion is to change the latter's perception of the object-world itself, an object-world that is surpassed by the presence of the Other, as it were. Monk believes that this method of training results in the brushed birds' different response (compared to that of the barn birds) to the object-stimuli they face at the match. The question that remains is exactly how this different response is manifested in their behavior. Monk's answer to this question is that the birds "can see the flight line that no one else can see." We have to unpack this statement.

"The Whole World Is His"

Sartre's existentialist language seems only to reinforce our impression of the persecuted state of the pigeon's world. How in the world then do Monk's birds ooze with a megalomaniac confidence in none other than the hell-raising pigeon shoot arena? My answer to this question was heavily influenced by the following episode, which took place more than six months after Monk's enigmatic remarks above.

It was one of the very few occasions when I was at the clubhouse. Without Monk's "escort" and seniority, I could not have imagined myself venturing into that place alone. Even with his accompaniment, his prestige was not influential enough to keep loud curses and grumbles from reaching my ear. It was a little more bearable this time because Keefer was with us. Since Keefer's aforementioned open confronting of me had been witnessed by many, his presence now had the added desirable effect of causing puzzlement on the part of the crowd. In time, for reasons I do not know, Keefer's antagonism toward me softened.

We placed ourselves at the bar, which was an even more daring move. We had our usual Yuenglings[6] and talked about pigeons. At one point, I raised the issue of the pigeon's "courage" to stand up to the hawk. I had read about it somewhere. That topic took on a life of its own, thanks to the crowd's forgetting who had started the subject. Virtually everyone tried to chime in about this important matter. Suddenly, I found myself sitting in the middle of the entire bar full of heated conversation—teeming with pride.

Opinions varied a little, but in general there was a consensus: the majority thought it happened when pigeons were flying in a flock of a substantial size, a minimum of two thousand pigeons. In a large flock, each bird's chance of becoming prey decreased, hence the resulting emboldenment. When that happens, the majority continued, the dominant males of the flock can gang up against the hawk in pursuit, and so forth. But there was a minority opinion, which silenced everyone else due to the seniority of its members. On this issue, there was a clear generational gap. Older men—not more than five—rallied around Monk's authoritative dismissal of the majority. I knew Monk savored silencing a noisy debate with his feeble, trembling voice. This was such a moment. In his usual shrill and measured pace, he said something like this: A pigeon in a flock is extremely jumpy. It is because pigeons "see too much." They constantly watch for the movement of the color pattern on their fellows' necks. That's the purpose of white neck-rings in many subspecies. They do that particularly as they are concentrated on feeding on the ground. The constant bobbing movement of their neighbors—signaled by the neck color pattern—gives them comfort. But when one fellow senses danger, its neck will prop up and freeze. All the other birds immediately see this freezing-stop of a neck pattern, and the flock takes flight. But the lone male, Monk continued, has "nothing to see." And so he is not jumpy and can "stand up to the hawk."

This statement of Monk's is odd indeed: ornithologically, it is a travesty; logically, a sophistry with nothing but feigned erudition. But that was that: it was he who spoke and his verdict carried the day. Clearly, Monk missed the point of the conversation: we were talking about pigeons in the natural state and he seemed to be talking about brushed ones. But despite the eccentricity, this intervention of his could not but bring a smile to my face because the general drift bore Monk's signature all over it. Let me dwell on this signature a bit before returning to existentialism.

It is clear that in his mention of the "loneness" of the brave pigeon—against the contemptible gregariousness—Monk tries to disrupt a certain individual-collective relationship assumed by the majority opinion. We may call the majority opinion communitarianism, which is a commonplace in ethological literature (for example, Johnston and Janiga 1995). According to the majority, there seems to be a degree of equity in nature in that the weak and the preyed-upon are equipped with multiplicity: pigeons are prey but gregarious, with many watchful eyes. Their weakness is compensated for by number. This may very well be, scientifically speaking. But scientific veracity does not diminish ideological attraction: a morally uplifting tale of the majoritarian power, this thesis appeals to our democratic sensibility. The tale celebrates a symphonious call of instinctive agreement between the individual organism and the collective body. This unmediated rapport, in turn, purportedly avails the animal nature's wisdom of co-survival—the wisdom that is magically retrieved in the scientist's calculations and the marvels of gun-club gossip. By "wisdom," of course, I have in mind the statistical probability: a bird in a larger flock somehow "knows" his decreased chance of becoming a prey. From this thesis we can problematize at least three different sites where this statistical knowledge is registered: the individual animal, the collective body, and the human observer. The presumed unity between the three subtends the thesis.

Once again, this may very well be, ornithologically speaking. But what is notable is how the presumed unity between the three sites conveniently bridges our democratic sensibility with scientific observability: the immediate rapport between individuality and collectivity is a precondition for theorizability. In other words, individual anonymity subsumed under collectivity enables scientific objectivity. Were the former to be otherwise—that is, if the individual-collective rapport cannot be assumed, as in Monk's theory of the "lone male"—the rightful site of the statistical information would immediately become problematic. (How about the predator? Would the predator be another site where this statistical knowledge is registered?) By assuming the general availability of the statistical knowledge, the thesis presupposes that a totalizing, abstract perspective on the size of the flock is equally available to all three—the scientist, the collective, and the individual. It is this logic that Monk's figure of the "lone male" disrupts. As if to augment the logic he is about to refute, Monk first volunteers a fuller clichéd explanation of individual-collective connectivity: individual awarenesses are serially relayed (by the reading of the neck color pattern from the fellows) to that of the collective. The relay is seamless and the space in which the communication takes place homogeneous and immediate. Not surprisingly, visual mimicry is mobilized to describe this subhuman gregariousness (see Taussig 1993: chap. 7). By the contemptuous insistence on "nothing to see" in his lone male, Monk attacks the heart of the seamless individual-collective connectivity. But the price of this disruption on Monk's part is the other half of this refuted logic: the rhetoric of empirical ("scientific") observation. As will be elaborated below, Monk remains defiantly silent on how his brushed pigeons or "lone males" differ empirically at matches.

Clearly, it is unfair to treat gun-club gossip as a full-blown thesis on animal behavior. But an important difference in opinion on animal sociality seemed to be at stake that afternoon, a difference that separates the bootlegger generation from others. Monk's intervention speaks to the individual animal's direct relation with the predator, about which the "majoritarian" narrative is silent. In the latter, the relationship with the predator is always mediated by the (serially related) collective awareness. Apprehension of the predator, in the latter view, cannot be an individualized, ontological experience, but only an *imitation* of the fellow creature. Sociality, in this view, avails in positive agreements (whether between individuals or between the individual and the collective) and mutual mirroring. In contrast, Monk's figure of the lone male predicates a different kind of sociality, one that requires an intervention of difference rather than the repetition of sameness; one that requires an individual's direct reckoning with the predator. It is as though in Monk's world, a prey's creaturely dignity subsists not in his relation with fellow preys, but directly in none other than the power of its predator. Sartre's existentialism fully warrants such thinking.

The Space of Freedom Opens Up

Sartre's existentialism is not only about human limitation, a sort of romantic indulgence in finitude (see Badiou 2003:25–27). It can also be about "empowerment." More specifically, it is about an immediate trafficking, or a paradoxical equation, between limit and freedom, disempowerment and empowerment, and persecution and election. His thesis on the Other's look is much more complex than the usual thesis on how the Other's gaze (say, that of the Panopticon) "objectifies" us, interpellates us into a restricted set of "identities," and limits our freedom—as was popularized in film theory (for example, Crary 1990, Metz 1982) and in whiteness studies (for example, hooks 1992, Fanon 1967[1952]).[7] True, Sartre also affirms that the Other's look regards me as part of the object-world: as I have done to that Other, the Other can also, in turn, locate me as an object "beside the benches, two yards and twenty inches from the lawn." However, this is not all. For him, our very awareness of the fact that we are so rendered an object by the Other is the evidence that we are not equal to our objectness. Why?

First, we have to clarify the meaning of what it is to "be" an object for Sartre. To be an object means that an exhaustive sense of what I am cannot be available to myself. Otherwise, we get caught in an absurd logic, whereby I can be both the subject of perception and what appears to it. As long as there is another subject of experience—which is a necessary presupposition in order to affirm the existence of culture or society—there is a "part" of me that falls out of my own purview and we call that part an object. And that objectal part of me "belongs" to the Other's look. For the Other is an Other because, as has been established, its purview or its horizon is by definition unavailable to me. When the Other apprehends me as an object, I cannot access that object "seen" by the Other—for, once again, "I cannot apprehend [an object] as it appears to the Other" (Sartre 2001[1956]:232). Sartre makes the same point succinctly as follows: "It is in and through the revelation of my-being-object for the Other that I must be able to apprehend the presence of his [the Other's] being-as-subject" (232). Just like any other object, my-being-an-object acquires another "face," which is turned toward the Other. This is the reason he writes: "I cannot be an object for myself" (246). Self-possession is ruled out.

If so, an enigmatic object becomes part of the subject's constitution. The subject, as it is conceived in this way of thinking, can be said to consist of two components. Instead of mind/body, the two components are first, the enigmatic "object" whose "face" is registered in the Other; second, a consciousness that—instead of being the master of its experience—"suffers" this object as an enigma, divided from itself. In sum, the subject is this being that is dislocated from its own being-an-object. The emergence of the Other's look renders me unequal to my objectness. In fact, the more "objectified" I become in the gaze of the Other, the more "unequal" I become to my status as an object. To put it more paradoxically: the more objectness that the Other takes away from me, as it were, the less objectifiable I become; there is more of "something else" that escapes from my objectness. This "something else" that is other than my-being-an-object Sartre calls freedom. For Sartre, we can experience our splitting of ourselves from ourselves-as-objects in the first place because of the existence of our freedom; were we to be equal to ourselves as objects, we would not experience this splitting, or even apprehend the Other's look in the fashion that Sartre describes.

Then, a very counterintuitive point we have to draw from this reasoning is this: "this concrete proof of [Other's] freedom which I can effect myself is the proof of my freedom; every concrete apprehension of a consciousness [any consciousness other than my own] is consciousness of my consciousness" (247). In short, the very fact that I am aware of the existence of the freedom/consciousness of the Other—outside of myself—is indubitable evidence that I, likewise, have freedom/consciousness.[8] Then, as long as I reject the idea that there is nothing but objects in the world, I have to admit that I have a freedom. Hence, the paradoxical equation of unfreedom and freedom: what seemed like a "disempowerment" at first due to the advent of the Other leads to an awareness of "empowerment." The persecutor—to bring back the idea of testimony in the Introduction—is "for me," enlisted in my service.

Matters of Choice

Going where it is possible to go would not be a displacement or a decision.

—Jacques Derrida, *On the Name*

So, how exactly do "lone males" and Monk's pigeons fly differently, empirically speaking? Isn't this a natural question? Isn't that the only thing that matters in the shooting arena, or in the prey-predator relationship in general? To be frank, these obvious questions were never resolved for me. Monk seemed rather irritated by my unwieldy empiricism and kept me suspended in mystery. I solicited hints from others. Only one was willing to try a theory, which I will discuss shortly. All of the others were unwilling, but they all reminded me of the bottom line. The bottom line is that Monk's pigeons were the most successful. . . .

Let me try to explain again the physics of the brushed bird's flight pattern. If you recall, the barn birds are said to react to every object-stimulus because they try to "see too much." Monk often replaced the latter phrase with "think too much." The resulting flight is erratic but hesitant and predictable. Brushed birds, in contrast, are supposed to dart through the "flight line that no one else can see." The implication is that the latter do not "see too much," and hence their flights are neither hesitant nor predictable. For Monk, the two contrasting patterns of flight ultimately come down to how the birds "choose," to use his own occasional word. In order to make sense of his idea of "flight line," and the kind of "choice" that it requires, allow me to introduce another important teaching of his. During my training sessions, Monk loved to sing the following mantra of a Zen-like refrain: "A good bird knows that going up is going down, going left is going right, going forward is going backward."

I once provoked him with these lines: "If a bird thinks all choices are the same [the word "choice" had been already established by then], he wouldn't choose. Then, how can he be the fastest or the most unpredictable?"

Although I got his usual response to this challenge—a grin and a dismissal—I think this refrain must be crucial in unpacking his idea of flight line. By association, we can conjecture that the flight line must present itself only to the kind of bird that "knows that going up is going down. . . . " It is about choice, and the kind of choice made by a "good bird" is supposed to result in the fastest and most unpredictable flight.

His instructions were often very brief, enigmatic, or downright incon- sistent. It was obvious that his pigeon language had never been shaped for pedagogy. I do not want to give the reader an impression that I eventually had answers for all of his enigmatic statements. To be truthful to the pre- dominance of confusion that surrounded my entire process of apprentice- ship, I want to include here—without an intention to fully explain—another enigmatic statement of his that gives us a glimpse of Monk's grotesque world of "choice": "For birds, there are only two kinds of people in the world; those who like 'em and those who don't."

I retorted, "How about those who don't care either way?"

"There are no such people," he said.

Both aphorisms or precepts—"going up is going down . . ." and "there are two kinds of people . . ."—testify to Monk's belief in the fundamental im- possibility of choice as we normally understand the notion. The first precept, "going up is going down . . . ," informs an impossibility of choice as there are no meaningful distinctions between given choices. The second precept, "there are two kinds of people . . . ," informs an inevitability of choice as one is forced to choose. Although they seem diametrically opposed, these two precepts interrogate our commonsensical notion of choice in like fashion.

The proposition of the impossibility of choice in "going up is going down . . ." does not mandate a non-choice or non-commitment. As has been reported above, Monk himself eliminated that reading when he (silently) dismissed my conjecture that a bird living by that precept would not bother to choose at all. Rather, I think the precept presses home, in hyperbole, the fact that choices are never discretely independent from each other, but are inseparably intertwined. The same point can be drawn from the second pre- cept, "there are two kinds of people. . . . " According to the second, the world is a stifling place exhausted by two camps, those who like pigeons and those who do not. The two choices here also are not discretely independent from each other, but are inseparably intertwined albeit in the mode of negation. One camp is an inverse version of the other as though they resided on oppo- site sides of a Möbius strip. Both precepts presuppose an extravagant world of exhaustive universality, where there is no "neutral" position to speak of. We may call this universe all-inclusive: whatever is "not-me" belongs to the

Other. We may even call the structure of "choice" that the two precepts touch on "chiasmic locking." For the chiasmic relation that we have established above is about how two entities are inseparably intertwined ("going up is going down . . .")—as one playing the role of condition of possibility for the other—precisely when they cannot "meet" ("there are only two camps . . ."). It seems that, for Monk, when it comes to matters of pigeons, everything comes in exhaustive two-ness. Here, binary scale overwhelms decimals.

This stifling logic of exhaustive (binary) universality is preposterous from the point of view of our usual idea of choice. For our ordinary notion of choice, by definition, requires a variety or multiplicity (to choose from). And when we normally speak of "having a variety to choose from," we imply that we also have a choice not to choose, that is, the non-choice or non-commitment. A choice is not really a choice without the option to abstain from choosing altogether.[9] Such is an indication of the fact that the notion of choice (in our usual understandings) requires the possibility of a *neutral* position (of non-choice or non-commitment). In painting an exhaustive world, Monk's precepts deny the possibility of such a neutral position for brushed birds. Then, the folly of barn birds, in contrast, must lie in their engaging in choice as we ourselves normally would: from a neutral position. But, I have to ask yet again: how does this manifest itself in their behavior? Let us take up the case of the barn bird first before we examine what the flight pattern resulting from Monk's kind of choice might look like.

One day, Monk volunteered to illuminate further why a bird "reacting to every disturbance" necessarily has to be hesitant. It was occasioned by my wondering aloud whether hesitation can also be an evasive move. His answer to this was an unhesitating "No." His reply went something like this: "You are not playing football, you see. Buckshots are not tackles." Then, he added this illuminating line: "A barn bird flies one way and thinks about the other way he didn't take."

I suppose this is what he meant when he said how barn birds "try to see/ think too much," hence the accompanying hesitation. It is not farfetched to think of a situation when we may extend the same advice to a fellow human being who regrets a choice made in the past. We may indeed advise that she or he "thinks too much," that she or he is hesitant for that reason, that she or he is not fully committed to a current project for the same reason, and so forth. We may even try a bit of theoretical erudition and suggest that our advisee is looking back at a choice she or he in fact never had in the first place. These are all likely scenarios. In so advising—particularly in the latter case—we import our sensible intuition that the idea of choice is somehow too artificial a construct to represent the messiness of real lives. For the idea of choice presupposes, shall we say, a level plateau of suspended time-space—whereby a multiplicity of choices present themselves before us fully, discretely, autonomously, independent from each other, and all at the same time as in a unified framework. The function of such a construct is to conceptually capture an imaginary virginal moment, *prior* to our agentive participation in the world, that is, our "messy" commitments. Only in such an arrangement can we entertain a neutral position, that is, the position of non-choice qua non-commitment.

Barn birds' failing in engaging "choice" as we normally understand, then, is an existential failure. In presupposing a level plateau of suspended space-time, the conventional idea of choice vitiates existentialism's deepest ontological grounding: the temporality of the always already. The existentialist subject finds itself arriving at choices "too late." At its most radical, then, as I have stated already, existentialism demands a whole new rethinking of our relation to the world of objects. How might we articulate the subject-object relation whereby the subject finds the world as though arriving at it too late—in the time of the always already—as though something or some encounter thereby is missing? How do we thereby render the elements of what is lost and absent relevant to our experience of the present and the positive? These questions are radical because they throw into crisis one of the most enduring epistemological ideologies of the West: the positing of subject-object relation under the proviso of reciprocal full presences. This ideology presupposes a certain synchronicity or unity in which both subject and object "show up" simultaneously, like two material things in collision. Here, the world of things (objects) is conceptually "placed before" the thinking subject, which in turn renders the latter also something of a thing that is locatable in the world (Weber 1996). The act of "placing before" requires an unequivocal differentiation between the thinking subject and the object thought. In questioning this, Monk, along with Sartre, calls for a revision of our very ideas of causality and objectivity.

How do brushed birds differ? If not our usual idea of choice, exactly what kind of choice do brushed birds engage in—so that for them "going down is going up . . ."? What act of choice is possible when a neutral position— the very essence of our usual idea of choice—is disallowed? I believe with the notion of "probability," Sartre describes precisely that kind of object-multiplicity that confronts us (for us to "choose") when the Other is taken into consideration.

Probability

Sartre designates the way the multiplicity of objects presents itself to us *prior* to our taking the Other into account "possibility" or "instrument-possibility." Without the Other, "my acts are commanded only by the ends to be attained and by the instruments to be employed" (Sartre 2001[1956]:239). But with the appearance of the Other, my instrument-possibility turns into probability:

> The dark corner in the hallway referred to me the possibility of hiding—as a simple potential quality of its shadow, as the invitation of its darkness. . . . But with the Other's look a new organization of complexes comes to superimpose itself. . . . [Now,] the potentiality of the dark corner becomes a given possibility of hiding in the corner by the sole fact that the Other can pass beyond it towards his possibility of illuminating the corner with his flashlight. This possibility is there . . . [but] I apprehend it through my anguish and through my decision to give up that hiding place which is "too risky." . . . [Thus] I apprehend my possibilities from outside and through him . . . somewhat as we objectively apprehend our thought through language at the same time that we think it in order to express it in language. . . . My possibility of hiding in the corner becomes the fact that the Other can surpass it towards his possibility of pulling me out of concealment, of identifying me, of arresting me. (239–40)

An instrument-possibility offered to me by a dark corner can be rendered so only in so far as I apprehend the Other's ability to negate it (causing me to determine it "too risky").[10] With this awareness, I am likely to begin to conceive the potential utility of the dark corner in terms of probability, not instrument-possibility. This is not merely because the same dark corner acquires another "face," turned toward the Other who, in turn, apprehends the object in terms of instrument-possibility. This is also because I become aware of the fact that my *act* of choosing the dark corner itself would be apprehended by the Other within its purview of instrumental-possibles. Probability, then, is a kind of instrument-possibility whose comprehending subject is, in turn, aware of the fact of its being apprehended as part of the

Other's instrument-possibilities. Probability, in short, belongs to the realm of a subject who is aware of having arrived at a scene "too late."

In the world of probability, the act of choosing itself would be apprehended by the Other as part of the workings of the object-world, that is, part of instrument-possibilities. The subject of choice here is no more a consistent, volitional site of mastery and discernment who reserves the option of non-choice or non-commitment. Rather, in the world of probability, we might say that the subject *"becomes" its choice*. Here, choosing to "go up," for example, is not a retractable sampling from a symmetrical and closed set of alternatives—which leaves behind "going down" as unchosen and untouched. There is no "other way he didn't take" left to "think about." Instead, every choice changes the "set" itself, as it were, and opens up the possibility of new "alternatives."[11] Therein, perhaps, lies Monk's "flight line." Flight line, then, is something that becomes visible only to a pigeon already in flight, only to an already engaged subject.

If not in so many words, I already got the drift of Monk's "philosophy" while in the field. Nonetheless, I could not suspend my curiosity as to how Monk's pigeons flew differently, empirically speaking. As I have hinted already, no one volunteered a theory but one: Keefer proved vulnerable to my manipulation of his status insecurity as the second in command at the club. He blurted out one day, as if in a hurry, that Monk's pigeons stagger in mid-flight for no apparent reason. If the flight line is a thoroughly subjectivized space, this makes sense; a pigeon in flight might react to what we don't see "objectively." But this is a fanciful scenario. I think Keefer made it up at my pressing. Deep down, I knew that my insistence on the empiricity of the issue was wrong-headed. I have criticized the "communitarian" thesis earlier for the same wrong-headed insistence. The thesis claims that the statistical probability (of the lessened chance of being preyed upon in a larger flock) is a "knowledge" shared by all parties involved: the individual bird, the collective bird, and, most conveniently, the human observer. Sartre had a name for such a statistical notion: instrument-possibility. If "probability" in the strict Sartrian sense is the only relevant "statistics" in a *socialized* world, my naïve empirical questioning must stop.

Human-Animal Relation beyond Representationality

In Chapter 6, I said I would introduce Monk as an individual who may pose that unmentionable question: why can't there be more than one humanity?

In front of Monk, I became terribly self-conscious about a certain presumed "us-humanness"—or "theyness"—in the question such as "can pigeons really do that?" In the field already, I vaguely felt that my insistence on the objective and empirical observability of difference in Monk's brushed pigeons was unfair. Suppose that the creatures Monk trained were football players. I am likely not to demand the same observability. If a football player is unusually successful in avoiding tackles, that's that; I am not likely to question how the manifest behavior and the player's "internal" thought process—that is, the idea "behind" the training—correlate. If the player professes to engage in particularly trained "choices" in the head, I would immediately take his word for it; his successful behavior is its direct proof. I fully grant a certain homogeneous and indivisible immediacy between the player's "internality" and "externality."

Then, what exactly am I presuming by asking all these questions regarding Monk's pigeons? Such is not merely a question about human-animal relationships. It is also a question about my disposition toward Monk's "beliefs." In short, it is also about intra-human or cultural difference. Monk's daily life, which is singularly devoid of human contact and replete with that with pigeons, testified to the arbitrariness of such a presupposed us-humanness. Besides, I could not decide which world was more opaque to me, Monk's or the pigeons'. In the face of his opacity, I lacked confidence to boast of Agamben's "unitary world" between us. Of course, Monk talked—that signature mark of division between humans and non-humans. But I had a hard time deciding whether Monk's speech added clarity or mystery. Increased time around Monk by and by disposed me toward readily entertaining an intra-human difference—or, shall we say, cultural difference—in equally abyssal terms (as we might with other species). This development was unexpected. Instead of an increased sense of rapport with pigeons, which I had presumed would happen, my time among pigeons sensitized me to the limits of rapport in general regardless of the species concerned. Perhaps Monk's solitude was rubbing off on me.

His misanthropy might have been too. Just like his "lone males," Monk in his person seemed to testify to the absence of any kind of smooth continuation between the individual human being and its collectivity. For Monk, homogeneity could not be assumed on either side, for humans or pigeons. In fact, he might have avowed more abyssal difference between brushed and barn birds than between humans and pigeons.[12] An ethologist's perspective could not be more different. A scientific statement on animals seems to necessitate a certain mutually opposing homogeneous frontier between humans and animals. Animals' "theyness" cannot possibly be posed without the correlating "us-humanness." In that sense, an ethological statement is always implicitly about humanity too. And both sides, in order to grant themselves a certain homogeneous indivisibility, assume an intra-group homogeneity, which in turn requires a certain individual-collective rapport.

In the end, I cannot claim that my bird phobia was cured after the apprenticeship. But, in retrospect, my expectations from Monk could have been persistently misplaced. I habitually resorted to the idea that the "cure" was about me, just as might happen with a therapist. But, perhaps, Monk was "brushing" me. Perhaps, he wanted me to learn the pigeon tricks, to become a lone male and find my own flight line. That way, I might turn off both the "third gaze" and the creaturely life it excites in me.

Self-Reflexivity and Finite Thinking

The fieldwork upon which this book is based was conceived during the time the so-called self-reflexivity movement was raging in the disciplines of ethnographic writing. It is not surprising that "seeing oneself seeing" became my central trope. I was partially attracted to the challenge of giving a "self-reflexive" account to already hyper-reflexive practices, be they "frivolous" hooliganism or the mimetic doubt in conspiracy theorizing. What is the relationship between this reflexivity and that reflexivity—one that "reflectively" stops the turn and the other that "irresponsibly" (in the sense developed in Chapter 5 per conspiracy theory) proliferates? Is the distinction as straightforward as Sartre's admonition to us to stay on the side of the "man of reason" (with self-reflective "openness"), as he characterized the person diametrically opposed to the passionate frivolity of anti-Semites (1986[1948]:28)? I want to dwell on this relation in this closing chapter.

There are two relevant trends to be considered as per the self-reflexivity movement's historical milieu. Anthropology's "reflexive turn" in the United States began in the mid-1980s along with two other trends: (1) the currency of Michel Foucault's motif of "the gaze" in the Anglo-theoretical scene; and (2) the appeal of the aesthetics of "white nihilism" in the wake of the civil rights struggle, which, according to one account, also concerns the gaze (Newitz 2001). Both left traces on anthropological reflexivity's visual trope of self-reflexivity. A reflection on the contemporaneous appeal of white nihilism occasions an insight into the reason why anthropological reflexivity was selectively influenced by Foucault's idea of the gaze made panoptic. I will associate this influence with the ideas of perversion and whiteness.

White Nihilism

Toward the end of the twentieth century, observes Annalee Newitz, self-loathing became one of the major tropes in white racial self-representation in the United States (2001:133). It was caused by the civil rights attacks on white privilege, and their effect was an internal contradiction in the white racial identity. According to Newitz, the contradiction consisted of, on the one hand, fears about the unavailability of a total "white power," and, on the other, guilt over white racism (133). Self-loathing was a symptomatic displacement of that contradiction. Its unspoken aim was "racial absolution and innocence," and its method involved renunciatory gestures of self-deprivation and self-shaming rituals. Newitz names as "white nihilism" this loose assemblage of exaggerated self-loathing aesthetics, which had come to permeate the popular culture of American white "working-class" youth beginning in the mid-1980s.[1]

At a deeper level, the discourse of self-loathing aims to render its speaker impervious to criticism (Newitz 2001:146–47). Its prime literary example Newitz finds in Fyodor Dostoyevsky's famed figure of the "underground man." The underground man "never allow[s] others to see him as humiliating himself *before* he sees himself in that way" (William Miller quoted in Newitz 2001:146). Notice that it is the gaze that announces itself as the figure's key. For "no one can insult you if you've insulted yourself first," Newitz quips, and she appropriately calls the strategy "preemptive self-hatred" (147): "Preemptive self-hatred can confirm one's sense of superiority. White supremacy and nihilism are mutually determining, contradictory, aspects of white-identity. . . . As a form of white self-naming, [self-loathing] certainly avoids the potential failures embedded in white supremacy" (2001:147).

Newitz's description of white nihilists seems intuitively persuasive; it is almost as if we are acquainted with *individuals* like that—such as hooligans at the Labor Day Shoot. I find this readily conjurable empirical concreteness—so much so that we can visualize individual human beings—an obstacle to whiteness studies. Indeed, the hooliganism in Hegins seems to realize Newitz's notion to perfection with its circular trajectory of seeing oneself seeing, with its shunning of the outsider's gaze, and with its exaggerated cruelty verging on self-humiliation. But my reservation is in her precipitous linking of self-humiliation with the rewards of superiority and supremacy. For the kind of "warrant" I have described, apropos the Labor Day Shoot, hooliganism was more ironic than self-righteous, more restless than "fully remunerated." After all, "frivolity" does not lend itself to self-certainty. I associated it with the feminine complaint. In the spirit of comparing two "reflexivities," I first turn to the anthropological reflexivity.

Seeing Oneself Seeing in Anthropological Reflexivity

By "reflexive anthropology," I do not necessarily mean the so-called textualist persuasion associated with inaugural names such as James Clifford, Stephen Tyler, or Vincent Crapanzano. My focus here is on the kind of reflexive move marshaled as a *criticism* of said textualism, especially in the name of political economy of power after Foucault. I am motivated by the peculiar way in which this criticism came to inhabit the loose discursive space known as "reflexive anthropology": simultaneously inside and outside, both as an internal criticism[2] and as a pervasive background (as it represented the emerging dominance of Foucauldianism across disciplines)—"like oxygen" by one estimate (Boyer 2003:58).

There, the figure of the Panopticon, implicitly or explicitly, became the staple of the mental landscape of anthropological reflexivity as Foucault's *Discipline and Punish* and *The History of Sexuality, Volume I* became de facto textbooks on matters of the gaze. The reigning figure there was, tentatively put, "seeing oneself seeing oneself" as a gesture of self-exposure on the part of the ethnographer-author. What needed to be rendered visible was the horizon of hegemonic frames that predetermined what could be made visible and invisible, while the horizon itself remained invisible. Revealing the culturally specific and historically contingent nature of such preconceits was the work of anthropological reflexivity par excellence. As an example, let me examine one of the trendsetters in this direction: Paul Rabinow's *Writing Culture* contribution, "Representations Are Social Facts" (1986).

After arguing for the relevance of Foucault for anthropology, Rabinow lists relevant research strategies: "Epistemology must be seen as a historical event—a distinctive social practice. . . . We do not need a theory of indigenous epistemologies or a new epistemology of the other. We should be attentive to our historical practice of projecting our cultural practices onto the other; at best, the task is to show how and when and through what cultural and institutional means other people started claiming epistemology for their own" (Rabinow 1986:241). He then goes on to advise James Clifford, the supposed representative textualist, that "representations are social facts"—that is, "a system of ordered procedures for the production, regulation, distribution, circulations of operation of statements" (240). The textualists' "blind spot," he continues, is none other than the "refusal of self-reflection" (251–52). In other words, what is lacking is the clear view of "in what field of power and from what position in that field any given author writes" (252). The implication is loud and clear: at worst, textualism is complicit with power. Rabinow's criticism shares its impulse with the present work to an extent: it is against the idea of self-reflexivity as some sort of textual technique deployable by an already formed author-subject. However, Rabinow's prescription of what the self-reflexive gaze should be radically differs from mine. Let me explain.

Apropos the Panopticon, Foucault treats the gaze as the very marker of the world-limit; *there is no other gaze "outside" that casts shadow on it.*[3] This inclination subtends Foucault's poststructuralist commitment to the radical finitude of the world, that is, the thesis of the impossibility of "metalanguage"—as in "all experience is an experience of signification." The gaze is thus the condition of possibility of the knowable world, and hence, its horizonal limit; it is the prison wall of an unsurpassable field of knowability that is positively sanctioned by the historically specific network of social and institutional relations. The question of truth is immediately that of the regime of truth, the positively identifiable/describable social organization involved in producing and distributing the truth. This militant prioritizing of the *positivity* of the social saw an immediate rapport with the social constructivism in anthropology.

Exposing, objectifying, and substantializing such a concealed gaze (of power) in the fashion of Foucault's aforementioned work has been the task par excellence of anthropological reflexivity. Rabinow's above intervention is paradigmatic. In a humbling gesture of self-exposure, the gaze of power is confessed to have been—I emphasize this—*coincident* with that of the anthropologist, and the reflexive anthropologist volunteers to capture the heretofore invisible anthropological eye "from behind," as it were. Thus, what is called for is a resituating and rendering visible of the "baggage" of the anthropological apparatus of power within a wider social and historical "context" (Kondo 1986:74). In short, "more context" was called for.

We may pause here and ask what might be the exact relationship between the Panoptic gaze and the self-reflexive gaze that professes to contextualize the former. And we can pose the question in a Kantian fashion (see Chapter 6): how can a subject at once coincide with the condition of possibility of the Panoptic gaze and become contextualized in it—that is, become what appears to it? Surely, such a subject would not experience power as an "objective" and externally confronting force.

Foucauldian Metaphysics

For Foucault (especially, of *History of Sexuality, Volume I*), "power" is the name of that which contrives the two Kantian dimensions to coincide; it is that which makes it possible for the subject to render itself visible to the process of self-surveillance. Power not only provides the subject with a gaze; the subject itself becomes visible to and by that very gaze. Power thereby forges a kind of loop between "seeing" and "being seen," as no subject's imagination can or even tries to reach beyond this frontier. To think otherwise for Foucault is an essentialism, an admittance of "metalanguage" beyond our acts of signification. "Truth of power" here directly equates with "power of truth" (Deleuze 1988:95).

In short, there is nothing outside of power. All differences and oppositions—say, that between Clifford and Rabinow—can be positively described within the context of power relations. For the Foucauldian Rabinow, then, power is the nominalist name of an absolutely immanent medium in terms of which self-reflection (which Clifford allegedly overlooked) qua contextualization is limitlessly possible. The effort that is worthy of the name reflexive anthropology, from this view, is a tireless amassing of contextualizations of the researcher's gaze within the political economy of knowledge.

But whence could a statement such as "nothing is outside power" issue from? From inside or outside power? The position that traverses both inside and outside at once Carl Schmitt designated as the "point of exception" and reserved it as a signature positioning gesture of the sovereign figure (Schmitt 1985). For, as we have seen in Chapter 6, the sovereign is the one who can utter: "I, the sovereign, who am outside the law, declare that there is nothing outside the law" (Agamben 1998:15). By thus situating itself both inside *and* outside, the sovereign (self-)grounds the very possibility of distinguishing the inside from the outside, the lawful from the unlawful. The sovereign figure, in other words, is the one who occupies the point of (extralegal) exception from which to declare that there is no metalanguage to legality. The point from which the legal authority issues is outside of, and invisible from, the nominalist legal reality thus predicated. Timothy Mitchell has observed a similar "logic of exception" operational at the level of institutional authority. For him, institutions self-legitimize, become both the agent of generative force and the object thus generated. Hence, an institution's authority issues as though from a transcendental beyond—and never just immanent in the positivity of institutional relations as Foucault had portrayed (Mitchell 1990:569). Thus, "the state needs to be analyzed . . . not as an actual structure but as the powerful, metaphysical effect . . ." (Mitchell 1991:94).

Metaphysics, according to Eric Santner, is an attempt to self-legitimize and self-possess from a point of exception (2001: chap. 1). Perversion is the name we have entertained for it in the Introduction. In this light, we may critically interrogate the anthropological motif of reflexively securing one's own gaze as a historically locatable object of inquiry. Anthropological reflexivity leaves the principle of the panoptic gaze unthought precisely to the extent that it renders its own gaze an object of inquiry; historicizing itself, anthropological reflexivity fails to theorize that captivating surplus "point of exception" from which the discipline's productive trade in the positivity of the social is organized. If ethics begins, for Kant, from the admittance of the fact that "what I see is never All" (see Chapter 6), seeking the point of exception is truly a "preemptive" kind of posture. In this anthropological posture, not among the hooligans of the Labor Day Shoot, Newitz's logic of white nihilism as prideful self-loathing is complete.

Toward "Totality"

It is worth asking why other schools of thinking have not isolated the issue of self-reflexivity as a disciplinary endeavor as in ours. The Francophone tradition poses a contrast. In the French tradition—as it heavily bore on German critical thinkers, such as Kant—being-with-others was to experience shadow qua limit, and to experience it was synonymous with self-reflexivity. And this "experience" included the anthropological kind of knowing. I want to offset this notion of self-reflexivity qua sociality against what one might label the Anglo-theoretical idea of self-reflexivity.

Nowhere is the Francophone idea of self-reflexivity more lucidly argued than in Lévi-Strauss's *Introduction to the Work of Marcel Mauss* (1987)—that is, despite my criticism of the author in Chapter 5. In the passage below, he makes explicit how the French way of conceptualizing society as "total social fact" was already a thesis on self-reflexivity; how it was already a commentary on the state whereby the researcher is part of the "picture" she tries to decipher: "To call the social fact total is not merely to signify that everything observed is part of the observation, but also . . . that in science in which the observer is of the same nature as his object of study, *the observer himself is a part of his observation*. ... [Thus, the social scientific object is] object and subject both at once; or both 'thing' and 'representation,' to speak the language of Durkheim and Mauss" (1987:29, some of the emphasis added). It is because "the observer himself is a part of his observation" that society is both "object" and "subject," or "thing" and "representation." Why? The reference here is not to the hermeneutics of a multifaceted objective world but the phenomenology of the *Other subject*. What is different from hermeneutics is how the Other subject renders the anthropologist an object. It is this additional fact that deems society both object and subject.

Lévi-Strauss's phenomenology of the Other is directly indebted to Jean-Paul Sartre as I wrote in Chapter 7 (2001[1956]:230). Recall that for Sartre, the Other's look/consciousness introduces into my world an orientation that is other than mine, but it is an orientation only in so far as my access to it is necessarily barred from me, hence opaque to me like an object. That orientation exerts its influence on me by announcing its existence without lending its "content." And among the inaccessible "content" is myself as object. To be an object, as we saw, means that an exhaustive sense of what I am cannot be available to me. Hence, insofar as there is the Other, "I cannot be an object for myself" (246). A paradoxical point Sartre derives from this is that the more "objectified" I become in the gaze of the Other, the more "unequal" I become to my body qua object. Hence, the more objectness that the Other takes away from me, as it were, the less objectifiable I become; there is more of "something else" that escapes from my objectness. This "something else," which is other than my being an object, Sartre calls "freedom." For Sartre, we can experience our splitting of ourselves from ourselves as objects in the first place because of the existence of our freedom; were we to be equal to ourselves as objects, we would not experience this splitting, or even apprehend the Other's look in the fashion that Sartre describes.

Lévi-Strauss derives his idea of sociality from this shared "dislocation" qua freedom. Society is possible for him here not because we share common positive characteristics (such as worldview)—again, despite the earlier criticism—but because of the shared negativity or shadow (see the Introduction), that is, an enigmatic part of myself that was given birth to on account of the existence of the Other consciousness/orientation. He calls such a shared enigma "unconsciousness," which for him is the only way through which self and other are connected in a form other than "already existing subjects." "[This is why] psychoanalysis allows us to win back our most estranged self, and in ethnological inquiry gives us access to the most foreign other as to another self. . . . Going down into the givens of the unconscious . . . is *not a movement towards ourselves*. . . . The unconscious would be the mediating term between self and other. . . . *We reach a level which seems strange to us*, not because it harbours our most secret self but because, without requiring us to move outside ourselves, it enables us to coincide with forms of activity which are both at once ours and other" (2001[1956]:35–36, emphasis added). For Lévi-Strauss, in this passage, then, society is neither in the self, nor in the other, but *outside both*. The society is "total"—both subject and object, representation and thing—in the sense that anyone participating in it needs to experience "dislocation"—desubjectification as much as subjectification. It is never an intersubjectively shared positive reality. Recall that, for Lévi-Strauss, the reality of total social fact became visible in the first place because of the self-reflexive nature of anthropological inquiry—that is, the researcher is part of the "picture." Self-reflexivity here is not a technique deployable by an already formed subject. Rather, it is a willing submission to dislocation and desubjectification, that is, a becoming-object to the Other's gaze. It is an ethical gesture of confronting one's own "enigma" as a social being. We called this self-loss or shame earlier.

The Enunciative Sociality

The inability to appreciate the "total" nature of the subjective-existential dimension of sociality Pierre Bourdieu called "objectivist bias" (for example, 1990:191–97). An objectivist fails to comprehend a degree of willful self-division from the representational knowledge on the part of the subject that is necessary for a successful consummation of a cultural practice. The subject, for Bourdieu, is a product not of a coincidence with the registering/anchoring point of the field of the gaze's horizon but of a certain non-coincidence, that is, to the extent of its *dislocation* from the prescribed representational "content." Thereby, Bourdieu tried to articulate the enunciative-onto-logical dimension of culture.[4] What we see "on the ground" of cultural practice is hardly ever a fully present agent, but an agent in the mode of a patient—who sees as if in the mode of being seen, chooses in the mode of being chosen. For this reason, one cannot give as a fully present subject. To do so would humiliate or to be perceived as proud. Rather, one gives as if already given.[5]

This is why, according to Jacques Derrida, gifting cannot be reduced to the *intersubjective* matters of exchange, contract, or debt. Rather, due to its ability to bracket or shadow agency, the act of gifting momentarily conjures into view a certain transcendental, anonymous "spirit" of sociality itself (1992:17). As mentioned in Chapter 6, Emile Durkheim may as well have called it the "real" of collective force (see Fields 1995). It is "real" in the sense of being an "illegible" Thing. On account of its Thingness, the collective whole that is posited here is without plurality of *contingent* parts; it is not some kind of positive global assemblage of apparatuses of power or regimes of truths. Rather, the "magic" here is that an individual event of enunciation is thought to directly "touch" the Totality—*without parts, without mediation*. How this is so is perhaps the reason for the continuing fascination with the practice of the gift: a mere object—a thing—is able to expropriate the subjective agency and make it seem as though it is the Totality of society itself that gives and receives.

Conspiratorial Disproportionalism

By "disproportionalism" in conspiracy theory in Chapter 5, I meant such an immediate trafficking between individual and society or between part and whole. The "illegible" (il)logic of a conspiracy theory is such that, as I wrote, the injury of displacement from the knowledge of the Other—its opacity and illegibility—somehow earns the "testifier" a right to directly "touch" that very Other's sinister power. The language deployed in conspiracy theory acts like the Durkheimian Thing in that it materially and eventally—as in "the tradition is dead and the Hegins shoot does not know it!"—bears the inscription of the Enemy's power. It actively assumes passivity. Then, the point I made about conspiracy in the end is a commonplace wisdom in the anthropological conventional—at least, what *used to be* the anthropological conventional. It is the ruse of the finite existence. My point simply is that the totalizing nature of conspiratorial knowledge—without parts and mediation—should be seen in the light of Lévi-Strauss's "totality." The researcher's reflexivity (the reflectivity of the "man of reason") is already part of such a "picture," fully taken into account.

Then, it is worthwhile to make note of why the Foucauldian analytics of power, and the anthropological reflexivity it informs, cannot make account of the enunciative-mimetic dimension of conspiratorial sociality. Conspiracy theorists are not essentialists despite themselves; they actively choose to be so. They are militantly uninterested in the ideas of "partial truths," of the contingency of meaning, of the Foucauldian wisdom that their version might be merely one of many "regimes of truth." For "disproportionality" is the name of conspiracy theory's logic.

Sacrifice as Self-Inadequation

After all, then, conspiracy theorizing around the Labor Day Shoot is not that different from the pigeon business. In Chapter 6, I spoke of the illogic that subtends the event: "There was a loss of the past . . . and so pigeons must be killed." Pointing out animals' abyssal difference, I also observed how it is that the animal tends to facilitate such a "jump in logic." It is time that I dwell on that point. I will identify similarities between the pigeon business at hand and how language is used in conspiracy theorizing.

So, let us say that the Labor Day Shoot is a case of sacrifice, as Bronner readily does (2005). How can we speak of what is at stake in sacrifice in terms other than those of representationalism? Let us bring back Jean-Luc Nancy's take on sacrifice. He observes that the West has never tired of censuring the so-called economism in the early sacrifice—as in "Here is the butter, where is the offering?" (2003). Western theologians' fitful reactions to economism received the earliest anthropological commentaries on the subject (for example, Frazer 1959:144; Harrison 1903:95). What proved most preposterous to the Western eye was a certain disproportionalism between the insignificant material surrendered and the boundlessness of the blessing requested. To the Western eye, nothing was really "sacrificed"; only its simulacrum (qua replica). As I have noted, this called for sublation, interiorization, or spiritualization into the figure of self-sacrifice.[6] At issue was a disproportional reciprocity, as it were, and the figure of self-sacrifice served as a corrective "balancing" of accounts.

As a parallel case, we saw Papuans/Melanesians' calling selling/buying or lending/borrowing by one name. Jacques Derrida pointed out this curious need to *mask* a gap that is also its *marking* (1992: chap. 2). "Marking" because one lexical sign is imposed to reveal, rather than conceal, the irreducibly imbalanced and syncopated operation that reciprocity inevitably is. By showing the representational inadequacy of the lexical sign, what is thus negatively marked is unmaskability itself, as it were. That way, *the inadequacy of the sign directly and immediately bears the imprint of the excess*

which it cannot possibly "represent." Derrida elsewhere names such an aspect
of the sign "self-inadequation" (1981:139). Coming back to sacrifice, we see
then what the ruse of the figure of self-sacrifice tries to achieve: what the
figure tries to mediate and close is the very "gap" that the early sacrifice
deliberately tries to leave open precisely by an untenable attempt to traverse
it—as in the formula, "Here is the butter, where is the offering?"

Hubert and Mauss's work on sacrifice perhaps speaks this analytical language of "disproportionalism" (apropos sacrifice's economism) with the most
numerical precision (1981[1964]: chap. 5). Indeed, the underlying aesthetic
impulse of their work on sacrifice cannot but be characterized as disproportionalism or imbalance. This is evident in their privileging of agrarian sacrifice as the paradigm of all sacrifices. For, there, we have the most dramatic
juxtaposition between what they called "concentration" and "diffusion" (78).
In the agrarian sacrifice, the extent of concentration is such that the victim
"receives the name or even the form of animal or man," they write (79). Upon
immolation, the victim becomes diffuse again, "vague and impersonal" (78).
At times, they further note, "the connexion with what it embodies becomes
so remote that it is sometimes difficult to perceive" (78). Perhaps herein lies
the "illegible" offense of economism: this leap from extreme concentration
to diffusion, from materiality to spirituality, and from particularity to gen-
erality—which is unbridgeable by any sensible representational reckoning.
It is this abrupt leap, this disregard for any sensible mediation, that Hubert
and Mauss call *apportionment* characteristic of sacrifice.[7]

This answers the question that drives their famed work: how is it that the
most diffuse can be accessed only through the most concrete, the most spiritual through the most material? This paradox touches on Emile Durkheim's
own most mature—and often unappreciated—attempt to overcome the sa-
cred/profane dualism. To paraphrase that formulation: the profane is none
other than the name for the sacred's inability to be fully itself. Likewise, materiality is the name for spirituality's inability to be fully itself. Seen this way,
the sacred needs the profane to be what it is; spirituality needs the material
to be what it is. Herein lies the most compelling reason for the existence of
religious rites. Within the same reasoning, Hubert and Mauss write that
in sacrificial rites, "the two worlds that are present [that is, the sacred and
the profane] can *interpenetrate and yet remain distinct*" (1981[1964]:100).
They "draw close to each other, without giving themselves to each other entirely" (100). We can speak of the gift in exactly the same terms: it is that

which draws together antithesis precisely in order to reveal unbridgeability. It masks *a* difference in order to reveal, so to speak, the "thing-in-itself" of Difference, which I previously referred to as unmaskability.

Finite Thinking

What simultaneously inspired and disturbed the Western sensibility about sacrifice, then, was its strange power to organize compossibility between opposites. It is a technique of the compossible that does not remain bound to the condition of the Lévi-Straussian mediation (qua univocal reproducibility of the same as seen in Chapter 5). It is rather closer to im-mediation; an im-mediation that institutes a transcendental form of mediation; a subtraction that paradoxically effects an excess. Such a subtractive "communication" Nadia Serametakis calls touch (1994). A subjective experience of touch is impossible except at the same time being-touched, to wit, without becoming an object of touch. To actively initiate touch is simultaneously to assume passivity. In this sense, touching is possible because the experience is always already other to itself—precisely because the subject cannot experience "all" of it. Touch as necessarily a shared experience epitomizes the moment when Self and Other, to repeat Hubert and Mauss, "interpenetrate and yet remain distinct." Although Hubert and Mauss do not use the notion of touch, their description of the sacrificial rite very much conjures its image. For the moment of the rite is when the sacred and the profane each becomes other to itself—as if touching each other. For this to happen, the absence of any intermediating mechanism is a requirement.

This brings us back to Nancy. His thesis on sacrifice appears in the monograph titled *A Finite Thinking* (2003). With the notion of finitude, Nancy envisions sociality that is freed from the ideas of representation, common sense, and empathy or sympathy. How else can we conceive of the sharedness of experience? How can we talk about communication that is other than a reproduction of the content of communication? His answer is finitude. The idea of touch looms large in that exposition. To experience touch, Nancy argues, is nothing other than to experience our limit, to experience ourselves as though we are already Other. Nadia Serametakis would agree (1994). Touching "communicates" not by externally appropriating the Other but by expropriating my own privative resource, by becoming an Other to myself. It is a familiar sagely wisdom according to which destitution, for sheltering nothing, immediately and directly accesses wealth. As such, finitude immediately accesses some kind of infinitude or transcendence; and disempowerment, empowerment.

As a case of finite thinking, Nancy invokes Georges Bataille's figure of looking into the night of darkness. Such is "the sight of nothing rather than a nothingness of sight," Nancy quips (2003:37). Because we are so deprived of the "content" of sight, what we begin to see is the act of seeing itself; that is, the thing-in-itself of sight: "seeing nothing and seeing that it sees nothing, it sees the faculty or the power of seeing reduced to itself" (38). Being alone with the faculty of sight . . . I wonder if this is the very aim of conspiracy theorizing, which is necessarily an experience of obstructed representation. Shall we call it a technique of partaking of the power of the unrepresent-able Other through an im-mediate touch, thus directly bearing its insidious inscription? As such, conspiracy theorizing is a work of magical transfor-mation of disempowerment into empowerment. "Seeing nothing and seeing that it sees nothing. . . . " Isn't this also the reason Monk cannot accept blind pigeons among his gallant troops?

Remnants of Whiteness

> Going down into the givens of the unconscious is not a movement to ourselves. . . . We reach a level which seems strange to us.
>   —Claude Lévi-Strauss,
>   *Introduction to the Work of Marcel Mauss*

> Whoever experiences shame is overcome by his own being subject to vision. . . . [Shame] is an experience of being present at one's own being seen, incapable of moving away and breaking from itself.
>   —Giorgio Agamben, *Remnants of Auschwitz*

One afternoon, I was back at Tom Klinger's place. My excuse this time was that I needed to fetch a tool in his possession for Bob Shade. Tom disap-peared into the garage for a good stretch of time, so I began sorting through a stack of albums on a coffee table. One of them stood out because pieces of yellowed paper were sticking out on the side. It was a scrapbook of some sort, a loose collection of photographic testimonials to life's precious moments of manly bravado—successful hunting expeditions, Tom baring a giant scar on his side, Tom with a pair of crutches, Tom's brother holding a fat cigar with his prosthetic hand, and so on. And there were newspaper articles on the Labor Day Shoot—lots of them. One big article attracted my attention because it had been carefully secured with tape, unlike the others. It was on a famous incident in 1991 when Tom got into a fistfight with a well-known buffoon of an animal rights activist from Chicago. I felt a sudden sense of camaraderie with this gruff man who was a fellow scrapbook buff documenting the shoot, and I asked him if he had more of those. He pretended not to hear me and immediately disappeared again. As he reemerged, I repeated my question. And Tom, perhaps sensing that I could not be easily ignored, groaned in a surprising sheepish manner: "Oh, I just happened to have these. . . . Some guys have a lot of these, not me; Jon's even got videos."

"You mean Jon Lubold?" I asked, and kept turning the pages.

At this, Tom suddenly came over and turned the album to the last page. I gasped and recoiled: there were dried pigeon parts, a head and a wing, flattened and secured like preserved mementoes of dried leaves.

"It's from last year," muttered Tom, grinning widely and putting the album away—deeply satisfied at the quick result of having me give up in disgust.

I did not get to see Jon Lubold's famed extensive collection, though he himself enticingly alluded to its existence. Like Tom, Jon also implicated other Labor Day hooligans in this seemingly inglorious practice. From Tom, Jon, and, later, others, I came away with a strong impression that such a collection evoked embarrassment, even shame.

It was a shock for me to discover the precious trophies of their media-directed passion side by side with pigeon parts, the violently reviled "rats with wings"—and mutilated pieces at that. I was at a loss as to how to reconcile this "hidden" trace of shame with the consistent triumphantalism I saw from the hooligans. In any case, I decided to take the scrapbook as a self-reflexive document of sorts.

But what kind of document was it? In order to differentiate it from the reflexive ethnography of the kind criticized heretofore, let me employ Foucault's category of archive from *The Archaeology of Knowledge* (1972). Foucault defines it as the positive fossilized dimension that abides by the imprint of the realm we have earlier referred to as enunciation (1972:130–33)— precisely the territory of his archaeology. It is a trace not of the text of discourse but of its taking place; not the positive biography of subjectivity but a negative imprint of the moments of "desubjectification"—in short, a shadow. Well, then, if an archive is a trace of that which necessarily "escapes capture," as I have described above, what sort of archaeological materialization is it? What exactly do we have to "collect"?

The temptation to avoid here is the sociological "striking of balance": an archive is not some kind of "unofficial" documentation whose addition would make our study more complete—in as much as enunciation is *not* an additional feature to semantics. Rather, an archive is that which bears witness to the experiences of being *subject to* desubjectification. According to Agamben, Foucault offered only one piece of material evidence to the notion of archive:

> This text is "The Life of Infamous Men," which was originally conceived as a preface to an anthology of archival documents, registers of internment or *letters de cachet. In the very moment in which it marks them with infamy, the encounter with power reveals human existences that would otherwise have left no traces of themselves.* What momentarily shines through these laconic statements are not the biographical events of personal histories . . . as suggested by the pathos-laden emphasis of a certain oral history but rather the luminous trail of a different history.[8] What suddenly comes to light is not the memory of an oppressed existence, but the silent flame of an immemorable ethos—not the subject's face, but rather the disjunction between the living being and the speaking being that marks its empty place. *Here life subsists only in the infamy in which it existed; here a name lives solely in the disgrace that covered it. And something in this disgrace bears witness to life beyond all biography.* (1999b:143, emphasis added)

Nothing more remains to be said about Tom's archive. I would only add that such is history without an objective *warrant* by the "third gaze"—of the nation, of the media, of the NRA, of the Ku Klux Klan. Such is history that is foreclosed of any possibility of self-possession. Whether such an archive still bears the name "whiteness," I really cannot tell anymore.

NOTES

Introduction

1. Pseudonyms are used for all field informants and some geographical names. The decision of the Supreme Court of Pennsylvania had opened the floodgate of possible lawsuits, in the face of which the organizers voluntarily stopped the event.

2. For a crucial conceptual distinction between "seeing," "looking," and "gaze," which is not my immediate concern here, see Zupančič 1996.

3. This requirement for joking/speaking on behalf of some consentaneous normativity, positing oneself as its instrument, would make the phobe a bad "joker," for the kind of "necessity" that the world of a phobe sustains (as seen above) is based on subjective singularity, the insistence of "for me."

Furthermore, this point is echoed in the frequent observations on racism's latent desire to solicit an organic community into existence. Lee Baker, for example, has shown a close link between the eruptive popularity of race theories in late nineteenth-century America and the rise of the professional middle-class "community" as the theories' main body of readership (1998). Etienne Balibar, in contrast, has called racism "spontaneous knowledge of the masses" in the sense that it promises an "imaginary transcendence of the gulf separating intellectuality from the masses" (1991:20). Race theory, particularly—without which, for him, racism does not exist—provides "immediate interpretive keys not only to what individuals are *experiencing* but to what they *are* in the social world" (19; emphases in the original). Both authors impart racism's hidden but ever present fantasy for an instantly available organic community—revealed either in the idealist hopes raised (among the professional middle class) for the communitarian potential of the new media apparatuses for propagating race theories (Baker 1998) or in the populist dream of the magical disappearance of all social divisions/antagonisms (Balibar 1991).

4. The philosopher Alain Badiou uses the phrase "subject-language" to refer to our perception of an event that is paradoxically *both* "more than the subject"—that is, more than a subjective illusion—*and* possible in the first place only to a "believer" who is already part of it—for example, the resurrection of the Christ (see Žižek 2000:135–36). I will take up this point again below under the theme of the "universalization of the particular."

Chapter One

1. The literature on the history of taming "cruel sports" in England and elsewhere is vast. See Burke 1978, Malcolmson 1973, Ritvo 1987, Thomas 1983, Thompson 1980[1963], and Yeo and Yeo 1981.

2. In the statewide coal-mining scene, between 1951 and 1962 the total number of employees in coal mining (anthracite and bituminous) decreased at the average annual rate of 34 percent; between 1963 and 1982 the decrease tapered to 10–15 percent. The figure began to climb again between 1983 and 1985—the latter of which is the year of the first protest at the Labor Day Shoot. The period saw the sharpest rate of decrease since 1962: 32 percent. U.S. Department of Commerce, Bureau of the Census, CBP-74-40).

3. I never overcame the impression that this suddenness aims for entrapping the unpatriotic elements among the crowd, as if to test the readiness of their allegiance. For the shoot supporters never tire of pointing out who moved about during the anthem. Needless to say, they are always "outsiders" largely, and "protesters" more specifically.

4. During the seven times I have attended at the shoot, I have seen two women shooters.

5. A similar line of images is mobilized by the animal rights activists against what they contemptuously call "the locals," whom they characterize as lazy and overweight "wife beaters," "alcoholics," "drunk drivers," and "smokers."

6. I am not here testifying from a moral distance. Needless to say, a birdphobe fails to distinguish the victim from the victimizer, the bird from its wonton slaughterer. The emotion I am trying to impart here is well captured in Alfred Hitchcock's film *The Birds*, which achieved an effect only a birdphobe might fully appreciate: birds first enter the frame from behind the camera, "as if materializing out of the mysterious intermediate space between the world of the spectator and the diegetic reality on the screen" (Žižek 1994). It is as if the birds swarm out of, and in spite of, "myself," the unsuspecting film-going spectator-voyeur.

7. Dan Nerle is exaggerating here. "Steve," though always the most impudent and colorful protester at the shoot, draped himself in a black martial arts uniform (and a black beret) for only a couple of years.

8. There was a general intensification of this trend during the time of my observation. But it was not a smooth development from its first introduction in 1989. Some years lapsed into violent clashes. The year 1991 was by far the most violent protest.

9. Tom has repeated this phrase on numerous occasions.

10. This information was acquired through participation at the leading animal rights organizations' annual convention for the shoot's protesters in Harrisburg the night before Labor Day. After a banquet, there are instructional sessions for the participating protesters, divided into different protest activities—mainly divided between "rescue" and "documenting." Since documenting acquired prominence, I availed myself of the training sessions for the reporters and photographers involved in the organization.

11. Similarly, when the Society for the Prevention of Cruelty to Children censored the appearance of children in staged performances in the late nineteenth-century United States, various reasons were cited, such as the danger of lightly clothed children catching cold on the stage or night performances getting in the way of proper bedtimes, but nothing was feared more than the possibility that those children would eventually abandon their families to run off with the troupe (Gilfoyle 1986).

Chapter Two

1. Certainly, mass mailing is a generalized phenomenon in twentieth-century American culture, from all sorts of "sweepstakes" to searches for missing children (see Ivy 1993). But when it comes to the concerns that amount to social movements, one might theorize a special affinity between direct mailing and non-human causes: of all the contemporary social movement issues in the West, animal rights activism and Greenpeace lead in the use of direct mail (Jasper and Nelkin 1992:74; cf. Godwin and Mitchell 1984:832). An organization's heavier dependence on mass mailing means that there is a deepening "division of labor" between its elite activists and its mass supporters, between a small cadre of committed, and paid, activists and that ghostly entity of passive, household-bound spectators whose individual influence on the cause thinly hangs on the checks they send in response to donation drives. A mailing-centered movement such as animal rights activism neither encourages mass participation nor provides social networking among its patrons but only asks for checks. In return, the elite activists promise to be a surrogate vigilant eye against possible cruelties toward animals, outside and away from home.

The rubric "professionalization" in social movement studies loosely captures this sharp division of roles between "performing" activists and (financially) "supporting" activists (for example, Gusfield et al. 1994, McCarthy and Zald 1973). But direct mailing has attracted only cursory attention from these studies as a mere "method" employed by social movement organizations to solicit financial support from the general public, as a mere carrier of ideology but not *the very form an ideology takes* (cf. Madison Social Text Group 1979:170). Neither do the theories of mass-media technology usually cover the "techniques" of mass mailing. Nonetheless, not only is direct mailing one of the core tactics of conservative politics in mass society (Madison Social Text Group 1979, Sabato 1983:160–64); its operation assumes and applies the same fundamental desires and anticipation regarded as essential to the workings of the mass media (see Ivy 1993). Foremost, a social movement organization designs solicitation mail specifically to be read in individual households. Moreover, direct mail is almost exclusively geared toward soliciting donations, and the "social problem" the organizations try to sell is unabashedly packaged as a commodity. Under these conditions, the messages are bound to be personal—even more so than television messages since mailings do not intend more than one reader per household. A celebrated political consultant craftily sums up this necessity for the intimate tone in direct mails: "[Use] the medium not as a large public address system but rather as a private undress system," "a door into your home" rather than a "window onto [sic] world" (Tony Schwartz quoted in Sabato 1983:157).

2. People for the Ethical Treatment of Animals was originally founded in 1980 by Alex Pacheco and Ingrid Newkirk. James Jasper and Dorothy Nelkin report that the Silver Springs case was a cornerstone not only for PETA but for the emerging animal rights movement generally (1992:30): "The publicity given to the case from 1981 to 1983 inspired the formation of animal rights groups around the country" (31). They further point out that through these images "PETA gained enough publicity—including coverage on the Phil Donahue Show—to build animal rights' first successful direct mail campaign" (31).

On PETA more generally, Jasper and Nelkin observe the following: "[PETA's] membership grew exponentially throughout the 1980s, reaching 8,000 members in 1984, 84,000 in 1987, and 300,000 in 1990. PETA's expansion reflects the rapid growth of the entire animal rights movement during this period. Although less wealthy than the large welfare organizations, PETA today is probably the richest of the new animal rights groups. . . . Almost all its revenues came from contributions and membership dues" (31).

3. The actual intruder to the lab did not identify himself as belonging to PETA but to Animal Liberation Front, which is an underground, cell-structured, guerrilla group whose members are widely suspected to be from major animal rights organizations.

4. Estimation from *Animal Times* (1994–95).

5. See Warner 1994 for a relevant discussion on "abstraction" in the disaster discourses of journalism (esp. pp. 393–94). In a similar line, Brian Massumi observes that "[the disaster in the mass media] exists in a different dimension of space from the human 'here,' and in different dimension of time. . . . It is everywhere by nature" (1993:11). He calls this tendency "a loss of the specificity of the landscape of fear" (23). See Benthall 1993 for a similar point made on the discourses of disaster relief organizations under late capitalism.

6. The newsletter often deliberately drops the distinction between the undercover agent and the whistle-blower as a narrative progresses, as though whistle-blowers are already half-way undercover operatives for PETA. Also, the newsletter habitually leaves ambiguous the identities of those helpers other than PETA agents (for example, an inspector from the USDA). This is applied in photographic techniques, too. Often, street demonstration scenes are shot in such a way that onlookers on the street blend with the PETA protesters. On closer inspection, one recognizes the same faces again and again from different pictures of what seem like mass uprisings (for example, PETA 1994–95:4).

7. See Ivy 1993:233 for the relevant literature on the growing perception of the breaking down of the family during the Reagan and Bush eras.

8. As Annette Kuhn observes, "Meanings do not reside in images . . . : they are circulated between representation, spectator and social formation" (Kuhn 1996:53).

9. The word "celebrity" is preferred to "star" for my purpose here since the latter

presumes the existence of an on-stage character in a restrictive sense. John Ellis even restricts the definition of star to the cinema. My use of the word "celebrity" veers toward that used by Joshua Gamson (1994). By focusing on the audience activities, or "celebrity watching," Gamson relaxes the requirements of "stage role" from the definition of the word and holds as its minimum requirement the fact that millions of eyes regularly behold the person.

10. In a related but a different sense, Alan Beck and Aaron Katcher observe that pet animals are "transitional objects," or thresholds between the outside and home" (1983:86).

11. Another celebrity-related discourse in PETA's newsletter is that of revealing the "secret" of a celebrity's vegetarian recipe. This further supports my point here: that celebrities are used by PETA to bring down the stars of mass publicity to the level of the mundane that the newsletter readers share.

12. For Doane, the coverage of catastrophe—for example, a plane crash—provides a moment of legitimating the referential credibility of television precisely by thrusting in disruption or indeterminacy to the normal televisual time and programming, where there is normally very little room for "accident" (1990:233). This moment of catastrophic disruption—when commercials stop, routine schedules are ignored, and anchors improvise—occasions a spontaneous, precarious, and unpredictable point of contact with reality, an irreducible testimonial to the Truth with a resounding message that "television was there." Such disruptive anchoring of referential validity, to paraphrase Doane, remedies television's signifying problematic caused by the perpetual deferral of contact with reality, a symptom of the impulse to regiment down to the minutiae in regular television programming (324).

13. However, underneath the bloodstained fur garment that the model scapegoats as gaudy glamour is a naked body that is itself an object of mass desire. In the name of uncovering the ugly side of the publicly sanctified glamour, PETA holds up this mass-idolized body-object as the utopian image of intimacy; by pretending to "undermine" the fashion industry, PETA celebrates the very mechanism it attacks. Just like the daytime television programs' gesture of "assault" on the primetime, PETA's campaign joins the celebration of a bigger mass-desire industry—while sacrificing the fur industry, whose glamour, arguably, had been fading anyhow—through the backdoor, as it were.

14. Ellis's citing of right-wing vigilantism as a case of "non-involvement" sounds ironic in the midst of the barrage of new right militancy in England and the United States in the 1980s and the 1990s. It seems that the more prudent question to ask with Ellis's findings is how such a systematic depraving of the audience's viewing power by the mass media allowed the right-wing pugnacity we witnessed at the time.

15. Peter Singer's book *Animal Liberation*, which many consider the bible of modern animal rights activism, was first published in 1975, and its sales peaked between 1984 and 1987 (Jasper and Nelkin 1992:177).

16. Singer defines speciesism as "a prejudice or attitude of bias in favor of the inter-

ests of members of one's own species and against those of members of other species" (1990[1975]: 6). The term was coined by Richard Ryder (1975).

17. The reason the MSPCA was initially founded sounds a bit outlandish to the contemporary ear. George T. Angell, the president of the society, recalled that it was to provide "better and more wholesome meats for our citizens, by improving the methods . . . practiced in slaughtering and transportation" (*ODA* January 1888:28). The first assignment of the society, thus, was the slaughterhouse monitor. It was iterated again and again in the early issues of the magazine that ill treatment of animals turned their milk and meat poisonous to humans (Angell 1888:114).

18. On this change, the *Annual Report* of the Illinois Human Society provides a clearer instance. Those who previously possessed the authority akin to police, for example, limited arrest warrant, in the humane organizations were simply called "agents." This title changed with the weakening of their power to "special police officers" in 1904, the label "police" self-consciously added precisely around the time they were losing police authority. In discussing the history of the American animal protection movement in the nineteenth century, it has to be noted that the American humane organizations did not go through the kind of power transition that occurred among their British counterparts, from the upper class to petty bourgeois members in organizations such as the Royal Society for the Prevention of Cruelty to Animals since the 1870s. Most British antivivisection organizations were established by the petty bourgeois members who split from the mother organizations largely run by aristocratic members. Antivivisection was not popular in England until 1881 (Ritvo 1987:161).

19. Also, see the Illinois Humane Society's *Annual Report* (1896:34).

20. The *Annual Report* of the American Society for the Prevention of Cruelty to Animals ranked the most cruel deeds in the following order: (1) cruelty by cab drivers; (2) cruelty during the transportation of animals; (3) exhibition of animals, such as P. T. Barnum's shows (1893:10)

21. This point is consistent with that of Michel Foucault. In *Discipline and Punish* (1979), he depicts the historical emergence of the humane discourse of "representation" in terms of efforts to abolish public displays of torture and execution, that is, in terms of what we might call the techniques of the humane observer (Crary 1990:15). For him, changes in the punitive measures of the judicial system were paralleled by progress in the discourse of humanely representing criminals as the victims of violent spectacles of punishment in the Old Regime. Hence, the reformers' outcry against public displays of punishment had been increasingly couched in terms of caring for the "humanity" of the criminals. He mentions two components that together organize the humane technique of observing cruelty: the "discourse of the heart" and the "spectatorial" distance (1979:91). A sort of "double-dealing" between both moments, it was the sentiment of those *middle* classes who had vested interest in distancing themselves both from the power of the king, which manifested itself in an excessive display of revenge upon the condemned body, *and* from the illegality of the criminal—both from the punisher

and the punished, or from the victimizer and the victim. In short, the technique of observing the spectacle of cruelty, which was increasingly voiced in terms of speaking for the "humanity" of the criminals, contained a bifold move. On the one hand, the humane representative feels for the criminal's torment as though "in the first person." From this vantage point, the savagery of the crime by proximity displaces itself to the executioner, and by extension to the power of the king, and the violence of the punishment becomes conflated with that of the crime (1979:9, 57). On the other hand, the representative is a "disinterested" third-person subject who, unlike the victim itself, has absolutely nothing at all at stake in the punishment displayed.

22. Another, widely accepted similar view regarding the European context is the argument that the issue of animal welfare was used to lay a firmer hand on the lower classes and to stamp out radical elements from them through stricter discipline (Ritvo 1987:132; Thomas 1983:185–86; Tester 1991:89).

23. One kind of "cruelty" that received attention in almost every issue of *ODA* was the "docking" of horses, a clipping of the tails of horses that was then in vogue in British high society. *Our Dumb Animals* jeered at this mimicking of the British upper class by the American wealthy and the privileged with more contempt than toward any other abuse of animals. This anti-aristocracy, anti-British stance is crucial in studying the American humane movement. As has been mentioned above, the first humane society, the ASPCA, which came into being in 1866, conscientiously tried to avoid the upper-class heritage of its British parent organization, the Royal Society for the Prevention of Cruelty to Animals, whose stormy clash with its petty bourgeois members shook and ended up splitting the organization in the mid-1870s.

24. The example Bhabha elaborates is the color of the skin in colonial racist discourse. Racism, as an instrumental regime of knowledge that contains and subjugates the difference of the colonial Other, "impedes the circulation and articulation of the signifier of 'race' as anything other than its fixity as racism" (1990:80), only as that marker of familiarity that tames the opacity of Otherness into transparently readable signs of inferiority/superiority. Hence, stereotypes of the Other race always vacillate between extremes, from the most desired to the most derided, from the loyal servant to Satan, and so forth. In this sense, a fetishistic knowledge always turns to the paradigm of the "primordial Either/Or," observes Bhabha (1983:27). Hence, "the black is both savage and yet the most obedient and dignified of servants; he is the embodiment of rampant sexuality and yet innocent as a child; he is mystical, primitive, simple-minded and yet the most worldly and accomplished liar, and manipulator of social forces" (85). In *ODA*, similarly, the working class is depicted *either* as those most viciously cruel to animals *or* as the kindest and most empathetic with animals to a fantastic degree (to the degree that the sight of kindness unites the anonymous urban masses of all classes "in a common tie of good feeling"); *either* working-class proximity with animals signals the apocalyptic image of human degeneracy *or* it holds redemptive potential. That is to say, the animal as a fetish in *ODA* articulates the maxi-

mum and the minimum of the possibility of the working class—either as the ideal humanity or its degenerate, bestial Other.

Chapter Three

1. Around the shoot controversy, visual and audio recording equipment was easily identified with the protesters and reporters for well-founded reasons. Hence, my carrying it became a liability for my safety. I dropped the camera altogether after it was kicked and smashed by an unknown assailant at a Labor Day Shoot (see Chapters 1 and 3). I kept carrying an audio recorder but used it only when among very trusted familiars. My quotations are generally from handwritten field notes of a tiny size. I will at times use quotation marks for non-verbatim quotes whenever clarity is called for. I will indicate what few quotes I can claim as verbatim.

2. In the Fund for Animals' analysis of the shoot in 1993, of the 75 percent of the total number of pigeons observed, 30 percent were "dead immediately," 47 percent were "injured and collected," 11 percent were "injured and not collected," and another 11 percent were "not injured."

3. As will be explored in Chapter 4, the majority of those registering for the post-1985--protest shooting competition are from outside the county, often out of state, and even from foreign countries. These outsider competitors are held in suspicion by the local supporters.

4. I use this term after British football hooligans. In the late 1960s, broadcast television cameras were first introduced to British soccer games. Along with the camera marched into the permanent landscape of the game the football hooligans, a cult of fan rowdies who appropriated the stands as their public arena for staging violent white working-class masculinities in the age of accelerating deindustrialization (Taylor 1982:154; J. Williams 1991). This historical coincidence stimulated the question of media-event interpenetration: Which induced which, hooliganism or television? Deviating from the causal and intentionalist explanation/accusation of "sensationalistic newsmaking" prevalent within the early Birmingham cultural studies group (Hall 1978:25; see Clarke and Clarke 1982), John Clarke has entertained a more semiotically dynamic view. He suggested that there came an unintended collusion between the media text and hooligan activities: On the one hand, television's re-packaging of the game for the detached and passive television viewership demanded an increased dramatization and "immediacy" of its image through highlighting the situated excitement of the stadium crowd; on the other hand, hooligans consumed the media's melodramatic representation of fan enthusiasm and then nostalgically re-presented in the space thus "illuminated" by media the now eroded working-class neighborhood fan-territorialism and masculine exploits (J. Clarke 1978:56). The significant value of this intervention for my inquiry is how Clarke, with this suggestion, has broken free from the dichotomous "encoding-decoding" model of mass communication (Hall 1980), and intimated the "participatory" and shifting relations of production/reception (see Berland 1992), the mass/the local, or media-text/eventhood.

5. On one Labor Day evening, during a group viewing of television news, I heard one hooligan interject a passing sarcastic remark about Jim Schaeffer, saying that he makes "tons of money" by representing the shoot, when news footage showed the attorney delivering a fiery rhetoric on communalism. Once outside Hegins Township, it is not uncommon to hear negative comments about the elites of the shoot, especially the attorney. Although local professionals are revered as the ones who are in the position to effectively and knowledgeably represent the regional society vis-à-vis the political and legal challenges of the "outside" mass society, for precisely the same reason, that is, their affinity to "city slickers," they are viewed with resentment and suspicion. See Vidich and Bensman 1968 for a similar observation.

6. Hooligans usually did not compete at the Labor Day Shoot, the minimum cost for participating in the shooting contest being $85, which can go up to $400 depending on the number of games one chooses to participate in. As I will develop in Chapter 4, hooligans tend to be rather contemptuous of those who compete at the Labor Day Shoot.

7. "Independent" here means self-employment, outside a contractual relation with big mining companies. Hence, these are small-scale coal holes, with no more than seven or eight laborers, frequently from the same extended family. Their work is rough and often extremely dangerous, for safety is not as rigorously monitored by the government. Independent miners are staunchly anti-unionist, many of them still believing that too much labor strife has cost the mining industry in Schuylkill County. Moreover, being "independent," they incline toward the values of small entrepreneurs and are militantly "producerist," and so tend to idealize manual labor and economic self-sufficiency, and antagonize merchants and creditors.

8. Upon being asked about occupation, the most common answer from the hooligans is "machinist" or "machine operator," which includes all kinds of blue-collar occupations. I have heard some farmers who are not landowners describe themselves this way. And a surprising number of people who label themselves with the term turn out to be descendants of miners. I have encountered very few full-time miners, or at least they tend to emphasize their secondary jobs. But since mining involves many other forms of work, for example, bulldozing or carpentry, the alleged secondary jobs usually turn out to be subservient to mining.

9. For example, information on the organized anti-Semitism within the county is not available.

10. For an explicit linking of British football hooliganism with white racism, see Ware 1997.

11. The actual coverage of this event by the national media has been intermittent: two appearances on the *NBC Nightly News* and a few editorials in *Newsweek* and *U.S. News and World Report*. But these and other well-known national media such as the *New York Times* maintain crews at the shoot every year, even when not reporting, perhaps in anticipation of a possible incident worthy of reporting. In 1995, a documentary film, *Gunblast: Culture Clash* (dir. Eddie Becker), was made about this event and was aired in the program titled *Weekend* at a station based in Washington, D.C.

Internationally, the shoot was a subject of German and Spanish television tabloid programs in 1996.

12. The overwhelming majority of the animal rights protesters participating at the Hegins demonstration are from major metropolitan areas, such as New York City, Philadelphia, Boston, Baltimore, Chicago, et cetera. They annually hold a banquet the night before Labor Day in Harrisburg, the location of their base camp. None stay within the Hegins region.

13. Hegins is located about ten miles west of Interstate 81, which runs north-south along the Appalachian mountain chain through Harrisburg. This four-lane highway becomes congested around the Hegins exit on Labor Day afternoon. Spectators gather from all over central and eastern Pennsylvania, but a look at the license plates of the vehicles parked indicates that the majority are from Schuylkill County.

14. The entrance is always a contentious spot. In order to make the protest difficult for the protesters, who need a great deal of back-and-forth movement between the park and its parking lot (where their makeshift headquarters is located), the shoot officials, beginning in 1994, imposed the fee of five dollars per admittance. For the general public, this was only a minor discomfort, since the fee can be reimbursed as food items from vendors inside the park. For vegetarians, however, this food stamp was worthless because of the total lack of meatless choices. Hence, frequent arguments break out with the protesters at the entrance, which was the reason for the reinforced security, armed with much machismo.

15. This is not the exact line, for I wrote it down a few days later.

16. Primarily concerned in these studies are broadcasts of royal weddings and coronations (Dayan and Katz 1985, Zelizer 1991), important sports events such as the Olympics (MacAloon 1984, Rothenbuhler 1988), and military parades and state funerals (Tsaliki 1995; also see Handelman 1990: appendix).

17. In Silverstein's words, "Tense involves only a relationship of simultaneity/ sequentiality of events" (1994:32), which is an *ordinal* concept that necessarily assumes a deictic situatedness. In contrast, the modern notion of clock-mensurable time that has evolved since the late medieval times in Europe was a journey from an ordinal to a *cardinal* notion, from that which was deictically anchored in authorizing reference points (such as the municipal lord's tower clock according to which all other timing devices were calibrated) to that implied by the abstract notion of duration, "portable" on any clock face (cf. Dohrn-van Rossum 1996, Landes 1983, Le Goff 1980). I owe this point to Michael Silverstein's seminar "Language and Discourses of Mensuration" held at the University of Chicago (spring 1998).

18. In this sense, the notion of media event presupposes a "success"—both for the event and its theorization—for the theory postulates, in the spirit of John Austin (1975[1962]), that an event's identity is self-defined by the "proclamation" at the ritual center. In Dayan and Katz's words, "media events have the power to redefine the boundaries of societies" (1992b:197); they prescriptively circumscribe territories while proclaiming the "identities" of the events for us.

19. I call the reader's attention back to Silverstein's criticism that Anderson, specifically his idea of social membership as equivalent to free and homogeneous spatiotemporal occupancy, reproduces the hegemonic ideology of the Standard Language. Along the same line, we can also problematize Anderson's borrowing, and his partial reading, of Walter Benjamin's idea of homogeneous, empty time. Has not Benjamin attacked the idea of "progression through homogenous, empty time" as the temporality of the ruling class (Benjamin 1968:xiii)? Against Stalinism's concept of the historical progress of mankind (a case of progression through homogenous, empty time) Benjamin conceived of the revolutionary history as "a structure whose site is not homogenous, empty time, but time filled by the presence of the now" (xiv), that is, the moment when the continuity of the winners is broken (Žižek 1989:143).

20. An example of non-citationality for Derrida would be John Austin's notion of the "performative," since Austin excludes from his definition of successful performatives "infelicities," such as deception, duplication, or mimicry (Austin 1975 [1962]:8–9).

21. Taussig's inspiration here is Walter Benjamin's observation on the "immediacy" of modern visual media (Taussig 1992, 1993). It was not identification but alterity, not technological transparency but primitive mimesis, that Benjamin regarded as pivotal to the workings of modernity's new imaging technologies (Benjamin 1968:217–51). It is not identification but a miming of the Other, not coevalness and simultaneity but primitivism, that defines the relation between the (Western) viewer and Nanook, and that constitutes the appeal of "immediacy." The viewer's taking up of the "authorial voice" of the primitivist colonial narrative in this image hinges precisely on Othering and the assertion of spatiotemporal *discontinuity*.

Here, we come to a seemingly paradoxical proposition that the frontierist rhetoric of "having been there" is predicated on an organization of spatiotemporal discontinuity. For Walter Benjamin, contact was the effect that modernist visual apparatuses privileged, but that being effected not through a rationalized perspectival technique of representing the truth of objects in space—that is, spatiotemporal continuity—but through the sensorial impact of "touch," whose intense ramification he observed from the "tactility" of Dadaist works (1992:143). Such a participatory and tactile contact he identified as mimesis and opposed it to the movement of signification such as the psychoanalytic sense of identification (Shaviro 1993:52). Building on Benjamin, Taussig suggests that mimesis is a magical realism that not only expresses but also manipulates reality, and likens it to the primitive sympathetic magic articulated by James Frazer and others, which mobilized both powers of imitation and contagion, similitude and contact (1993: chap. 4). For example, a hoof print used in sorcery is visually an "imperfect ideogram," a poor replication, but it partakes of the substance of the horse, a testimony to the fact that contact was made (1993:53–57, 220).

There are theorists of television who would argue that such a *mimetic* rhetoric of "having been there," not the literal sense of spatiotemporal continuity and synchronicity, is the central organizing technique of "live" television (for example, Doane 1990,

Ellis 1982, Feur 1983, Morse 1983, Stam 1983). It is now a commonsensical wisdom in media studies that television is the preeminent machine of decontextualization (for example, with its interruption of the solemnity of a funeral with commercials), of the "flattened" signification without depth, that requires a periodic compensatory validation of its referential authority vis-à-vis the "outside" reality and the unity of "real time." A media event, for the notion's advocates, occasions precisely such a compensatory recovery of authority and depth by way of tangibly displaying normally abstract entities such as the national public, owing to the power of live television that relays dispersed elements together on a "single" spatiotemporal plane. Meanwhile, a mimetic representation presses so close to the represented that it partakes in the substance of the latter, making the "medium" indistinguishable from the referent. For Mary Ann Doane, what television presses so close against to give the effect of immediacy is death, an ultimate Other (1990:222–39), for information threatened with annihilation transfixes the viewer. Thus television for her is a medium that mimes a constant flow of modulated catastrophic shocks: accidents, injuries, disasters, et cetera—a medium that subsists on the limits of technology rather than its prowess.

By miming catastrophe and death, Doane argues, television supplements its claim to transparency with a sensuous contact, with testimony to the fact of "being there." More specifically, it mimes the corporeality of bodies "on the scene": the fleshy mortality of victims, onlookers' tangible signs of emotions, or bodily situated on-site reporters (1990:233). These are precisely the images foregrounded in the coverage of the Labor Day Shoot. And just as our knowledge of the doomed primitive Other renders an image of first contact more arresting, more sensuously susceptible, the looming termination of the pigeon shoot "tradition" heightens the commodity allure of the shoot's televised image.

22. This exchange was accidentally audio-recorded, with the recorder "meant" for television.

Chapter Four

1. In North America, the perception of pigeons as agricultural pests has not been extensive. For example, a major American review of avian pest control excludes feral pigeons from a list of "the most common major bird pest species in the world" (Dyer and Ward 1977). On the same note, Johnston and Janiga declare that "feral pigeons are no longer agriculturally consequential in North America" (1995:265).

2. She is misinformed here, for it was only in the past that shotgun shells contained lead. Regardless of her accuracy, however, what is significant, as is to be developed below, is how she perceives the bird as no longer edible. Though I have not met anyone who claimed to still consume pigeons, the traces of past consumption are everywhere. For example, the traditional serving at the local Independent Miners' Picnic (see below) is the pig roast and the soup called "blind pigeon and sweet corn soup," with the substitution of chicken today. (No one could explain to me why it was called "blind.")

3. I have encountered some men who professed to have "stolen" dead pigeons at the Labor Day Shoot during the Great Depression and sold them by hiding in the bush behind the southern end of Hegins Community Park where "out of bound" but injured pigeons were likely to land.

4. The author of a sentimental memoir on the county's old pigeon shoot tradition (1993), Patrick Canfield is an unmatched pro-shoot zealot. The book concentrates on the miners' cult of pigeon shooting in Schuylkill County in the 1920s and 1930s. Written directly in reaction to the protest, its historical vision is highly selective. But the volume is the only written document to date on the leisure of the region's early miners, an important addition to the extensive area historiography that had paid disproportionate attention to work-related miners' cultures.

5. The poetic power of this stretch of reasoning is buttressed by another equation between outsider-protesters and pigeons, or pests generally. "We don't have very much use of pigeons in this area" is another widely used phrase around the Labor Day Shoot.

6. The conflation of "poisoning" and "drug" is prevalent in the discourse of the shoot's supporters, as can be heard from Herman Clemens's observation, "You don't see people who shoot pigeons shooting drugs." The logo of the official T-shirt of the 1990 Labor Day Shoot was "Shoot pigeons, not drugs." There is a widely held belief among the shoot's supporters that the animal rights protesters are predominantly drug addicts and homosexuals, and so one year they were nicknamed HIV. A false rumor and panic spread in 1996 that an animal rights activist, who was infected with HIV and had only six months to live, was coming to the shoot strapped to a bomb.

7. Due to grain transportation, train yards and shipping docks provide year-round feeding sites for the granivorous feral pigeons.

8. Dead pigeons are gathered in oil drums and transported to the Mopac Rendering Division in Elisabethville, Schuylkill County, to be turned into fertilizer. The shoot leaders are so proud of this "recycle" factor that the logo of the 1999 shoot T-shirt reads, "We recycle," with a cute cartoon of a shooter dropping his dead pigeon into a bin.

9. A systematic census of the feral pigeon population is reputed to be a hopelessly difficult task, and is a much-disputed issue. One study asserts that a census of visible birds would miss about 23 percent of the true total; another calls for the minimum of one year of observation (Johnston and Janiga 1995:229).

10. In the minds of the older generation of practioners, this teaming up seems to have a strong reference to the "buddy" system in coal bootlegging during the Great Depression.

11. The different way in which West Enders hold their guns from the rest was a perpetual source of disputes and fights throughout the matches chronicled by Patrick Canfield (1993). The non–West Enders called their rivals' way of holding the gun "high-gun position," and theirs, "fair-gun position." These refer to the different ways a shooter can hold his gun while waiting for a trap to open. Obviously, the closer the shooter has his sight to his eyes the quicker the firing, and the closer the target, will be. According to non–West Enders, the high-gun position was a sly invention that bent the ambigu-

ous pigeon shoot rule that the gun must be held "below the elbow" before the bird takes flight. Technically, the high-gun position keeps this rule by having the eyes already lined up with the sight but with the elbow unnaturally raised high above the gun.

12. The composition of the selected birds is extremely complex, an outcome of an elaborate game plan against the opposing shooter that takes into consideration each bird's personality and breed characteristics. Clearly, a description in terms of plumage only, as above, does not suffice.

13. Some pigeons were made to travel in a draped cage. They were the ones in the process of having their sun-oriented, physiological time reset for a particularly intended "surprise" maneuver on match day. For each bird's physiologic clock is reset at sunrise each day to accommodate the daily shift in the sun's position, and artificially manipulated day/night cycles can "clock-shift" the birds earlier or later than real time, which results in the shift in direction of their flight trajectory relative to the sun.

14. Regardless of the actual gender, pigeons are referred to as males in the pigeon shoot arena, in contrast to the animal rights protesters' reference to them as females.

15. An increasing number of trappers in the region are nowadays breeding pure albinos, but for a different use than trapping. Flying white "doves" for wedding pictures is in vogue of late in the area, providing an extra source of income for trappers.

16. This observation was easy because those who registered to compete in the Labor Day Shoot were given a separate parking lot in order to guard them from the protesters' vandalism.

17. The county had experienced the influx of garment manufacturers from New York City in the 1930s and 1960s, in concert with the waning mining industry during the same times. The mining-centered historiography of the region has scarcely looked into the history of the region's garment industry, which promises interesting insights on the gendered labor history.

18. In the region, the term "bootlegger" designates an illegal extractor of coal. For an account of an elaborate pigeon-shoot culture developed among this group especially around the Great Depression, see Canfield 1993.

19. The population of those of German ancestry within Hegins Township had been close to 90 percent throughout the twentieth century. It declined a little in the 1990s. For example, in 1990, residents of German ancestry numbered 2,793 out of 3,505 (*Census of Population and Housing* 1995). The *Citizen Standard* still runs a column in the "Dutch Language."

20. This has been confirmed by the photograph archive at the *Pottsville Republican*. For the historical linking of Jewish "conspiracy" to the tradition of witchcraft in the Middle Ages, see Barkun 1994:116.

Chapter Five

1. The talk was given to the Anthropology Department Colloquium, New School for Social Research, December 5, 2007.

2. Touch is a kind of subtraction that paradoxically effects an excess. Such a sub-

tractive "communication" is precisely what Nadia Serametakis articulates by the term "touch" (1994). A subjective experience of touch is impossible without becoming an object of touch. To actively initiate touch is simultaneously to assume passivity in being touched. In this sense, touching is possible because the experience is always already other to itself—precisely because the subject cannot experience "all" of it.

3. Like the "nerve weakness," they contend, conspiracy theory is "an embodied anxiety that articulates the stresses, contradictions, and dreams of redemption of a subject under the influence of diffuse and haunting . . . force fields" (Harding and Stewart 2003:264).

4. "Conspiracy theorists have an irrational tendency to continue to believe in conspiracy theories, even when these take on the appearance of forming the core of [a] degenerating research program" (S. Clarke 2002:131).

5. The opposing view I have in mind here is a ready identification of Descartes' cogito as an instance of the most egregious "cognitivism" in whose opposition the "body" or "habitus" is celebrated. See, for example, D. Clarke 2004 and Lau 2004.

6. The difference with Harding and Stewart's approach I am articulating here converges on the idea of the body. The Cartesian perspective I deploy here also summons the figure of the body as a central notional apparatus that commands the dissipation of rationalist impetus. But it is a body that is quite distinct from Harding and Stewart's prescription. Their body is a figure of unmediated mirroring of social influences, of the "nervous system" or of the "structure of feeling" (Harding and Stewart 2003:264). Although said to be reflective of societal contradictions, their idea of embodied mirroring itself is in the order of accord and the imaginary. The psychoanalytico-ethnological body, in contrast, is *not* a medium that enables an expression (even if of an instance of "contradiction"). As has been mentioned per cogito and the idea of witnessing, it rather actualizes, "gives body to," a certain "impossibility," cohering together only to reveal irreducible incoherences. In the Introduction, I called such a body "creaturely life" qua direct embodiment of "injunctional impossibility." I will pursue this linkage in the next chapter.

7. This particular example was originally authored by Jacques Lacan. I borrowed it here because Bateson's own example is not as concise. His own example for the play frame consists of three sentences: "All statements within this frame are untrue"; "I love you"; "I hate you." To this, he appends the following explanation: "The first statement within this frame is a self-contradictory proposition about itself. If this first statement is true, then it must be false. If it be false, then it must be true" (2000[1972]:184). He includes non-human animals in this, if not linguistic, capacity.

8. By the expression "the ones that self-write the condition of their own enunciation," I have in mind the kind of ethical gesture implied in Foucault's prescription of ethnology. Necessarily apropos the singular individual (not social), Foucault's ethnology belongs in the realm of historicity rather than that of history. "We must always start over," quips Jacques Derrida, referring to the similar gesture founded on faith's singular individuality in Kierkegaard (1995:80).

9. The literal referent in Derrida's passage here is the Greek god of "writing." In the pages referenced here and in many other parts of the essay, Derrida uses the words "writing" and "mimesis" almost interchangeably.

10. Dominic Boyer very usefully captures the complex proximity this way: "anthropology of conspiratorial knowledge often takes the form of a process of exposition of ideological reason by critical reason, a process that seeks to validate the former's basic rationality even while asserting the latter's powers of rational correction or perfection" (2006:31).

11. In Derrida's original, the Greek word *pharmakos* replaces the scapegoat. The quoted passage, which is originally that of J. P. Vernant, is lifted from the pages in which Derrida equates *pharmakos* with the scapegoat (Derrida 1981:130–33).

12. For what proved most preposterous to the Western eye, according to Nancy, was a disproportionalism between the insignificant material surrendered and the boundlessness of the blessing requested. Hubert and Mauss tried to capture this aspect by the term "apportionment" (1981[1964]). (The term is in the French original *prélèvement* [1899].) It captures a certain disproportionalism between the material concreteness of the sacrificed "victim" and the abstract "spirituality" of the wished-for effect. One might say that the efficaciousness of a sacrificial rite calls for the reversibility of opposites—from the concrete to the abstract, from the material to the "spiritual," from particularity to universality, and so on. Such a reversal is different from replacement or substitution, which belongs to the order of resemblance or equivalence. It is rather, if I continue to follow Hubert and Mauss, a paradoxical technique of availing the most diffuse through the most concrete, the most spiritual through the most material. As Nancy notes, thus, to the Western eye, nothing was really "sacrificed," only its simulacrum. To the Western eye, the early sacrifice thus called for sublation, interiorization, or spiritualization. The sublated Western versions he mentions are those of Socrates and Jesus Christ; the Westernized sacrifices were self-sacrifices.

Chapter Six

1. The subject for the final two sentences is "the West" in the original. Contextually, Nancy uses it interchangeably with "representation" (see 1993:1).

2. This normative binarism is challenged by the presence of the Baumans (see Chapter 4). Instead of analysis, Bronner subsumes this challenge as an "irony": "The irony is that the original protest of the event was instigated by a resident of the region" (Bronner 2005:435–36).

3. Darnton implies a connection of this episode with the violence of the French Revolution half a century later. Some suggest a similar pigeon connection. In the seventeenth century, French aristocrats kept very large flocks of dovecote pigeons, which foraged in the agricultural countryside. But farmers were prohibited from killing the birds, contributing to the accumulating animosity that erupted during the Revolution (Cooke 1920).

4. In the same article, Darnton also turns to other "cultural idioms" of the period,

such as the witch hunt, charivari, and carnival mock trial. However, his reference to
the theories of Leach and Douglas remains as an implicit warrant for his other, ancil-
lary explorations. See Fernandez 1988 for a critical assessment of Darnton's use of
anthropological theories.

5. I owe this point to Valerio Valeri's *The Forest of Taboos: Morality, Hunting, and
Identity Among the Huaulu* (2000). Page references below are to the manuscript. To
paraphrase his argument at hand here: Leach simultaneously talks about taboo as
repressing boundary percepts that lie between verbal categories and as applying to
categories which are anomalous with respect to clear-cut oppositions. Therefore, there
is a slippage from a theory of taboo as repression of intermediate (and thus uncatego-
rized) percepts to a theory of taboo as "applying" to what is in fact categorized and has
not, therefore, a purely perceptual, interstitial reality (2000:30).

6. I owe James W. Fernandez for this summary formulation of what was initially
a messy idea.

7. As I will elaborate below, it was Sigmund Freud who in his *Totem and Taboo*
most powerfully showed the subject/object ambiguity in the "law" of prohibition: the
violator of taboo himself becomes a taboo. Freud held up this aspect against the view à
la Douglas and Leach that the law of prohibition *precedes* human participation.

8. More specifically, the notion of homology shows a strong impetus toward invent-
ing a singular unifying system of meaning. This was especially conspicuous in Darnton,
whereby even "incompatible cultures," with their directly conflicting "grids" of classification, found themselves legible to each other within the universalizing conceptual apparatus, "commonplaces of French Folklore." The notion of "ambivalence" summarizes
that impetus in that its equivocation allows even conflicting attitudes—say, toward the
cat—enumerable from one and the same classificatory grid.

9. The relevance of Valeri's work for my overall purpose proves limited. First of
all, despite Valeri's naming of his theory of taboo "negative morality," his overall reference to the tradition of critical theory or psychoanalysis is tangential. For example,
although he makes a cursory reference to the Freudian notion of repression, his theory of the subject is far from being centered on lack or decenterment. Instead, Valeri
deems the economy of desire as entirely translatable into the politics of the permeating
body. That is, for him, the problem of identity is that of the body politic. Hence, moral
principles (that is, the ideas of pollution or taboo) only concern the maintenance of
bodily integrity against external threats of disintegration. He writes that "the loss of
[the subject's symbolic] integrity is represented in bodily terms, and viewed on the
model of disease—that is, as a vulnerability of the body to external agents capable
of invading it . . . —[this] is due to the fact that the subject exists in concrete form
principally in the body and through the body. In other words, the subject is symbolically constituted, first and foremost, by symbolically articulating the body with other,
external bodies" (2000:97). My criticism is not that Valeri reifies the body as such. He
does allow a wider ethical meaning of the body, as when he says: "pollution, although
focused on the subject, and modeled on the body's permeability to external objects,

and principally concerned with the substances and processes where this permeability is located, may stray very far from them" (99). For example, "an embodied subject necessarily tends to embody itself beyond the limits of its body. This is particularly true of powerful people" (98). However, what he assumes is the subject's *awareness* of his or her body, upon which moral principles are metaphorized. Nothing could be further from the Kantian point of view that I espouse here.

10. Recall that, for Bronner, the idea of ambivalence—qua pigeon as both sacred and profane—is the pivotal conceptual device that secures his central theoretical task: of synthesizing symbolism with history, unity with difference. His thesis is that the pigeon was initially an ambivalent category in the ancient folkways that was subsequently polarized in history—supporters taking the profane aspect and protesters the sacred. For him, the source of "ambivalence," then, is only one: the biblical world of ancient folk ways, which is, as will be demonstrated by contrast, an empirical category.

11. See Fields 1995 for the very similar Durkheimian idea of society as "the Real."

12. In point of fact, John Zammito accuses Kant—the patron saint of anti-metaphysics—of being a metaphysician at heart (2002).

13. Kant may as well have said that the moderns continue to be in thrall to these categories precisely by being good constructivists and representationalists. Intellectuals of his time were drunk with the optimism of representationally synthesizing the then burgeoning natural science with everything else, such as theology and philosophy. Moral philosophy was no exception: there was a tireless drive toward aligning the secular idea of nature with ethics. The effect was opposite for Kant: the more morality was understood in terms of phenomenal praxis, not transcendentally, the less they understood it. The more the moderns believed in the power of the individual as the representationalist hero, the less they understood the hold transcendentally presupposed categories such as modernity, the West, or society had upon us. The more "enlightened" the moderns became, the more mythical the hold of their signature social form, the nation-state, and so forth, became.

14. The inherent impossibility of consistency or coherence in law is well known. According to Eric Santner, Franz Rosenzweig saw it as stemming from the inherent incompatibility between law and "life": law is only about precedents when life is about novelty (Santner 2006:67).

15. In formulating how this self-splitting—which "isolat[es] the nonhuman within the human"—is realized with the advent of the metaphysico-representationalist regime, Agamben closely follows what I deemed above as Kantian thinking. Agamben maintains that the condition of being included through an exclusion (a descriptor for modern citizenship) is equivalent to "being in relation to something from which one is excluded or which one cannot fully assume" (1998:26–27). This precisely describes the predicament of the Kantian moral subject who, by being burdened with existence as an object, with pathological particularities, relates to itself only negatively vis-à-vis the moral universality. Echoing Kant, Agamben says that the cipher of such a capture of life in law (only as an exception) is not sanction but *guilt*, as being-in-debt (26).

Guilt in Kant, as we have seen, rises because of the necessary discord between the positive, object-dependent particularities of the human subjective existence and the inner voice of the law that stays empty as a categorical imperative.

Chapter Seven

1. I note here in passing for now that this "troublemaker" image accompanied trapping even before the current controversy began. I suspect that that is related to trapping's close association with coal bootlegging during the Great Depression, which is the subject of a piece titled "Boredom in the Great Depression: Lack as a Protagonist of History" that I am preparing for the journal *Radical History Review*. In fact, Monk's oldest son has told me that he was once fired from a construction job because his boss spotted trapping equipment on his truck bed.

2. Then, what happens if a real hawk shows up? That would certainly undermine the golden rule that the hawk should not visually materialize for the birds. I posed this question to Kenny. After multiple attempts on my part, he whispered that everyone around the trap scene knows that hawks should be shot immediately when spotted, which is illegal.

3. The term "flight line" among the British pigeon hunters—often called "pigeon shooters"—means quite the opposite of what Monk seems to mean here. Among the former, the term refers to a predicted route of travel. Pigeons are known to be very susceptible to the comfort of familiarity. And within a few square miles of a flock's territory, the birds are likely to repeat the routine routes of flights.

4. I borrow the image of the Möbius strip from the many works of Slavoj Žižek (2000: chap. 2).

5. Note that he is not merely observing the fact that other consciousnesses are not available to me. Philosophy calls such thinking skepticism. Sartre is not merely saying that the world as perceived by the Other "escapes me." The difference is that the world that "escapes me" is also the world "in which I take part." What does this entail? If skepticism problematizes the limits of our thinking, existentialism begins from the premise that our thinking is also an "object" that "takes part" in the world, hence subject to being registered as such by another thinking/consciousness. Skepticism is only (pessimistically) concerned with how much our thinking can capture the world that always already exists "out there" as a finished form. Existentialism, in contrast, is about the emergency of the "disappearance" of the world; it asks how our relation to the object-world actually changes by dint of the fact that we are always already "caught" in (or "thrown" into) others' thinking or address. A comparison to Monk's understanding of his birds' existential plight seems to be apposite.

6. The Yuengling (pronounced Yingling) brewery is indigenous to the area and is located in the county seat, Pottsville. It is the oldest brewery in the nation. The name is that of the family that started the brewery and still owns the make. Many local residents raised false hopes that I, an Asian, might finally shed light on what the Chinese-sounding name "means."

7. In the conventional view of whiteness studies, the gaze is generally said to ir-redeemably fix its patient's presence in the awareness of being abandoned to a look. Franz Fanon, for example, famously wrote of whiteness in terms of discriminating vision that is hyper-sensitive to the sameness and difference occurring in someone else's body in relation to one's own. The gaze is here understood as an agentivized, voy-euristic, and unilateral domination of its object, even as its owner is disembodied, that is, a pure subject of the gaze, seeing but not being seen. One of the problems with this view of the gaze, as a unilateral domination, is that the "whiteness" of the disembodied subject of the gaze is given, as if whiteness is about being a white person or Caucasian, as if whiteness is about a self-conscious valuation of an always already racialized body, at the level of some possessible content. It is a short step from here to draw a simple opposition between Self and Other, which is so deeply entrenched in cultural studies as well as in postcolonial studies on racial consciousness.

8. The radically social, anti-individualistic nature of Sartre's thesis cannot be over-looked. Here, the Other is not a fully formed external *factum brutum* of the "objec-tive" reality in relation to whose resistant encounter the subject constitutes itself as an "interior" and private recess. Sartre's Other constitutes the subject's own horizon of experience, that is, its condition of possibility (not resistant impossibility). But, as has been established, it does so not in a "positive" sense but as a negative horizon whose presence the subject must acknowledge but whose "content" forever remains inacces-sible to the latter. It is a negative horizon whose inaccessibility warrants the fact that a subject's experience is not solipsistically isolated. How does this work? How is it at once a necessary part of the non-solipsistic, socialized subjective experience and yet "inaccessible" to the latter? The (suspected) existence of the Other's look constitutes the subject as part of the world of objects: "for me the Other is first the being for whom I am an object; that is, the being through whom I gain my objectness" (2000[1956]: 246). But that object—Sartre equates it to the body—because it is a product of the Other, to repeat, also has a "face," which is turned away from me just like any other objects.

Such a notion of sociality continued through the Francophone tradition. For Claude Lévi-Strauss, for example, sociality equals an impossibility of self-possession on account of the self-division caused by the other subject (see Song 2006:474–75). Society is possible for him not because we share common positive characteristics, such as a worldview, and mirror each other, just as in the above communitarian view of ani-mal sociality, but because of the shared negativity, that is, to put it in Sartre's language, an enigmatic part of myself that was given birth to on account of the existence of the Other consciousness/orientation. For Lévi-Strauss, then, society is neither in the Self nor in the Other but *outside both*. The society is "total"—both subject and object, rep-resentation and thing (Lévi-Strauss 1987)—in the sense that anyone participating in it needs to experience self-division—desubjectification as much as subjectification.

9. In the language of set theory, such a "set" (of multiplicity) must have among its "members" an element whose value is empty (see Hallward 2003:64–66).

10. "My relation to an object or the potentiality of an object decomposes under the

Other's look and appears to me in the world as my possibility of utilizing the object, but only as this possibility on principle escapes me; that is, in so far as it is surpassed by the Other toward his own possibilities" (Sartre 2001[1956]:240).

11. What is at stake here can be put in the ethical language of Bernard Williams:

> What one does and the sort of life one leads condition one's later desires and judgments. The standpoint of that retrospective judge who will be my later self will be the product of my earlier choices. So there is no set of preferences both fixed and relevant, relative to which the various fillings of my life-space can be compared. . . . The perspective of deliberative choice on one's life is constitutively *from here*. Correspondingly the perspective of assessment with greater knowledge is necessarily *from there*, and not only can I not guarantee how factually it will be then, but I cannot ultimately guarantee from what standpoint of assessment my major and most fundamental regrets will be. (B. Williams 1981:34–35)

12. According to Jacques Derrida (2003), debates on the difference between human intelligence and that of the animal in the West have unfolded largely around a pair of concepts: response versus reaction. Among those thinkers who believed in an unbridgeable difference between humans and animals, he continues, response and reaction are qualitatively different: humans "respond" (through a system of signaling) but animals only "react" (to stimuli). One of such proponents, Jacques Lacan—whom Derrida criticizes—further distinguished the two abilities in the following manner. Humans can "respond" to a situation because they can "pretend to pretend"; animals only react to a situation because they can only "pretend" (Derrida 2003:131). Say, the "situation" of concern here is where both are hunted by a predator (qua the Other) in a field of snow. According to Lacan, an animal can be cognizant of the fact that it is being followed and hence engage in an evasive or "pretending" dance or choreography (Lacan quoted in Derrida 2003:130). But unlike humans, animals are not capable of leaving false tracks or covering the tracks they already made (131). Derrida's points of objection to Lacan's theory are of no concern to us here. What is of concern is what Lacan's view—which Derrida portrays as exemplifying the dominant view in the West—implies in relation to Monk's distinction between barn birds and brushed birds. When Monk characterizes the barn bird's behavior at a match as something like an impetuous reaction to "every disturbance" is he not drawing a parallel to Lacan's theory of the (non-human) animal?

Conclusion

1. Newitz does not commit herself to a precise timing as I have here. But the majority of popular culture examples she assembles to make the point fall roughly in the mid-to-late 1980s.

2. Paul Rabinow's dissenting title "Representations Are Social Facts" (1986) was included in the inaugural volume *Writing Culture*.

3. My criticism of Foucauldianism here owes greatly, if not to Foucault himself, to Copjec 1994.

4. Enunciation, as Foucault articulates in *The Archaeology of Knowledge*, refers to the event of discourse, not to its "content"; to its *taking place*, not to the text of what is stated (1972:130–33). Thereby, Foucault tried to reserve the subject-experiential dimension that is reducible neither to representationality specific to sociohistorical contexts nor to the biographical attributes of the speaking subject. Once again, consider the statement "I am lying" (see Chapter 5). At the referential level, this statement does not make sense, but we know that it does. This is because the subject of the statement emerges as "more than the statement." Here, a deliberate relinquishing of propositional validity of a referential statement gives birth to a surplus meaning that escapes capture by power.

5. On this point, see Mauss's elaboration on the etymology of the term *don* (2000[1990]). "A visit is always repaid or returned even when it is the first. This language of restitution is necessary even for services that one 'gives' for the first time" (Derrida 1992:39).

6. Concerning Socrates' self-sacrifice, Derrida notes it as a gesture that founds the law or *eidos*: "The eidos is that which can always be repeated as *the same*" (1981:123).

7. The term in the original French is *prélèvement* (1899).

8. See Ingham 2007 for a detailed analysis of what could be the effect of "pathos" mentioned here.

REFERENCES

Acland, Charles R. 1995. *Youth, Murder, Spectacle: The Cultural Politics of "Youth in Crisis."* Boulder, Colo.: Westview Press.

Adams, Carol. 2000[1990]. *The Sexual Politics of Meat: A Feminist-Vegetarian Critical Theory.* New York: Continuum.

Agamben, Giorgio. 1998. *Homo Sacer: Sovereign Power and Bare Life.* Trans. D. Heller-Rozen. Stanford, Calif.: Stanford University Press.

———. 1999a. *Potentialities, Collected Essays in Philosophy.* Trans. D. Heller-Rozen. Stanford, Calif.: Stanford University Press.

———. 1999b. *Remnants of Auschwitz: The Witness and the Archive.* Trans. D. Heller-Rozen. New York: Zone Books.

———. 2004. *The Open: Man and Animal.* Trans. K. Attell. Stanford, Calif.: Stanford University Press.

American Society for the Prevention of Cruelty to Animals (ASPCA). 1873–76. *Annual Report.* New York.

Anderson, Benedict. 1991[1983]. *Imagined Communities.* Rev. ed. London: Verso.

Ang, Ien. 1985. *Watching "Dallas": Soap Opera and the Melodramatic Imagination.* London: Methuen.

Animal's Agenda. 1992, November-December.

Animal Times. 1995, January-February. Pp. 14–17

Aurand, Harold, and William Gudelunas. 1982. "The Mythical Qualities of Molly Maguires." *Pennsylvania History* 49:91–105.

Austin, John L. 1975[1962]. *How to Do Things with Words.* 2nd ed. Ed. J. O. Urmson and M. Sbisà. Cambridge, Mass.: Harvard University Press.

Badiou, Alain. 2003. *Ethics: An Essay on the Understanding of Evil.* Trans. P. Hallward. London: Verso.

Baker, Lee D. 1998. *From Savage to Negro: Anthropology and the Construction of Race, 1896–1954.* Berkeley: University of California Press.

Balibar, Etienne. 1991. "Is There a 'Neo-Racism'?" In *Race, Nation, Class: Ambiguous Identities,* trans. E. Balibar and I. Wallerstein, ed. E. Balibar and C. Turner. London and New York: Verso, 17–28.

Barkun, M. 1994. *Religion and the Racist Right: The Origins of the Christian Identity Movement.* Chapel Hill: University of North Carolina Press.

———. 1998. "Conspiracy Theories as Stigmatized Knowledge: The Basis for a New Age Racism?" In *Nation and Race: The Developing Euro-American Racist Subculture*, ed. J. Kaplan and T. Bjorgo. Boston: Northeastern University Press, 71–93.

———. 2003. *A Culture of Conspiracy: Apocalyptic Visions in Contemporary America.* Berkeley: University of California Press.

Barthes, Roland. 1981. *Camera Lucida: Reflections on Photography.* Trans. R. Howard. New York: Hill and Wang.

Bateson, Gregory. 2000[1972]. *Steps to an Ecology of Mind.* Chicago: University of Chicago Press.

Beck, Alan M., and Aaron H. Katcher. 1983. *Between Pets and People: The Importance of Animal Companionship.* New York: G. P. Putnam's Sons.

Benjamin, Walter. 1968. *Illuminations, Essays, and Reflections.* Trans. H. Zohn. Ed. H. Arendt. New York: Schocken Books.

Benthall, Jonathan. 1993. *Disasters, Relief, and the Media.* London: I. B. Tauris and Co. Ltd.

Berger, John. 1980. *About Looking.* New York: Pantheon Books.

Berland, Jody. 1992. "Angels Dancing: Cultural Technologies and the Production of Space." In *Cultural Studies*, ed. L. Grossberg, C. Nelson, and P. A. Treichler. New York: Routledge, 38–55.

Bhabha, Homi K. 1983. "The Other Question...Homi K Bhabha Reconsiders the Stereotype and Colonial Discourse." *Screen* 22(4):18–36.

———. 1986. "Foreword: Remembering Fanon; Self, Psyche and the Colonial Condition." In *Black Skin, White Masks*, by Frantz Fanon, trans. C. L. Markmann. London: Pluto Press, vii–xxv.

———. 1990. "The Other Question: Difference, Discrimination, and the Discourse of Colonialism." In *Out There: Marginalization and Contemporary Culture*, ed. R. Ferguson. Cambridge, Mass.: MIT Press, 71–87.

Blatz, P. K. 1994. *Democratic Miners: Work and Labor Relations in the Anthracite Coal Industry, 1875–1925.* Albany: State University of New York Press.

Bourdieu, Pierre. 1990. *The Logic of Practice.* Trans. R. Nice. Stanford, Calif.: Stanford University Press.

———. 1997. "The Work of Time." In *The Logic of the Gift: Toward an Ethic of Generosity*, ed. A. D. Schrift. London: Routledge, 190–204.

Boyer, Dominic. 2003. "The Medium of Foucault in Anthropology." *Minnesota Review* 58–60:265–72.

———. 2006. "Conspiracy, History, and Therapy at a Berlin *Stammtisch.*" *American Ethnologist* 33(3):327–39.

Bratich, Jack. 2002. "Injections and Truth Serums: AIDS Conspiracy Theories and the Politics of Articulation." In *Conspiracy Nation: The Politics of Paranoia in Postwar America*, ed. P. Knight. New York: New York University Press, 133–56.

Bronner, Simon J. 2005. "Contesting Tradition: The Deep Play and the Protest of Pigeon Shoots." *Journal of American Folklore* 118(470):409–52.

Brunette, Peter. 1994. "Electronic Bodies/Real Bodies: Reading the Evening News." In *Thinking Bodies*, ed. J. F. MacCannell and L. Zakarin. Stanford, Calif.: Stanford University Press, 181–94.

Brunsdon, Charlotte, and David Morley. 1978. *Everyday Television: Nationwide*. London: British Film Institute.

Burke, Peter. 1978. *Popular Culture in Early Modern Europe*. London: Temple Smith.

Campbell, C. 1972. "The Cult, the Cultic Milieu, and Secularization." In *Sociological Yearbook of Religion in Britain*. Vol. 5. London: SCM Press, 193–222.

Canfield, Patrick M. 1993. *Growing up with Bootleggers, Gamblers, and Pigeons*. Wilmington, Del.: Interlude Enterprises.

Chicago Sun Times. 1993, November 30.

Citizen Standard. 1989, August 30.

Clarke, Alan, and John Clarke. 1982. "'Highlights and Action Plays'—Ideology, Sport, and the Media." In *Sport, Culture, and Ideology*, ed. J. Hargreaves. London: Routledge and Kegan Paul, 62–87.

Clarke, David. 2004. "The 'Field' as Habitus: Reflections on Inner and Outer Dialogue." *Anthropology Matters* 6(2):1–10.

Clarke, John. 1978. "Football and Working Class Fans: Tradition and Change." In *"Football Hooligans," the Wider Context*, ed. R. Ingham, S. Hall, J. Clarke, P. Marsh, and J. Donovan. London: Inter-Action Inprint, 37–60.

Clarke, Steve. 2002. "Conspiracy Theories and Conspiracy Theorizing." *Philosophy of Social Sciences* 32(2):131–50.

Clifford, James. 1988. *The Predicament of Culture: Twentieth-Century Ethnography, Literature, and Art*. Cambridge, Mass.: Harvard University Press.

Coleman, Sydney H. 1924. *Humane Society Leaders in America*. Albany, N.Y.: American Humane Association.

Cooke, A. 1920. *A Book of Dovecotes*. London: Foulis.

Copjec, Joan. 1994. *Read My Desire: Lacan against the Historicists*. Cambridge, Mass.: MIT Press.

———. 2004. *Imagine There's No Woman: Ethics and Sublimation*. Cambridge, Mass.: MIT Press.

———. 2006. "May '68, the Emotional Month." In *Lacan: The Silent Partners*, ed. S. Žižek. London and New York: Verso, 90–114.

Copleston, Frederick. 2006[1952]. *History of Philosophy*. Vol. 6, *The Enlightenment: Voltaire to Kant*. London: Continuum International Publishing Group Ltd.

County Business Patterns. U.S. Department of Commerce, Bureau of the Census, CBP-74–40.

Crary, Jonathan. 1990. *Techniques of the Observer: On Vision and Modernity in the Nineteenth Century*. Cambridge, Mass.: MIT Press.

Darnton, Robert. 1984. *The Great Cat Massacre and Other Episodes in French Culture History*. New York: Basic Books.

———. 1986. "The Symbolic Element in History." *Journal of Modern History* 58(1): 218–34.

Davis, J. M. 1975. "Socially Induced Flight Reactions in Pigeons." *Animal Behaviour* 23:567–601.

Dayan, Daniel, and Elihu Katz. 1985. "Television Ceremonial Events." *Culture and Society* (May-June):60–66.

———. 1992a. "Media Events and Ceremonial Politics." *Intermedia* 20(4–5):16–17.

———. 1992b. *Media Events: The Live Broadcasting of History.* Cambridge, Mass.: Harvard University Press.

de Cordova, Richard. 1990. *Picture Personalities: The Emergence of the Star System in America.* Urbana and Chicago: University of Illinois Press.

Deleuze, Gille. 1988. *Foucault.* Trans. S. Hand. Minneapolis: University of Minnesota Press.

Derrida, Jacques. 1981. *Dissemination.* Trans. B. Johnson. Chicago: University of Chicago Press.

———. 1988. "Signature Event Context." In *Limited Inc.* Evanston, Ill.: Northwestern University Press, 1–21.

———. 1992. *Given Time: I. Counterfeit Money.* Trans. P. Kamuf. Chicago: University of Chicago Press.

———. 2003. "And Say the Animal Responded?" In *Zoontologies: The Question of the Animal,* ed. C. Wolfe. Minneapolis: University of Minnesota Press, 121–46.

Doane, Mary Ann. 1990. "Information, Crisis, Catastrophe." In *Logics of Television: Essays in Cultural Criticism,* ed. P. Mellencamp. Bloomington and Indianapolis: Indiana University Press, 222–39.

Dohrn-van Rossum, Gerhard. 1996. *History of the Hour: Clocks and Modern Temporal Orders.* Chicago: University of Chicago Press.

Dolar, Mladen. 1996. "At First Sight." In *Gaze and Voice as Love Objects,* ed. R. Salecl and S. Žižek. Durham and London: Duke University Press, 129–53.

Douglas, Mary. 1966. *Purity and Danger: An Analysis of Concepts of Pollution and Taboo.* London: Routledge and Kegan Paul.

———. 1975. *Implicit Meanings: Essays in Anthropology.* London and Boston: Routledge and Kegan Paul.

Dyer, M. I., and P. Ward. 1977. "Management of Pest Situations." In *Granivorous Birds in Ecosystems,* ed. J. Pinowski and S. C. Kendeigh. Cambridge: University of Cambridge Press, 102–19.

Dyer, Richard. 1979. *Stars.* London: British Film Institute.

Eherenreich, Barbara. 1989. *Fear of Falling: The Inner Life of the Middle Class.* New York: Pantheon Books.

Ellis, John. 1982. *Visible Fictions: Cinema, Television, Video.* London and New York: Routledge.

Fanon, Franz. 1967[1952]. *Black Skin, White Masks.* Trans. C. L. Markmann. New York: Grove Press.

Fenster, Mark. 2008[1999]. *Conspiracy Theories: Secrecy and Power in American Culture*. Minneapolis: University of Minnesota Press.

Ferguson, Sarah. 1994. "Strike a Pose." *New York* 7:60–66.

Fernandez, James W. 1988. "Historians Tell Tales: Of Cartesian Cats and Gallic Cockfights." *Journal of Modern History* 60:113–27.

Feur, Jane. 1983. "The Concept of Live Television: Ontology as Ideology." In *Regarding Television: Critical Approaches—An Anthology*, ed. A. Kaplan. Los Angeles: University Publications of America, Inc., 12–22.

Fields, Karen E. 1995. "Translator's Introduction: Religion as an Eminently Social Thing." In Emile Durkheim, *The Elementary Forms of Religious Life*, trans. K. E. Fields. New York: Free Press.

Fish, Stanley. 1997. "Boutique Multiculturalism, or Why Liberals Are Incapable of Thinking about Hate Speech." *Critical Inquiry* 23(2):378–89.

Flieger, Jerry Aline. 1997. "Postmodern Perspective: The Paranoid Eye." *New Literary History* 28(1):87–109.

Foucault, Michel. 1970. *The Order of Things: An Archaeology of the Human Sciences*. New York: Vintage Books.

———. 1972. *The Archaeology of Knowledge*. Trans. A. Sheridan. New York: Pantheon Books.

———. 1978. *History of Sexuality*. Vol. 1, *An Introduction*, Trans. R. Hurley. New York: Random House.

———. 1979. *Discipline and Punish: The Birth of the Prison*. Trans. A. Sheridan. New York: Vintage Books.

Frankenberg, Ruth. 1993. *White Women, Race Matters: The Social Construction of Whiteness*. Minneapolis: University of Minnesota Press.

———, ed. 1997. *Displacing Whiteness: Essays in Social and Cultural Criticism*. Durham, N.C., and London: Duke University Press.

Frazer, J. G. 1959. *The Golden Bough*. New York: S. G. Philips.

French, Richard. 1975. *Antivivisection and Medical Science in Victorian Society*. Princeton, N.J.: Princeton University Press.

Freud, Sigmund. 1964[1905]. *Jokes and Their Relation to the Unconscious: The Standard Edition of the Complete Psychological Works of Sigmund Freud*, vol. VII. Trans. and ed. J. Strachey. London: Hogarth Press.

———. 2000. *Totem and Taboo: Resemblances between the Psychic Lives of Savages and Neurotics*. Trans. A. A. Brill. Amherst, N.Y.: Prometheus Books.

Frykman, Jonas, and Orvar Löfgren. 1987. *Culture Builders: A Historical Anthropology of Middle-Class Life*. Trans. A. Crozier. New Brunswick, N.J.: Rutgers University Press.

Gamson, Joshua. 1994. *Claims to Fame: Celebrity in Contemporary America*. Berkeley and Los Angeles: University of California Press.

Geertz, Clifford. 1973. "Deep Play: Notes on the Balinese Cockfight." In *The Interpretation of Cultures*. New York: Basic Books, 412–53.

Gilfoyle, Timothy J. 1986. "The Moral Origins of Political Surveillance: The Preventive Society in New York City, 1867–1918." *American Quarterly* 38:637–52.

Gledhill, Christine. 1991. "Signs of Melodrama." In *Stardom: Industry of Desire*, ed. C. Gledhill. London: Routledge, 207–29.

Glitz, M. L. 1959. "The Problem of Bird Damage to Ohio." *Proceedings of North Central Branch, Ecological Society of America* 14:47–48.

Godwin, R. Kenneth, and Robert Cameron Mitchell. 1984. "The Implications of Direct Mail for Political Organizations." *Social Science Quarterly* 65(3):829–39.

Goodwin, D. 1983. *Pigeons and Doves of the World.* Ithaca: Cornell University Press.

Gusfield, Joseph R., Enriques Larana, and Hank Johnston. 1994. *New Social Movement: From Ideology to Identity.* Philadelphia: Temple University Press.

Habermas, Jürgen. 1989. *The Structural Transformation of the Public Sphere.* Cambridge, Mass.: MIT Press.

Hacking, Ian. 1991. "The Making and Molding of Child Abuse." *Critical Inquiry* 17(2):255–68.

Hall, Stuart. 1978. "The Treatment of 'Football Hooliganism' in the Press." In *Football Hooliganism: The Wider Context*, ed. R. Ingham, S. Hall, J. Clarke, P. Marsh, and J. Donovan. London: Inter-Action Inprint, 15–37.

———. 1980. "Encoding/Decoding." In *Culture, Media, Language*, ed. S. Hall, D. Hobson, A. Lowe, and P. Willis. London: Hutchinson, 128–38.

Hallward, Peter. 2003. *Badiou: A Subject to Truth.* Minneapolis and London: University of Minnesota Press.

Handelman, Don. 1990. *Models and Mirrors: Towards an Anthropology of Public Events.* Cambridge and New York: Cambridge University Press.

Harding, Susan, and Kathleen Stewart. 2003. "Anxieties of Influence: Conspiracy Theory and Therapeutic Culture in Millennial America." In *Transparency and Conspiracy: Ethnographies of Suspicion in the New World Order*, ed. H. G. West and T. Sanders. Durham, N.C.: Duke University Press, 258–86.

Harrison, J. E. 1903. *Prolegomena to the Study of Greek Religion.* New York: Meridian.

Hendrick, George. 1977. *Henry Salt: Humanitarian Reformer and Man of Letters.* Urbana: University of Illinois Press.

Hill, Mike. 1997. *Whiteness: A Critical Reader.* New York and London: New York University Press.

Hofstadter, Richard. 1967. *Paranoid Style in American Politics, and Other Essays.* New York: Knopf.

Holden, Constance. 1981. "Scientist Convicted for Monkey Neglect." *Science* 214: 1218–20.

hooks, bell. 1992. *Black Looks: Race and Representation.* Boston: South End.

Hubert, Henri, and Marcel Mauss. 1899. "Essai sur la nature et la fonction du sacrifice." *L'année Sociologique* (1897–98): 29–138.

———. 1981[1964]. *Sacrifice: Its Nature and Functions.* Trans. W. D. Halls. Chicago: University of Chicago Press.

Husting, Ginna, and Martin Orr. 2007. "'Dangerous Machinery' Conspiracy Theorist as a Transpersonal Strategy of Exclusion." *Symbolic Interaction* 30(2):127–50.

Illinois Humane Society. 1896. *Annual Report*.

Ingham, John. 2007. "Matricidal Madness in Foucault's Anthropology: The Pierre Rivière Seminar." *Ethos* 35(2):130–58.

Ivy, Marilyn. 1993. "Recovering the Inner Child in Twentieth-Century America." *Social Text* 37:227–52.

Jasper, Dorothy, and James M. Nelkin. 1992. *The Animal Rights Crusade: The Growth of a Moral Protest*. New York: Free Press.

Johnston, R. F., and M. Janiga. 1995. *Feral Pigeons*. New York: Oxford University Press.

Kant, Immanuel. 1970. "What Is Enlightenment?" In *Political Writings*, trans. H. Reiss, ed. H. B. Nisbet. Cambridge: Cambridge University Press.

Karatani, Kojin. 2003. *Transcritique: On Kant and Marx*. Trans. S. Kohso. Cambridge, Mass.: MIT Press.

Katz, Elihu. 1980. "Media Events: The Sense of Occasion." *Studies in Visual Anthropology* 6:84–89.

Katz, Elihu, and Daniel Dayan. 1985. "Media Events: On the Experience of Not Being There." *Religion* 15:305–14.

Kaufmann, W. 1968. *Existentialism from Dostoevsky to Sartre*. Cleveland: Meridian Books.

Kondo, Dorienne. 1986. "Dissolution and Reconstitution of Self: Implications for Anthropological Epistemology." *Cultural Anthropology* 1(1):74–88.

Kroskrity, Paul. 2000. *Regimes of Language: Ideologies, Politics, and Identity*. Santa Fe: School of American Research Press.

Kuhn, Annette. 1996. "The Power of the Image." In *Media Studies: A Reader*, ed. P. Marris and S. Thornham. Edinburgh: Edinburgh University Press, 50–54.

Lacan, Jacques. 1978. *The Four Fundamental Concepts of Psycho-Analysis*. Trans. A. Sheridan. Ed. J. Miller. New York: W. W. Norton.

———. 1993[1981]. *The Psychoses 1955–1956: The Seminar of Jacques Lacan, Book III*. Trans. R. Grigg. Ed. J. Miller. New York: W. W. Norton.

Laclau, Ernesto, and Chantal Mouffe. 1985. *Hegemony and Socialist Strategy: Towards a Radical Democratic Politics*. Trans. W. Moore and P. Cammack. London: Verso.

Lacoue-Labarthes, Philippe. 1989. *Typography: Mimesis, Philosophy, Politics*. Trans. C. Fynsk. Stanford, Calif.: Stanford University Press.

Landes, David S. 1983. *Revolution in Time: Clocks and the Making of the Modern World*. Cambridge, Mass.: Harvard University Press, Belknap Press.

Lau, R. K. W. 2004. "Habitus and the Practical Logic of Practice." *Sociology* 38(2): 369–87.

Leach, Edmund. 1964. "Anthropological Aspects of Language: Animal Categories and Verbal Abuse." In *New Directions in the Study of Language*, ed. E. H. Lenneberg. Cambridge, Mass.: MIT Press, 23–63.

———. 1971. "Kimil: A Category of Andamese Thought." In *Structural Analysis of Oral Tradition*, ed. P. Maranda and K. E. Maranda. Philadelphia: University of Pennsylvania Press.

Le Goff, Jacques. 1980. *Time, Work, and Culture in the Middle Ages*. Chicago: University of Chicago Press.

Levi, Primo. 1988. *The Drowned and the Saved*. Trans. R. Rosenthal. New York: Vintage International.

Lévi-Strauss, Claude. 1963. *Totemism*. Boston: Beacon Press.

———. 1976. *Structural Anthropology*. Vol. 2. Trans. M. Layton. Chicago: University of Chicago Press.

———. 1987. *Introduction to the Work of Marcel Mauss*. Trans. F. Baker. Routledge and Kegan Paul.

MacAloon, John. 1984. "Olympic Games and the Theory of Spectacle in Modern Societies." In *Rite, Drama, Festival, Spectacle: Rehearsals toward a Theory of Cultural Performance*, ed. J. MacAloon. Philadelphia: Institute for the Study of Human Issues, 241–80.

Maclean, N. 1994. *Behind the Mask of Chivalry: The Making of the Second Ku Klux Klan*. New York: Oxford University Press.

Madison Social Text Group. 1979. "The New Right and the Media." *Social Text* 1(1):169–80.

Malcolmson, Robert. 1973. *Popular Recreations in English Society, 1700–1850*. Cambridge: Cambridge University Press.

Mandarini, Matteo, and Alberto Toscano. 2006. "Antonio Negri and the Antinomies of Bourgeois Thought." Translators' introduction to Antonio Negri's *Political Descartes: Reason, Ideology, and the Bourgeois Project*. New York and London: Verso.

Marsh, Ben. 1987. "Continuity and Decline in the Anthracite Towns of Pennsylvania." *Annals of the Association of American Geographers* 77(3):337–52.

Massumi, Brian. 1993. "Everywhere You Want to Be: Introduction to Fear." In *The Politics of Everyday Fear*, ed. B. Massumi. Minneapolis: University of Minnesota Press, 3–37.

Mauss, Marcel. 1967. *The Gift: Forms and Functions of Exchange in Archaic Societies*. Trans. I. Cunnison. New York: W. W. Norton.

———. 2000[1990]. *The Gift: The Form and Reason for Exchange in Archaic Societies*. Trans. W. D. Halls. New York: W. W. Norton.

McCarthy, John D., and Mayer N. Zald. 1973. *The Trend of Social Movements in America: Professionalization and Resource Mobilization*. Morristown, N.J. : General Learning Press.

McDowell, R. D., and H. W. Pillsbury. 1959. "Wildlife Damage to Crops in the United States." *Journal of Wildlife Management* 23:240–41.

Metz, Christian. 1982. *The Imaginary Signifier: Psychoanalysis and Cinema*. Trans. C. Brittan, A. Williams, B. Brewster, and A. Guzzetti. Bloomington: Indiana University Press.

Meyrowitz, Joshua. 1985. *No Sense of Place: The Impact of Electronic Media on Social Behavior.* New York: Oxford University Press.

Mitchell, Timothy. 1990. "Everyday Metaphors of Power." *Theory and Society* 19: 545–77.

———. 1991. "The Limits of the State: Beyond Statist Approaches and Their Critics." *American Political Science Review* 85(1):77–96.

Moores, Shaun. 1993. *Interpreting Audience: The Ethnography of Media Consumption.* London: Sage.

Morley, David. 1986. *Family Television: Cultural Power and Domestic Leisure.* London: Comedia.

Morse, Margaret. 1983. "Sport on Television: Replay and Display." In *Regarding Television: Critical Approaches—An Anthology,* ed. A. Kaplan. Bethesda, Md.: University Publications of America, 44–66.

Nancy, Jean-Luc. 1993. *The Birth of Presence.* Stanford, Calif.: Stanford University Press.

———. 2003. *A Finite Thinking.* Ed. S. Sparks. Stanford, Calif.: Stanford University Press.

Nash, Roderick F. 1989. *The Rights of Nature: A History of Environmental Ethics.* Madison: University of Wisconsin Press.

Newitz, Analee. 2001. "White Savagery and Humiliation, or a New Radical Consciousness in the Media." In *White Trash: Race and Class in America,* ed. M. Wray and A. Newitz. New York and London: Routledge, 131–54.

New York Times. 1991, September 3.

Newsweek. 1984, August 27.

Norris, Andrew, ed. 2005. *Politics, Metaphysics, and Death: Essays on Giorgio Agamben's* Homo Sacer. Durham, N.C.: Duke University Press.

Olson, Kathryn M., and G. Thomas Goodnight. 1994. "Entanglements of Consumption, Cruelty, Privacy, and Fashion: The Social Controversy over Fur." *Quarterly Journal of Speech* 80(3):249–76.

Our Dumb Animals (ODA). 1888–1900. Selected issues. Published by the Massachusetts Society for the Prevention of Cruelty to Animals (MSPCA).

Pacheco, Alex, and Anna Francione. 1985. "The Silver Springs Monkeys." In *Defense of Animals,* ed. P. Singer. New York: Blackwell, 135–47.

Palladino, G. 1991. *Another Civil War: Labor, Capital, and the State in the Anthracite Regions of Pennsylvania, 1840–68.* Urbana: University of Illinois Press.

Perez, Berta Elena. 1990. "Ideology of Animal Rights Movement." Ph.D. diss., University of Minnesota, Minneapolis.

PETA. 1993. "Join Us and Make a Difference for Animal Rights." Brochure.

———. 1994–95. *Annual Review.*

Pottsville Republican. 1989, September 5.

Rabinow, Paul. 1986. "Representations Are Social Facts: Modernity and Post-Modernity in Anthropology." In *Writing Culture: The Poetics and Politics of Ethnography,* ed. J. Clifford and G. E. Marcus. Berkeley: University of California Press, 234–61.

Rasmussen, Birgit Brander, Eric Klinenberg, Irene J. Nexica, and Matt Wray, eds. 2001. *The Making and Unmaking of Whiteness*. Durham, N.C., and London: Duke University Press.

Regan, Tom. 1983. *The Case for Animal Rights*. Berkeley, C.A.: University of California Press.

Ritvo, Harriet. 1987. *The Animal Estate: The English and Other Creatures in the Victorian Age*. Cambridge, Mass.: Harvard University Press.

Rogin, Michael Paul. 1987. *Ronald Reagan, the Movie: And Other Episodes in Political Demonology*. Berkeley: University of California Press.

Rothenbuhler, E. 1988. "The Living Room Celebration of the Olympic Games." *Journal of Communication* 38:61–81.

Ryder, Richard D. 1975. *Victims of Science: The Use of Animals in Research*. London: Davis-Poynter.

Sabato, Larry J. 1983. "Political Consultants and the New Campaign Technology." In *Interest Group Politics*, ed. A. J. Cigler and B. A. Loomis. Washington, D.C.: Congressional Quarterly Press, 145–68.

Santner, Eric. 2001. *On the Psychotheology of the Everyday Life: Reflections on Freud and Rozenzweig*. Chicago: University of Chicago Press.

———. 2006. *On Creaturely Life: Rilke, Benjamin, Sebald*. Chicago: University of Chicago Press.

Sartre, Jean-Paul. 1986[1948]. *Anti-Semites and Jew*. Trans. G. J. Becker. New York. Schocken Books.

———. 2001[1956]. *Being and Nothingness: A Phenomenological Inquiry on Ontology*. Trans. H. E. Barnes. New York: Citadel Press.

Schmitt, Carl. 1985. *Political Theology: Four Chapters on the Concept of Sovereignty*. Trans. G. Schwab. Cambridge, Mass.: MIT Press.

Scott, James C. 1985. *Weapons of the Weak: Everyday Forms of Peasant Resistance*. New Haven, Conn.: Yale University Press.

———. 1990. *Domination and the Arts of Resistance: Hidden Transcripts*. New Haven, Conn.: Yale University Press.

Schuylkill Economic Development Co. 1995

Seramatakis, Nadia. 1994. "The Memory of the Senses: Historical Perception, Commensural Exchange and Modernity." In *Visualizing Theory: Selected Essays from Visual Anthropology Review, 1990-1994*, ed. L. Taylor. New York: Routledge, 214–29.

Seshadri-Crooks, Kalpana. 2000. *Desiring Whiteness: A Lacanian Analysis of Race*. London and New York: Routledge.

Shaviro, Steven. 1993. *The Cinematic Body*. Minneapolis: University of Minnesota Press.

Shell, Marc. 1993. *Children of the Earth: Literature, Politics, and Nationhood*. New York: Oxford University Press.

Shils, Edward. 1975. *Center and Periphery: Essays in Macrosociology*. Chicago: University of Chicago Press.

Silverstein, Michael. 1994. "Whorfianism and the Linguistic Imagination of Nationality." In *The School of American Research Advanced Seminar, "Language Ideologies."* Rev. version. Santa Fe: School of American Research.

Singer, Peter. 1990[1975]. *Animal Liberation.* New York: Avon Books.

Song, Hoon. 2006. "Seeing Oneself Seeing Oneself: White Nihilism in Ethnography and Theory." *Ethnos* 71(4):470–88.

Sperling, Susan. 1988. *Animal Liberators: Research and Morality.* Berkeley: University of California Press.

Stallybrass, Peter, and Allon White. 1986. *The Politics and Poetics of Transgression.* Ithaca, N.Y.: Cornell University Press.

Stam, Robert. 1983. "Television News and Its Spectator." In *Regarding Television: Critical Approaches—An Anthology*, ed. A. Kaplan. Los Angeles: University Publications of America, 23–43.

Süskind, Patrick. 1988. *The Pigeon.* Trans. J. E. Woods. New York: Alfred A. Knopf.

Tambiah, S. J. 1969. "Animals Are Good to Think with and Good to Prohibit." *Ethnology* 8(4):423–59.

Taussig, Michael. 1992. *The Nervous System.* New York: Routledge.

———. 1993. *Mimesis and Alterity: An Alternative History of the Senses.* New York: Routledge, Chapman, and Hall.

Taylor, Ian. 1982. "On the Sports Violence Question: Soccer Hooliganism Revisited." In *Sport, Culture, and Ideology*, ed. J. Hargreaves. London: Routledge and Kegan Paul, 152–96.

Tester, Keith. 1991. *Animals and Society: The Humanity of Animal Rights.* London: Routledge.

Thomas, Keith. 1983. *Man and the Natural World: A History of the Modern Sensibility.* New York: Pantheon Books.

Thompson, E. P. 1980[1963]. *The Making of the English Working Class.* Harmondsworth: Penguin.

Tsaliki, Liza. 1995. "The Media and the Construction of an 'Imagined Community': The Role of Media Events on Greek Television." *European Journal of Communication* 10(3):345–70.

Tsing, Anna. 1993. *In the Realm of the Diamond Queen: Marginality in an Out-of-the-Way Place.* Princeton, N.J.: Princeton University Press.

Tuan, Yi-Fu. 1984. *Dominance and Affection: The Making of Pets.* New Haven, Conn., and London: Yale University Press.

Turner, James. 1980. *Reckoning with the Beast: Animals, Pain, and Humanity in the Victorian Mind.* Baltimore: Johns Hopkins University Press.

Valeri, Valerio. 2000. *The Forest of Taboos: Morality, Hunting, and Identity among the Huaulu.* Madison: University of Wisconsin Press.

Vidich, Arthur, and Joseph Bensman. 1968. *Small Town in Mass Society: Class, Power, and Religion in a Rural Community.* Princeton, N.J.: Princeton University Press.

Wallace, Anthony. 1987. *St. Clair: A Nineteenth-Century Coal Town's Experience with a Disaster-prone Industry.* New York: Knopf.

Ware, Vron. 1997. "Island Racism: Gender, Place, and White Power." In *Displacing Whiteness: Essays in Social and Cultural Criticism,* ed. R. Frankenberg. Durham, N.C., and London: Duke University Press, 283–310.

Warner, Michael. 1994. "The Mass Public and the Mass Subject." In *Habermas and the Public Sphere,* ed. C. Calhoun. Cambridge, Mass.: MIT Press, 377–401.

Washington Post. 1992, September 8 and 12.

Weber, Samuel. 1996. "Objectivity and Its Others." In *Massmediauras: Forms, Technics, Media,* ed. A. Cholodenko. Stanford, Calif.: Stanford University Press, 36–54.

Weil, Robert. 1986. "Inhuman Bondage." *Omni* 9:65.

Whorf, Benjamin Lee. 1956[1939]. "The Relation of Habitual Thought and Behavior to Language." In *Language, Thought, and Reality: Selected Writings of Benjamin Lee Whorf,* ed. J. B. Carroll. Cambridge, Mass.: MIT Press, 134–59.

Williams, Bernard A. O. 1981. *Moral Luck: Philosophical Papers, 1973–1980.* New York: Cambridge University Press.

Williams, John. 1991. "Having an Away Day: English Football Spectators and the Hooligan Debate." In *British Football and Social Change: Getting into Europe,* ed. J. Williams and S. Wagg. Leicester: Leicester University Press, 160–84.

Willman, Skip. 2000. "Spinning Paranoia: The Ideologies of Conspiracy and Contingency in Postmodern Culture." In *Conspiracy Nation: The Politics of Paranoia in Postwar America,* ed. P. Knight. New York: New York University Press, 21–39.

Woolard, Kathryn A. 1998. "Introduction: Language Ideology as a Field of Inquiry." In *Language Ideologies: Practice and Theory,* ed. B. Schieffelin, K. A. Woolard, and P. Kroskrity. New York: Oxford University Press, 1–45.

Yeo, Eileen, and Stephen Yeo. 1981. *Popular Culture and Class Conflict, 1590–1914: Explorations in the History of Labour and Leisure.* Sussex: Harvester Press.

Zammito, John H. 2002. *Kant, Herder, and the Birth of Anthropology.* Chicago: University of Chicago Press.

Zelizer, Barbie. 1991. "From Home to Public Forum: Media Events and the Public Sphere." *Journal of Film and Video* 43(1–2):69–79.

Žižek, Slavoj. 1994. *The Metastases of Enjoyment: Six Essays on Women and Causality.* New York and London: Verso.

———. 2000. *The Ticklish Subject: The Absent Center of Political Ontology.* London and New York: Verso.

Zupančič, Alenka. 1996. "Philosophers' Blind Man's Bluff." In *Gaze and Voice as Love Objects,* ed. R. Salecl and S. Žižek. Durham, N.C., and London: Duke University Press, 32–58.

INDEX

ACKNOWLEDGMENTS

I want to thank Ilana Gershon and Dominic Boyer for turning their deaf ears to my endless protests of self-doubt. The two patiently indulged my flickering sense of relevance to academia . . . and to everything else. Jeongwon Joe shared a life with me and held my hand through the most pathetic fits. Teri Silvio was a constant presence albeit from afar. Marshall Sahlins kept me legal throughout. I know of his heroism on my behalf in a way that not many are acquainted with.

I dedicated my very first work to the "enigmatic vigor" of Michael Silverstein. The memory of that vigor lives on here. Around the time of my first acquaintance with it, Marilyn Ivy stormed onto my horizon with the promise of phantasmic intellectual possibilities. Whatever got to live in me ever since I met Michael and Marilyn is the true author of any good that might have found its way in the foregoing.

I thank my first mentors-at-employment: Joel Kuipers, Roy Richard Grinker, and Veena Das. I am grateful for their high hopes for me and apologize for the modest outcome. The same must be said to the kind folks in the Department of Anthropology at Cornell University, who tirelessly wagered on my abilities time and again. Besides Dominic Boyer, I want to single out Andrew Willford, Magnus Fiskiső, and Viranjini Munasinghe. I thank Steven Sangren, Terence Turner, and the numerous graduate students there whose names I cannot enumerate for their dependably spirited engagements. Hugh Raffles at the New School is another person I should mention in the same breath with much gratitude.

Colleagues in the Department of Anthropology at the University of Minnesota, Twin Cities, gave me the bliss of a home abundantly worthy of the name. David Valentine and Charlie the department dog made this bliss into a domestic kind too. I am grateful for their existence. For their inspiring professional rationality and their irrational advocacy on my behalf, I single out Kat Hayes, Karen Ho, Jean Langford, David Lipset, and Stuart McLean.

Thanks to Gloria Raheja, Karen-Sue Taussig, and Steve Gudeman for their model mentorship in professionalism, and Bill Beeman for his humane and bountiful leadership as the benevolent head of the department. Laura Hauff generously lent to this book her balanced intellect as a biological anthropologist. I am blessed to have militant and loyal intellectual co-conspirators in my past and present students: Murat Altun, Xenia Cherkaev, Avigdor Edminster, Christopher Kolb, David Schrag, Gun Shin, and Melor Sturua.

The College of Liberal Arts and the Institute of Advanced Study at the University of Minnesota provided invaluable resources for the completion of the present work. I thank librarians at the Schuylkill County Historical Societies at Pottsville and Harrisburg and at the Pottsville Public Library.

My editor, Peter Agree, heroically endured the tedium of the tortuously long time it took to write this work. He gallantly carried for me the fidelity and focus that I myself often could not. Christine Sweeney may very well be the best copyeditor ever. Ju-Young Lee, Matthew Carlson, and Erik Heimark collectively gave me invaluable editorial assistance at the last minute. The final thanks go to my parents, who never stopped marveling at the fact that I have made a small career writing about pigeons.